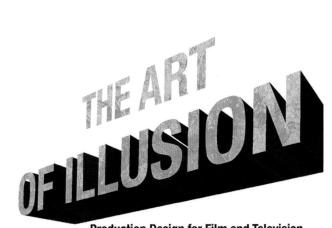

THE ART OF ILLUSION

Production Design for Film and Television

THE ART OF ILLUSION

Production Design for Film and Television

TERRY ACKLAND-SNOW
with WENDY LAYBOURN

THE CROWOOD PRESS

First published in 2017 by
The Crowood Press Ltd
Ramsbury, Marlborough
Wiltshire SN8 2HR

enquiries@crowood.com

www.crowood.com

This impression 2024

British Library Cataloguing-in-Publication Data
A catalogue record for this book is available from the British Library.

ISBN 978 1 78500 343 1

Frontispiece: A miniature cathedral ready for filming with lights, camera and crew in place.

Typeset by Jean Cussons Typesetting, Diss, Norfolk

Printed and bound in India by Thomson Press India Ltd.

CONTENTS

FOREWORD
by Chris Kelly, Producer

Invariably, media attention is focused on the stars, for obvious reasons. It's their faces that appear on posters, their names that, it is assumed, sell films and television programmes. However, for anyone with a genuine love of the business, the real heroes and heroines are the unsung ones; the problem-solvers, the imaginative engine room behind the visual experience. Chief among these are the Production Designers and Art Directors.

For decades, Terry Ackland-Snow has been among the best of British. As a producer, I've had the good fortune to work with him on many occasions. Unflappable, resourceful, indefatigable, cheerful and loyal, he has been more than equal to every challenge we've thrown at him. Before the ubiquity of CGI, Terry's inventive skill enabled him to turn the most fanciful or demanding script into plausible visual reality; on time and on budget. Five words that are music to a producer's ears.

It is typical of his generosity of spirit and love of his craft that, instead of hanging up his drawing board, he is devoting his considerable energies to passing on his secrets to a younger generation, the Oscar-winners of tomorrow. Typical too that despite the industry's increasing reliance on the computer, Terry continues to stress the fundamental importance of draughtsmanship. No one is better qualified to teach and inspire.

DEDICATION

In memory of my brother, Brian Ackland-Snow, 1940–2013

At the time of his death in 2013, my brother Brian hadn't worked for fourteen years due to the cruel illness, Alzheimer's Disease. However, his humour, compassion and generosity still shone through. He was a very unselfish man in the workplace and as a husband and father.

Brian loved drawing, art and modelmaking from an early age, but, at our father's insistence, he had to complete his carpentry apprenticeship with the family business before he started in design. After this, he joined the Art Department at the Danziger Studio in Elstree as an Art Department Assistant, subsequently working on his first film, *The Road to Hong Kong*, at Shepperton Studios, under Production Designer Roger K. Furse.

He went on to work on many films and television programmes from 1962 until he retired, having won an Oscar in 1987 for Best Art Direction and a BAFTA for Best Production Design for *A Room with a View*, and a Primetime Emmy for Outstanding Individual Achievement in Art Direction for the mini-series *Scarlett*.

Brian's film and television credits include: *Without a Clue*; *A Room with a View*; *Superman III*; *The Dark Crystal*; *McVicar*; *Dracula*; *Death on the Nile*; *Cross of Iron*; *The Slipper and the Rose*; *There's a Girl in My Soup*; *Battle of Britain*; *2001: A Space Odyssey*; *The Quiller Memorandum*; *The Road to Hong Kong*; *The Magnificent Amersons*; *Animal Farm*; *Kidnapped*; *Scarlett*; *Cadfael*; *The Man in the Brown Suit*; *Hart to Hart*.

ACKNOWLEDGEMENTS

Within this book we acknowledge all who are sadly no longer with us, but who, through their outstanding innovations from the early days of film design to the present day, have left their legacy for the benefit of all filmmakers.

A very special thank you to Lauren Crockatt, Davina Harbord, Emma James, Miranda Keeble and Ciara Sheridan, whose dedication to the cause, combined with attention to detail, kept us focused throughout all the difficult times!

Special thanks to the following: Andrew Proctor – Art Department and Visual Effects; Terry Apsey – Construction Manager; Dominic Ackland-Snow – Construction Manager; Ken Barley – Head of Department Plaster; Adrian Start – Head of Department Paint; Darcey Crownshaw – Set Decorator and Founder of Snow Business; Leigh Took – Special Effects Supervisor and founder of Mattes and Miniatures Visual Effects; David Sproxton – Animator and co-founder of Aardman Animations; Terry Bamber – Production Manager and Assistant Director; Jamie Anderson – Director of Anderson Entertainment; Dayne Cowan – Visual Effects Supervisor; Robin Vidgeon – Director of Photography; John Glen – Director; Chris Kelly – Producer; Peter Young – Set Decorator; Tony Pratt – Production Designer; Peter Murton – Production Designer; Simon Murton – Concept Artist; Harry Lange – Production Designer; Carol Ackland-Snow – Photography and Sketch Department; Bill Stallion – Storyboard Artist, thanks to his family; Keith Ackland-Snow for providing information on the Ackland-Snow family; and Paul Isaacs for providing a selection of story boards for the book; and story board artist Martin Asbury.

Thanks to the following for illustrations: Warner Brothers – Batmobile Photograph; Universal Studios; Henson Productions – Muppet Storyboards; MGM – James Bond Photographs; Disney Art Department – photographs of *The Dark Crystal* and *Labyrinth*; EON – photographs of James Bond, *The Living Daylights*; Columbia Pictures – *The Deep*; 20th Century Fox – *The Rocky Horror Picture Show*; Paramount Pictures EMI – *Death on the Nile*; The Imaginarium.

PREFACE

By Wendy Laybourn

Wendy Laybourn.

What is illusion? The *Collins English Dictionary* defines it as a 'deceptive impression of reality'. Nowhere is this definition so relevant as in film production. In order to transport the audience to wherever the script leads, the Art Department uses illusion to create whatever style is needed to produce the appropriate backdrop for the performers and the rest of the film crew to work with. If you read through the 'Film Crew Breakdown' below, you will fully appreciate the number of people involved in any production and will better understand what a critical contribution the Art Department has in the finished film or television programme.

The film crew uses light, colour, sound and movement to transform the script into a drama, a musical, a flight of fantasy, or a blood-curdling horror movie. So never forget, as you become deeply involved in the latest tricks or technologies, that you are an entertainer first and foremost, putting images up on a screen for the enjoyment of an audience and following in the traditions set by the earliest filmmakers.

The creation of film technology was not originally meant for artistic expression, but began simply as a commercial extension of live 'theatrical' events, recording them much like the modern documentary. The practitioners soon found that portraying a story on screen was quite different from that of a theatre production. There are major qualities available to filmmakers that are difficult, if not impossible, to achieve on stage. For example, the close-up of faces and objects in order to achieve emphasis was first used by D.W. Griffith in 1907. The ability to use the camera lens to zoom in and out of any particular aspect of a scene gives the Director, Designer and Cinematographer enormous scope to add depth and quality to the action.

The controlled use of sound over action and vice versa was first used in 1926 when it was found possible to link both sound and picture together on celluloid. In addition to giving the Director the ability to emphasize the dialogue, this technology gave rise to sound design and atmospherics, as well as a specifically written and arranged music track that augments the action and creates the style and feel of the film.

When film was in its infancy it was essentially just a series of animated photographs, but then the 'showmen' stepped in to work with the photographers and began the process of what is now taken for granted as 'film production'. However, the essence of filmmaking has not really changed since those early days and it is important to remember that the early filmmakers were working with very basic and unsophisticated equipment and materials. Nonetheless, the creativity of the entire crew and their passion for telling the story is the same as ever, it is just the technology that has grown over the decades so that the tricks and scenic illusions have become more and more exotic, making the seemingly impossible now a practical reality.

The Production Designer and the Art Department are involved with all aspects of the actual sets, either in the studio or on location. Joining together with the Director, Cinematographer (Director of Photography), Construction Manager and all the other Heads of Department, they produce the 'land of magic and illusion, which the audience sees on the screen.

Production Design is way beyond aesthetics and interior design, with the Production Designer and Art Director being two of the key creators involved in any production. Given the practical and economic framework that governs the whole production, the Art Department has to be able to make the designs work around the physical restrictions of the shooting schedule. This is where the 'teamwork' of production comes into play and where the Art Department is expected to produce the best of creative work. Film production is not only highly creative, it is also a business that handles many millions of pounds or dollars, so any production is constricted by time, budget and constant changes of concept and ideas, combined with the sheer physicality of the actual construction process. Only a crew that works together like a well-oiled machine will be able to reach their target and satisfy not only the viewing public but, very importantly, the producer and the investors.

Set construction at the Shepherd's Bush Studios in the 1920s. At the Debrie camera are Freddie Young (left) and St Aubyn Brown. Freddie Young BSC went on to win three Oscars for his cinematography on Ryan's Daughter, *Doctor Zhivago and* Lawrence of Arabia.

Within this team, the Production Designer, who will almost always have risen through the ranks of the Art Department, is the creative force behind every aspect of the design and is the person who imagines and recreates, in drawings and sketches, exactly what mood, colour palette and style the Director has visualized for the production. In essence, the Production Designer is the link between the Director and the extended Art and Construction Departments.

From the Production Designer's drawings and sketches, it is the Art Director's job to turn them into perfect blueprints and technical drawings, which the Construction Crew will use to build and fabricate the actual sets. Not only does the Art Director have to use his or her considerable creative and technical talents as an architect and artist, but also needs a good working knowledge of building materials and methods, as well as a vice-like grip on the finances. The Art Department is responsible for the budget of the entire Construction Crew, which is why this budget is a separate sector of the main production budget and is the largest 'below the line' budget on any feature film.

Art Directors are artists who can adapt their style to any number of different types of production. They integrate themselves and their team into the mood and feeling of a particular project, whether it is a comedy, a musical, a costume drama or a science fiction extravaganza. The range of materials used and the scope of the design will test their imagination and skills to the utmost. During the pre-production and production periods, they will have constant discussions with the Construction Manager and together they will make decisions about the suitability of the materials and locations involved – as well as incorporating the restraints of time and economics.

In this book, which is aimed at anyone wanting to make a career in film, Terry Ackland-Snow will take you through the processes involved in creating a film set. All of the tips, tricks and techniques described in the book have been used and refined over many decades and, although the technology might have changed, the essence of filmmaking is still the same.

Film sets have developed through time from the canvas backcloths used in theatres through to their present and highly sophisticated form. Each year, the development of technology and visual processes makes film sets more exciting and the Art Director has to be abreast of every innovation. In film production the learning process never ends and the film crew is like a mobile and ever-changing life force, so even the most experienced Production Designer and Art Director will find each new project a challenge!

FILM CREW BREAKDOWN

Production Office including Director

The Producer has overall control of every aspect of the production process, working with the Director, the Scriptwriters, the Director of Photography (Cinematographer), Production Designer, Special Effects Supervisor and Visual Effects Supervisor in a careful planning process to bring the film to the cinema screen.

Art Department including Construction, Props and Set Dressing

The Production Designer, Art Director, Construction Manager, Props and Set Dresser work together to construct and create the style and atmosphere of the sets, both in the studio and on location.

Camera and Lighting including Grips

The Director of Photography, the Camera, Lighting and Grips crews work closely with the Director and Production Designer to maintain the consistent 'look and feel' of the film.

Hair and Make-Up including Prosthetics

The Hair and Make-up Designer and team work with the Director, the Production Designer and the Costume Designer to create the look that the Director wants to match to the period and content of the production using prosthetics, wigs and many other tricks and techniques.

Costume Department

The Costume Designer and team are responsible for all items of clothing worn by every performer appearing on screen. The Designer works closely with the Director, the Production Designer and Hair and Make-Up to set the style, character and overall tone of the production.

Production Sound Crew

The Sound Mixer, Boom Operators, Assistants and Technicians are responsible for recording all dialogue and sound effects on set.

Second Unit

The Second Unit (there can be more units on a large or stunt-driven film) is a fully operational and highly specialized shooting crew that looks after the filming of scenes, involving such things as special physical effects, stunts, action and aerial shots, motion capture, mattes and miniatures – in fact, anything out of the ordinary.

Special Physical Effects

The Special Physical Effects Supervisor and crew are highly skilled technicians and will work with the Director and Stunt Co-ordinator during pre-production and production to create the physical effects for the film – pyrotechnics, stunts and action, working models, mechanical and atmospherics.

Visual Effects

The Visual Effects Supervisor is a skilled VFX technician and will work closely with the Director and Art Department throughout pre-production, production and post-production to oversee all visual effects work carried out by the post-production facilities, with their highly skilled and creative teams.

Picture Post-Production including Visual Effects

The Post-Production Supervisor, with a team of Editors, works with the Director, Director of Photography, Sound and Visual Effects Supervisors to bring together all the elements of the film.

Sound Department including Post-Production, Sound Design and Music

The Sound Designer – or Supervising Sound Editor – works with the Post-Production Supervisor, the Director and the Composer to provide the film with its distinctive atmosphere for the complete audience experience.

Cinema Exhibition

This is the final stage for the finished feature film. There is a range of global cinema outlets from independent screens to major cinema chains.

Support Facilities

Throughout the film production world there is a whole range of companies that supply essential Equipment, Stock, Hardware and Software, Facilities and Service, Location Caterers, Location Transport, Freight Shipping and Travel, Specialist Materials and Chemicals. These support companies and their employees are highly skilled in their particular professions, although they are rarely mentioned in the credits.

INTRODUCTION

ABOUT THE AUTHOR

It was fifty years ago when I took my first steps into the film industry at Danziger Studios in Elstree. The first major studio I worked at was MGM, closely followed by Pinewood, which inevitably led to location projects – making the world my studio!

My family has a significant history within the film industry. My father, Frank Ackland-Snow, followed the steps of his older brother, Percy, and joined the film industry as a carpenter at Shepperton Studios. In the mid-1940s, the film industry went into depression due to World War II, so, in 1950, Frank and

Percy started a construction company called Ackland-Snow Limited. They worked on many shows, including *Doctor Who* and *Day of the Triffids*. Later on, when Art Director Scott McGregor asked my father if one of his sons could join him on a production, he suggested my brother Brian. Fortunately for me, although Brian went on to be a well-respected Production Designer, he was unable to commit at this time, so I eagerly took the job and began a long and rewarding career in film design. My son Dominic has since followed me into this wonderful industry, working as a Construction Manager on films such as *Kingsman 2* and *Alice Through the Looking Glass*, and my daughter is now a successful Graphics Artist.

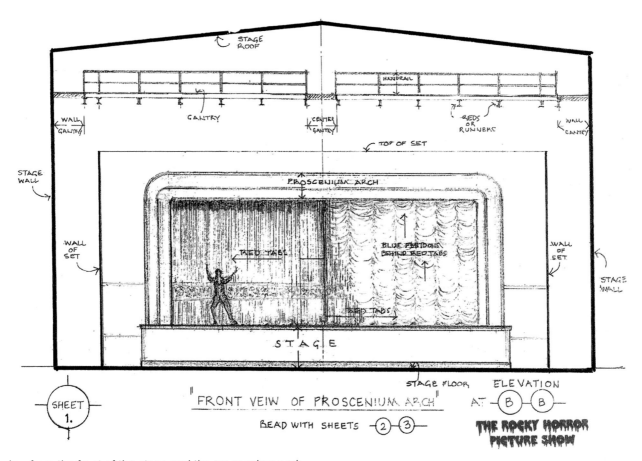

The view from the front of the stage and the proscenium arch.

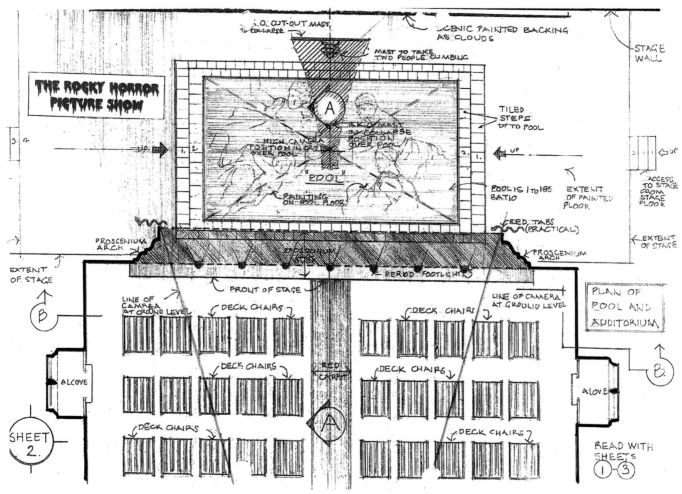

Sketch of the overhead aspect of the swimming pool and stage.

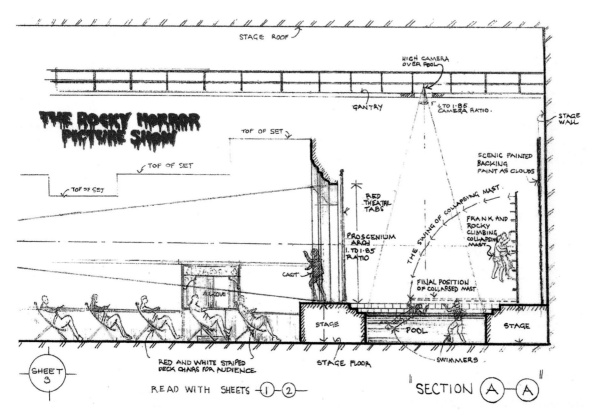

Showing the elevation of the swimming pool scene.

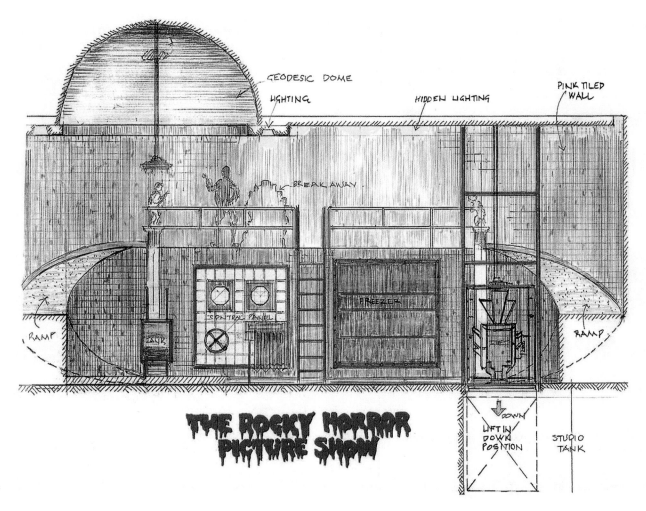

Sketch of Dr Frank-N-Furter's laboratory, showing the location of the freezer, the ramp and the breakaway wall – note the geodesic dome as part of the ceiling.

The Rocky Horror Picture Show

Rocky Horror was my first stint as an Art Director and, as such, is a good example of the responsibilities of this role and the types of methods I will be discussing in the book. The film became a classic and the impact of the design we produced speaks for itself as it is continually replicated to this day.

In 1975, I was settling into my job as Art Department Assistant on *The Rocky Horror Picture Show*, when I was called to a meeting advising me that the Art Director had left the picture due to other commitments. The discussion around the table was centred around who was going to take his place. The answer, much to my surprise, was 'Terry is!' So I was dropped into a senior role at the tender age of twenty-nine, in what was to become an iconic film. What luck! Not only was I quite young to take on such responsibility, but I found myself having to employ people who had, on previous productions, been my employers.

We filmed at Bray Studios, near Windsor, with a separate location in Oakley Court, which is an old manor house next to the studio. Bray was constructed by Hammer Film Productions around an eighteenth-century country house called Down Place in 1951. Hammer made its final film there in 1966, but the Studio and Oakley Court continued to be used by Special Effects teams for such productions as the St Trinian's films, *Half a Sixpence*, *Murder By Death*, the 1970s *Dr Who* television series, Gerry Anderson's *Space 1999*, as well as *The Rocky Horror Picture Show*.

One of the film's more memorable sequences features a character called Eddie crashing on a motorcycle through a block of ice in a giant freezer into the Doctor's laboratory. This needed a stuntman and clever work by the camera and grips to make it appear that the actor, Meatloaf, was actually on the bike. The original idea was that the motorbike and rider would be speeding around inside a Wall of Death – a fairground attraction built to resemble the inside of a huge drum or barrel where the bikes ride around at speed manoeuvring up and down the 'wall'.

This was deemed too dangerous, so I designed the idea

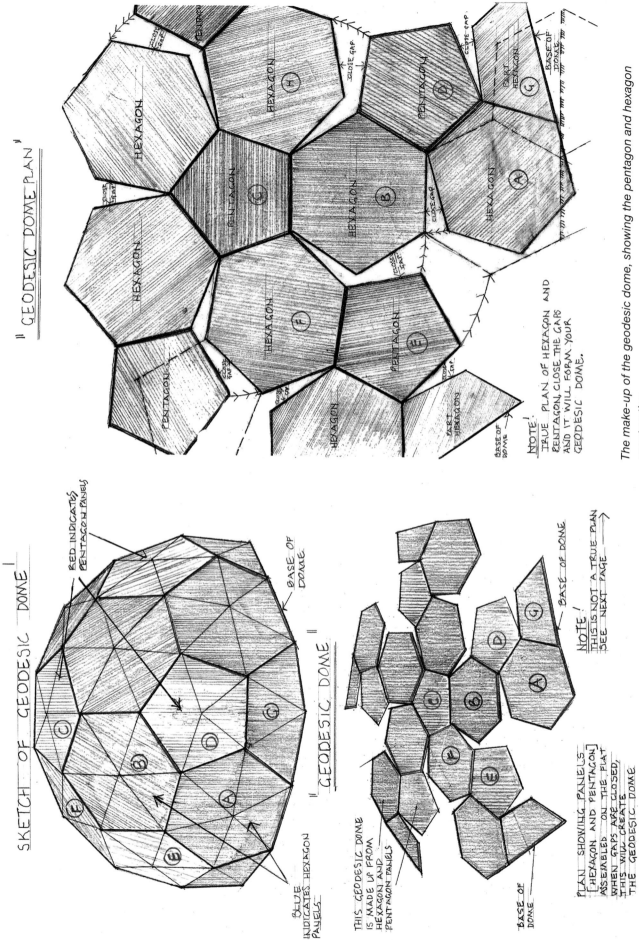

The make-up of the geodesic dome, showing the pentagon and hexagon construction.

The plan of Frank's laboratory, showing the freezer ramp down which the motorcycle enters the set and the Narrator's wheelchair.

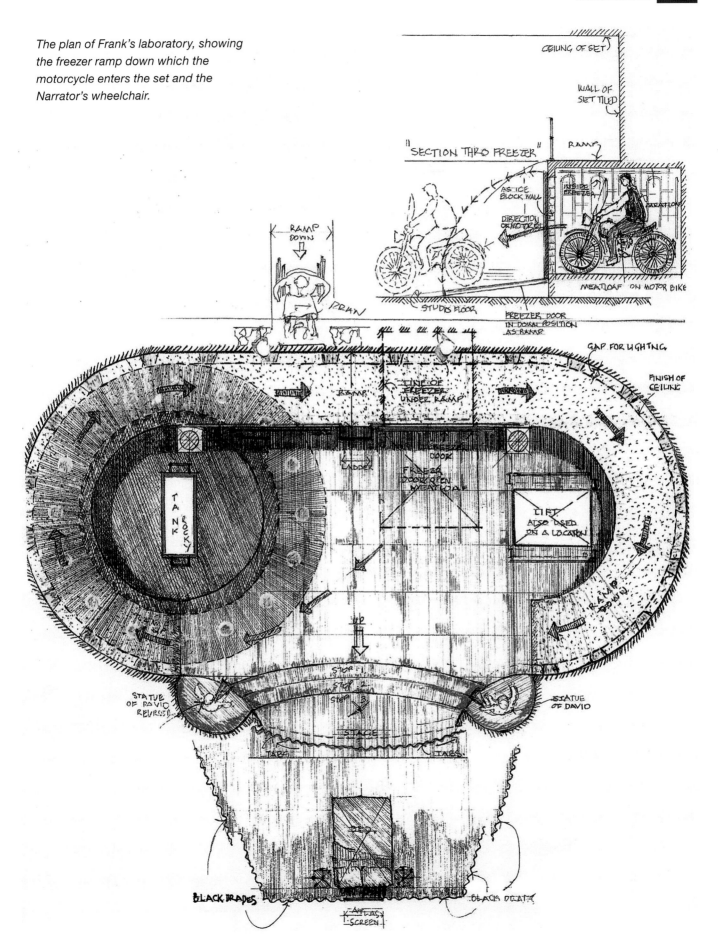

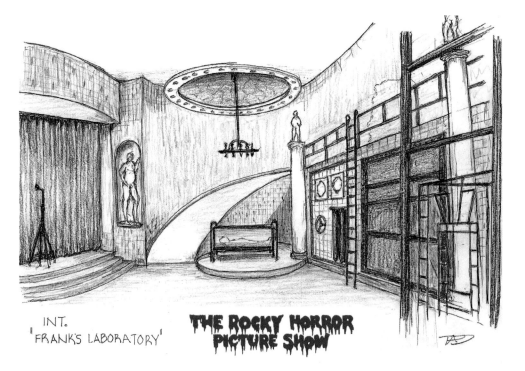

INT.
"FRANK'S LABORATORY"

THE ROCKY HORROR
PICTURE SHOW

Sketch of the interior of Frank's laboratory.

of a ramp in the laboratory, which would be much safer. This set-up was agreed, along with the colours of red and pink for the walls. I had the pink tiles made out of hardboard squares and painted in different shades of pink, applying the shades at random on the walls, which was the look I wanted to achieve. The freezer indicated on the plan and the elevation is where the performer rode the motorbike out of the freezer. We frosted both bike and actor with wax, which proved very effective.

A laboratory was constructed for Dr Frank-N-Furter, the main character. He also had a bed on a small stage as shown on

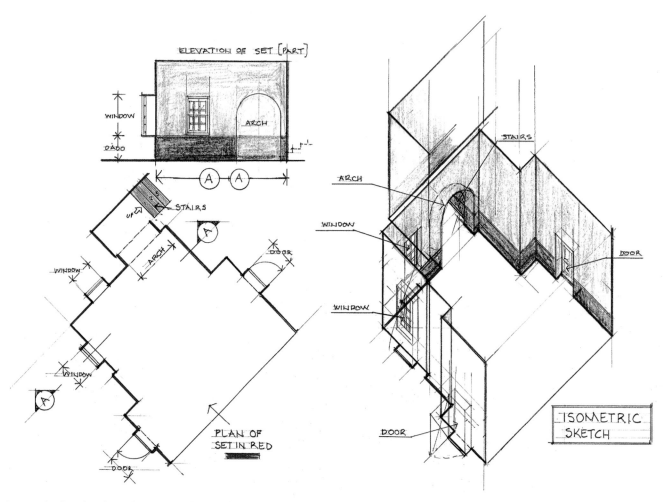

Isometric drawing from the plan and elevation. This can help to work out action on the set.

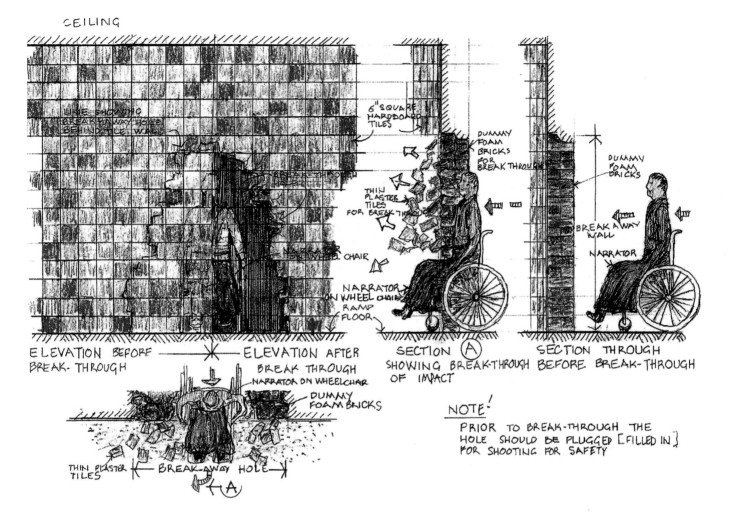

Sketch showing the construction of the breakaway wall and the progress of the wheelchair.

the plan, which had a breakaway wall. The tiles for this were made of thin plaster so that they would shatter easily and were painted in shades of pink to match the hardboard tiles. To build this, we first had to cut the breakaway area out of the flat, fill the hole with dummy bricks and then apply the pink tiles to match the existing ones. This breakaway is where the Narrator comes crashing through the wall on a wheelchair.

As part of the set there was a modified model of the Statue of David. There were two statues, one with the correct stance and another that was the opposite way round. The term for this mirror image is 'handed'.

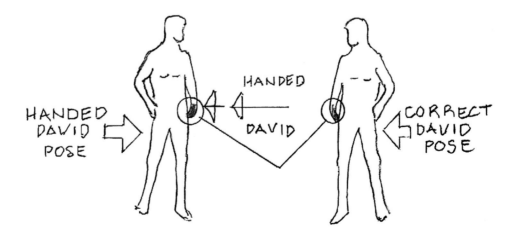

Explanation of the David 'handed' pose.

The street scene under construction at Pinewood.

The street under construction starting to be partially dressed.

Supergirl

Following *Rocky Horror*, I worked as Art Director on many films, including *Papillon*, *Death on the Nile*, *Aliens*, *Superman II* and *III*, *Supergirl*, *Labyrinth*, *Batman* and my favourite, as Underwater Art Director, *The Deep*, which we filmed on location in the Caribbean. Part of the job was learning how to dive – absolute heaven!

In every production, the Art Department has to be absolutely flexible and open to all influences from the outside world, which can be refined and redesigned to create the illusion the Director wants the viewing audience to experience. For *Supergirl*, we had to create Smallville, a mid-American town, with the appropriate built-in perspective. I went to the USA to recce in the mid-West and so realistic was our set when it was finished on the Pinewood Backlot that an American, who had come from a Texas fast-food franchise as a Set Dresser, got so engrossed in his job that he tried to walk off the edge of the set! Luckily there wasn't far to fall.

Later on, a prominent fuel company did not want its name used when a gas station was blown up for a stunt, so my initials are now immortalized on the screen as 'TAS Gas'. Every part of a film crew is utilized to their utmost during the production of a film and you have to be ready with answers, solutions and skills.

The street fully dressed with shop fronts and American vehicles.

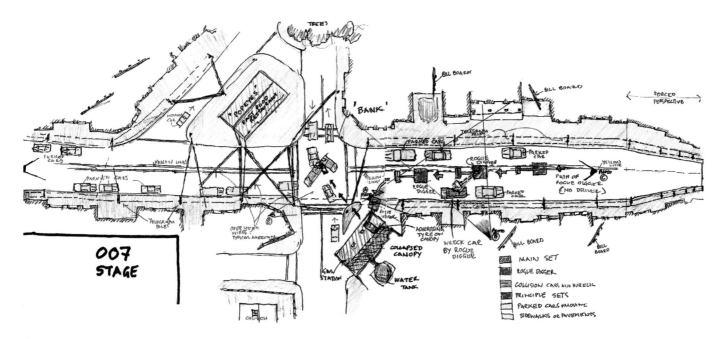

A draft sketch of the Supergirl *crash scene with the camera angles. Note that the street was ended in perspective to give the illusion of length.*

Zaltar's palace under construction.

The card model of the Smallville set with left to right: Art Director Terry Ackland-Snow, 'Supergirl' Helen Slater and Production Designer Richard MacDonald.

LEFT: One of the vehicles used in the crash scene, with left to right: Storyboard Artist Mike Ploog, Art Director Terry Ackland-Snow and Concept Artist Simon Murton.

BELOW LEFT: A celebratory drink on the set, with left to right: Director Jeannot Szwarc, Art Director Terry Ackland-Snow, Production Designer Richard MacDonald and Storyboard Artist Mike Ploog.

BELOW RIGHT: Ever immortalized as 'TAS Gas'. Note the crane in the middle of the street, which was used for the 'Supergirl' flying rig and Selena's Rolls-Royce.

TEACHING FILM DESIGN

In 2001, I started Film Design International in Pinewood Studios to offer draughtsmanship courses for the film and television industry. The courses are aimed at a wide range of Art Department professionals and university graduates who seek specific training in order to further their careers. Students are encouraged to 'go back to basics' and learn the traditional art of draughting and making scale models and miniatures, as well as CAD instruction (Computer-Aided Design) and an understanding of how a film crew works – especially in respect of construction and cinematography.

I really believe that, in order to maintain the art of draughtsmanship, existing practitioners should bridge the generational gaps between the traditional and the newer ways of doing things. The best way to achieve this is to have young people taught by the practitioners themselves, passing on their knowledge and experience gained over many years of working in the business. Those starting out in the industry must fully understand the role of the Art Director and the Art Department through basic knowledge in design, camera operation, direction and editing techniques – plus the all-important scheduling and budgeting requirements. The Art Department is unique within the film crew in that it runs its own budget during a production. So, to be a successful Art Director, not only do you have to be able to create and visualize, as well as control and inspire a team of people, but also have a full understanding of the financial and planning aspects involved.

This is a practical guide to Production Design – a term which has been credited to Producer David O. Selznick to describe the larger than life designs of William Cameron Menzies for the 1939 film *Gone with the Wind*. It literally means the creation of the physical world surrounding a film story.

Production Design uses the expertise and experience gained over many years to work out how the story of the script can be told in the space and time available, working to the Director's very specific instructions – and all this has to be achieved within the financial and scheduling restrictions put in place by the Producer. Although a background in art or design with an ability to sketch is a great advantage, this is only part of the job. Everyone in the Art Department must, to some degree and according to level of experience, have a working knowledge of the effect of lighting on the shade and saturation of the colours used on set on the costumes, make-up and construction materials. They also need to know how the camera will see the scene and how the various lenses will affect the picture and how much of it will be in focus. For example, with a telephoto lens, the foreground, middle or background pieces may be out of focus, so you might need to change the design choices. Accordingly, this book covers not only the skills and responsibilities of the Art Department, but also those of all the crews with which it comes into contact.

It has always been my aim to make sure that the new generation of filmmakers is fully apprised of the art of creating illusion on film. Having been in this industry long enough to witness all the changes myself, I believe it is so important to continue the outstanding work of the Art Department that has been developing over the last century. I also truly believe that, in order to make best use of the incredible technology available in today's market, the basic skills that created so many classics have to be absorbed and understood.

THE AUTHOR'S FILM AND TELEVISION CREDITS FROM 1962–2002

Film: *Masters of Venus; Richard the Lionheart; The Pink Panther; The Haunting; In the Cool of the Day; The Yellow Rolls-Royce; Carry On Cleo; A Shot in the Dark; Operation Crossbow; The Liquidator; On Her Majesty's Secret Service; Lady 'L'; Fahrenheit 451; Eye of the Devil; Blue Max; Half a Sixpence; 2001: A Space Odyssey; The Anniversary; Battle of Britain; Hoffman; Mr Forbush and the Penguins; Up Pompeii; The Man Who Had Power Over Women; Papillon; Tommy; The Rocky Horror Picture Show; The Return of the Pink Panther; Barry Lyndon; Sky Riders; The Deep; Death on the Nile; Medusa Touch; Arabian Adventure; Nijinsky; Superman II; The Great Muppet Caper; The Dark Crystal; Krull; Superman III; Pirates of Penzance; Supergirl; Spies Like Us; King David; Aliens; Living Daylights; Consuming Passions; Batman; Rainbow Thief; Doomsday Gun; Get Real; Bourne Identity; Dad's Army* (original film)*; It's all Happening; The Quest; Rocket to the Moon; Take Me High; Rebel Zone; Papa.*

Television: *The Avengers; Danger Man; Harry's Girls; Black Beauty; Shirley's World; Dick and Julie in Covent Garden; Dopple Clanger; Alternative 3; Inspector Morse Series 2, 3 and 5; Soldier, Soldier Series 1–6; Closing Numbers; Kavanagh Q.C.; SOS; Monsignor Rénard; Without Motive; Nell Gwynn* (theatre).

CHAPTER 1

THE ART DEPARTMENT

Feature film production is an industry full of multi-talented artists and artisans, but it is also a heavily financed and controlled business in every sense. It is not a career to enter into light-heartedly, so it is important to understand the pressures that will come with being part of a film production crew.

A professional film crew is a well-practised and creative machine where everyone shows up to work knowing exactly what to do and when to do it. In film production, every artist to some extent is a technician, using technology to turn ideas into reality. An educational environment is 'safe' by design, free from the unpredictable situations that working life throws at you and free from the need to make a living. There are very few people who can leave education fully capable of working in the professional film world as an accomplished creative or technician. That takes life experience, which can only be gained once you start working.

There are so many facets to the process of producing a film or a television drama that jobs, skills and technologies are very often intertwined. This book is all about working in the Art Department, which houses the people who create a film's look. They build sets and dress them. They have the skills of an architect, an artist, an interior designer and a world-class shopper. However, everyone in the Art Department must have a working knowledge of the skills and responsibilities of all the crews they come into contact with, because they will have a direct influence on the design process.

Essentially, the Art Department is the 'hub' around which the film crew works. It provides the creative template on which the other departments depend, providing a base for the exchange of creative ideas, where opinions and options are discussed and formalized. The work and planning undertaken in the Art Department enables the crew to build and create the illusion that the audience will see on the screen.

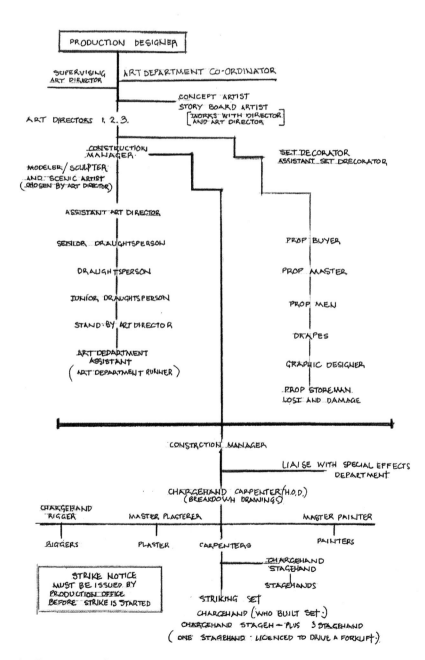

Art Department Structure.

THE ART DEPARTMENT STRUCTURE

The head of the Art Department is the Production Designer, who is fully supported by the Art Director. These two roles are often confused, so what is the difference? The Production Designer is in charge of everything artistic. He or she will have been chosen by the Director in the early days of pre-production as the most suitable for and the most compatible with the Director's vision for the film. They will work with the Director and the other Heads of Departments from pre-production right through until the final scene is captured.

The Art Director works directly for the Production Designer and looks after the Art Department on a day to day basis, including the Construction Crew, which can number 200–300 craftsmen and women on a major feature film.

Both the Production Designer and the Art Director will have worked their way through the various levels of the Art Department and, essentially, both will have a firm understanding of architecture and materials. However, the Production Designer does not necessarily need to have the same technical qualifications as the Art Director. The Production Designer creates the detailed sketches and drawings, both of interiors and exteriors, which then fall to the Art Director and his team to extend into blueprints for the Construction Manager to work from.

Within the Art Department, the Art Director is the leader, the translator of sketches and drawings into working blueprints, the intermediary between the Production Designer, Director and Construction Crew, as well as the protector of everyone working in his department. He will, in return, demand absolute loyalty and discretion from those around him.

The Director is the absolute 'boss' of the creative film crew, but how an individual Director interacts with the Art Department will depend on their personality. Some will only be concerned with the performances and the action on set and will leave much of the overall design and construction to the Production Designer and the Art Department, whilst others will be more 'visual' and want to have a hands-on approach. Whichever version of Director is in control of the film, the Art Director will have to be the ultimate diplomat, whatever the challenges.

The Production Designer and the Art Director are co-dependent. In any argument between the Designer and the Director regarding, for example, last-minute location or set changes

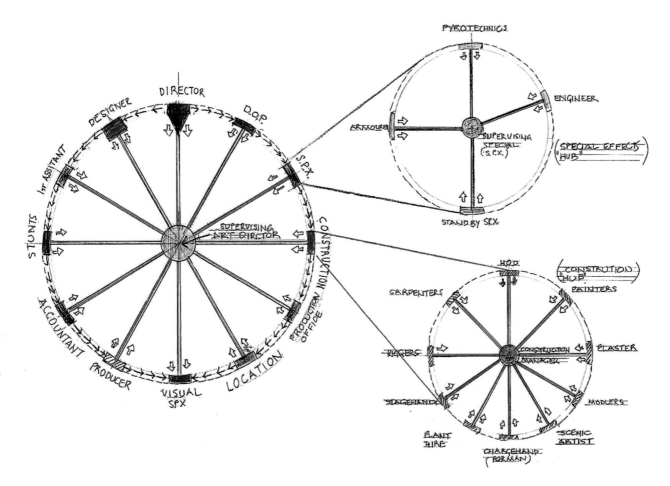

Art Department Structure showing how the Art Department 'hub' interacts with Special Physical Effects and Construction.

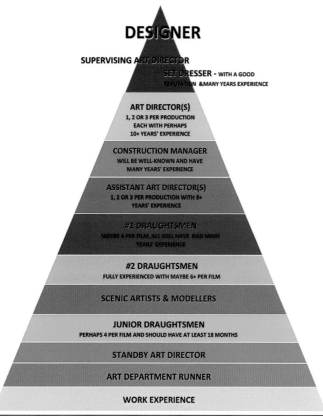

DESIGNER

SUPERVISING ART DIRECTOR

SET DRESSER – WITH A GOOD
REPUTATION &MANY YEARS EXPERIENCE

ART DIRECTOR(S)
1, 2 OR 3 PER PRODUCTION
EACH WITH PERHAPS
10+ YEARS' EXPERIENCE

CONSTRUCTION MANAGER
WILL BE WELL-KNOWN AND HAVE
MANY YEARS' EXPERIENCE

ASSISTANT ART DIRECTOR(S)
1, 2 OR 3 PER PRODUCTION WITH 8+
YEARS' EXPERIENCE

#1 DRAUGHTSMEN
MAYBE 4 PER FILM, ALL WILL HAVE HAD MANY
YEARS' EXPERIENCE

#2 DRAUGHTSMEN
FULLY EXPERIENCED WITH MAYBE 6+ PER FILM

SCENIC ARTISTS & MODELLERS

JUNIOR DRAUGHTSMEN
PERHAPS 4 PER FILM AND SHOULD HAVE AT LEAST 18 MONTHS

STANDBY ART DIRECTOR

ART DEPARTMENT RUNNER

WORK EXPERIENCE

LARGE FEATURE FILM
APPROXIMATE BREAKDOWN OF ART DEPARTMENT
CREW REQUIRED FOR A FILM PRODUCTION WITH A
BUDGET OF SAY £200m UP TO MANY MILLIONS

Breakdown of crew for a large-budget feature film.

that are already designated and well under way and which may be costly or tricky to reorganize, the Art Director should, very diplomatically, support the Designer with quick sketches, original material and, very importantly, budget and scheduling information, to back up the Designer's argument.

The final responsibilities of the Art Department are to the studios and locations where the sets will be constructed. Within the studio complexes, there will be specific rules and regulations that have to be taken into consideration. The same applies to locations, so the Art Director, with the Location Manager, has to have a basic knowledge of that country's laws, as well as the specific needs of the local regulations.

Many factors contribute to every image seen by the audience on the cinema screen and each department of the film unit bears responsibility for a particular aspect of the content. All will make their individual and collective contribution to the convincing portrayal

of the action and the story, bearing the responsibility of making sure that the overall concept adds to the cinematic illusion, so the relationship which the Designer and Art Director develop with the Director and the other Heads of Department is of critical importance.

There are many things to assimilate when you start working in film. Every production is a work of illusion, created over a period of time by a multitude of artists and craftsmen. The Art Department is going to be your home and the people working in and around it your family for the duration of the shooting process, so be prepared to work in close contact with this crew for twelve to eighteen hours a day, six to seven days a week, anywhere from three to six months in any one year. The ability to 'get on' with everyone is essential, not only to make your life as part of the crew easier, but a pleasant and willing personality makes you a much more employable asset to the Art Director when he chooses the crew for his next film.

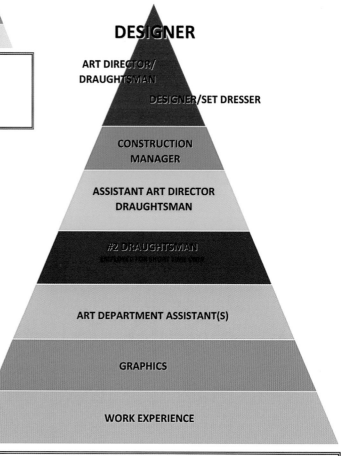

DESIGNER

ART DIRECTOR/
DRAUGHTSMAN

DESIGNER/SET DRESSER

**CONSTRUCTION
MANAGER**

**ASSISTANT ART DIRECTOR
DRAUGHTSMAN**

#2 DRAUGHTSMAN
EMPLOYED FOR SHORT TIME ONLY

ART DEPARTMENT ASSISTANT(S)

GRAPHICS

WORK EXPERIENCE

MEDIUM BUDGET FILM PRODUCTION
APPROXIMATE BREAKDOWN OF ART DEPARTMENT CREW
REQUIRED FOR A MEDIUM BUDGET PRODUCTION WITH
PERHAPS A COST OF £16m TO £20m

Breakdown of crew for a medium-budget film.

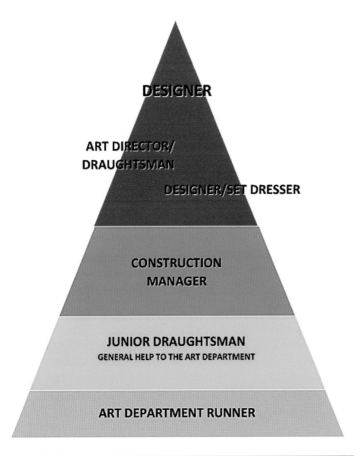

DESIGNER

ART DIRECTOR/ DRAUGHTSMAN

DESIGNER/SET DRESSER

CONSTRUCTION MANAGER

JUNIOR DRAUGHTSMAN
GENERAL HELP TO THE ART DEPARTMENT

ART DEPARTMENT RUNNER

SHORT FILM PRODUCTION

DEPENDING ON THE BUDGET, IT COULD BE A TWO DAY OR TWO WEEK SHOOT

Breakdown of crew for a low-budget short film.

UNDERSTANDING THE JOBS IN THE ART DEPARTMENT

Although initially working alone with the Director, the Designer will have to determine what resources he needs to realize the design necessary for the film. After the initial reading of the script, he will have a rough idea of the basic technical problems he will face and the Director's own interpretation will present other problems – such as insisting on using distant locations or extensive special effects.

However, the Designer will have a very skilled team of technicians and craftsmen and women to help him. The following is a list of the primary categories of these professionals and a breakdown of their responsibilities.

* Please note that the following titles marked with an asterisk are generic terms and are used to describe both male and female practitioners. All roles can be filled by either a man or a woman and references to 'he' are for convenience only.

Production Designer

As a major Head of Department, the Production Designer works very closely with the Director, Art Director, Construction Manager, Costume and Make-up Designers and the Director of Photography, playing a crucial role in helping the Producer and Director to achieve the visual requirements of the film.

A great deal of work and imagination from the Art Department goes into constructing the appropriate backdrop to any story and into selecting and constructing the appropriate sets. Working from the script or screenplay, the Designer assesses the visual qualities that will create the right atmosphere for the performers to bring the story to life. After preparing a careful breakdown of the script, Production Designer meets with the Director to discuss how best to shoot the film – whether to use studio sets and/or locations; what should be built and what could be adapted; whether there is a visual theme that recurs throughout the film; whether there are certain design elements that may give an emotional or psychological depth to the film; and when and where special physical effects and visual effects (CGI) should be used. These discussions are followed by an intense period of research, during which the Production Designer and his Specialist Researchers source ideas from books, photographs, fine art and the internet.

In the pre-production stage, the Production Designer illustrates his vision for each set and location with sketches and models as a guide. These illustrations will outline a colour palette, period, texture and tone to which everyone adheres. Working closely with the Producer and Director, the Designer narrows down the requirements and sets the Art Department budget.

During principal photography, the Production Designer acts as a co-ordinator to maintain the overall aesthetic vision. They influence decisions made by the Lighting, Wardrobe, Hair and Make-up and Special Effects Departments.

Supervising Art Director

The Supervising Art Director acts as the 'eyes and ears' of the Production Designer and the Art Department on big-budget films. The sheer complexity of the work and the speed of feature film production mean that it is often unrealistic for the Production Designer to depend on one Art Director to cover all the sets. Big science-fiction epics or action films might have several locations, using second and third shooting units, plus models and miniatures and action sequences, all of which may require dedicated Art Directors, who will work under the watchful eye of the Supervising Art Director.

Construction Manager

The Construction Manager is the Head of Department for the Construction Crew and is responsible for interpreting the Art

Department's plans and designs to establish the number of sets required, their size, design, colour and texture – and to turn those blueprints into fully functional film sets.

Hired by the Production Designer to oversee the entire process of set building, from initial planning through to the final coat of paint on the finished sets, they will employ Heads of Department for Carpentry, Scenic Painting, Ornamental Plastering and Rigging. These will usually be people with whom the Designer will have worked on many films and for many years, trusting them implicitly to do the best job. The Heads of Department, in turn, will employ their own crews. (*See* Chapter 3 for full Construction Crew Breakdown.)

The Art Director

The Art Director is essentially the Project Manager of the Art Department and works directly for the Production Designer, the Head of Department. They need to have a good eye for decoration and detail, the ability to think visually, to conceptualize ideas and be able to bring these ideas into tangible form. Art Directors must understand fully how sets and props will interact with the cast, as well as with lighting, special effects and roving cameras. They have to find practical solutions to creative problems, whilst simultaneously monitoring the budget and a large crew, often over multiple studio sets and locations. This is a job that demands a highly qualified and very creative person, who is also a very effective and respected leader.

The Art Director's work starts in pre-production, working closely with the Production Designer to analyse the script so that blueprints are produced, which the Construction Manager will use to assess the level of crew and materials needed for the construction and dressing of the various sets, both in the studio and on location. This information is vital for the Art Department budget, which the Producer and his team need to assess in order to determine the overall finances required for the production.

Assistant Art Director

Working directly for the Art Director, the Assistant's responsibilities will vary according to the size of the production. On smaller films, they help the Art Director with a wide range of jobs including Art Department research, finding props, surveying locations, modelmaking and helping to produce blueprints. Big-budget films will involve the design and build of many complicated sets, both in the studio and on location, so a number of Art Directors may be employed, all working on individual sets throughout pre-production and production, each with their own teams.

Art Department Co-ordinator

The Co-ordinator is the link between the Production Office and the Art Department. Working with the Production Manager, he performs a crucial role in making sure that the Art Depart-

ment budget is kept under control, as well as providing the day to day administration and support to keep the department running efficiently. If you are just as comfortable around spreadsheets and budgets as with a sketch pad and pencil, then this is the job for you!

*Chief Draughtsman

The Chief Draughtsman is in charge of all the draughting and will be well versed in the use of lenses and the layout of the sets and construction, with knowledge of engineering and decorative detail. He will be able to lay out matte shots and create models.

*Draughtsman (UK) or Draftsman/Drafter (USA)

This is the person who makes the detailed technical drawings or plans for any structure on set. In the USA, the 'Drafter' may also be referred to as 'Set Designer', but this is not to be confused with the Production Designer.

In film production, the Draughtsman's drawings and blueprints provide visual and structural guidelines for the Construction Manager and the Construction Heads of Department, specifying dimensions and materials, using additional drawings, sketches, specifications and calculations.

The Draughtsmen will have to use their knowledge of standard building techniques to produce details of the structure, but they will also have to be creative enough to adapt the Designer's concept into a very practical form, as most film sets will be required to carry the full weight of people and equipment. They will be asked to create technical drawings for many unexpected things – from moving sets to accommodate action sequences to imaginary vehicles and machinery for science fantasy and fiction films.

A Draughtsman must have excellent technical drawing skills. A working knowledge of architecture, fine art and graphics is essential and experience in Theatre Production Design is also useful. Once fully trained, the Draughtsman will be expected to have expert knowledge of all building materials and construction techniques, including a good comprehension of period buildings and the techniques involved. He should also have a thorough understanding of what Directors and Directors of Photography require from film sets in terms of light and camera angles.

*Junior Draughtsman

A Junior Draughtsman will initially be given specific construction details to look after. These could be details around windows and doors, or perhaps helping to build the card miniature that the Designer, the Director and the Cinematographer might need in order to work out camera angles and so on.

Standby Art Director

This role is usually a Junior Art Director who monitors the Art

Department's work on set during filming on behalf of the Art Director. As such, they are responsible for dealing with any changes or improvements to the set during shooting. They work closely with the Set Decorator and the Standby Construction Crew to co-ordinate these alterations with the Art Department. The Standby will be ready to organize any repair, alteration or replacement as necessary, often at the direct request of the Director or the Cinematographer, who may need something changed very quickly before a scene is shot, or repaired if any damage has been caused by the action during the shoot.

Art Department Assistant

As with most jobs in film production, the best way to gain knowledge is to begin with hands-on experience, working at junior levels as an Art Department Assistant. This gives you time to understand properly how film production works, as it's a very different environment to any 'domestic' job. This is the entry-level role for this highly creative team. Being an Assistant or Runner in any of the departments is a brilliant job, as it is the only time in your career when you will have the opportunity to watch the professionals at work, to ask all the basic questions and to absorb as much information as possible, without having a massive amount of responsibility.

Sketch Artist (Storyboard Artist)

The Sketch/Storyboard Artist is to the Director what the Concept Artist is to the Production Designer. First used in the epic *Gone with the Wind* in 1939, the Storyboard Artist is now an integral part of the feature film production team. They tell the story in pictures and help the Director to show his team what he is planning, what the team will need to do and what they are going to try to achieve. So, the Storyboard Artist has to be very skilled, perceptive and 'quick on the draw'.

In many ways, comic books are the art form that most closely resembles cinema – they both tell stories in a primarily visual form. Think of the way a comic book tells a complex story by using a sequence of static images in a very stylized way. This is exactly what the Director needs in order to plan action that cannot be left to on-set improvisation.

The Storyboard Artist translates screenplays, or sequences from screenplays, into a series of illustrations in this comic-book form. These illustrations have two functions – to help the Director to clarify exactly what he wants to achieve and to illustrate to all other Heads of Department exactly what is required, for example prosthetics for Make-up, visual effects, special physical effects and props for the Art Department.

Set Dresser/Decorator

The Set Decorator is responsible for converting the blank canvas of the set into a space that feels authentic, lived-in and believable. They deal in the details – the fine touches that reveal the personalities of the people who live in the country house, the Eastern palace, or the broken-down beach hut on a Pacific island.

It is the small details that often tell the audience most about the characters and the style of the production, such as pictures hanging on the walls, the contents of the fridge or bathroom cabinet, the books and the treasured objects that are kept in a box in the desk drawer. All this is created by the imagination and creative flair of the Set Decorator, who researches, prepares and oversees the dressing of every set and adapted location. In television or on commercials, they are called Stylists.

The props that the Set Decorator provides are non-structural. They include:

- Dressing Props – wall hangings, drapes, flooring
- Hand Props – anything picked up or held by the actors
- Hero Props – objects central to the action
- Stunt Props – replicas made of soft material such as furniture or bottles that will be smashed
- Mechanical Props – anything that might move or be illuminated.

All of these help to bring characters to life, or to give a certain atmosphere and sense of period to a set.

*Property Master/Prop Master

The Property, or Prop Master, heads up the Property Department and is responsible for any and all hired, manufactured or purchased props. The Property Department procures and makes dressings for the set – interiors and exteriors such as furniture, equipment, machinery, farm, garden and rural items, as well as the smaller paraphernalia. The Set Dresser, Property Master, Property Buyer and Greensman work as a team and are always in close contact with the Art Director, Director and Assistant Director.

The work begins during pre-production when the Prop Master joins the preliminary design meetings with the Director, Production Designer, Costume Designer and other Heads of Department to establish the aesthetic of the production and to ensure a cohesive look throughout the film. The script is then broken down, scene by scene, to identify the props required, which props can be rented or purchased and which must be specially fabricated – and so the props budget is calculated.

During principal photography, the Prop Master and his Assistants direct their crew in staging props (laying out items in preparation for a scene) and distributing necessary props to the cast. After a take, the crew might reset the props for another take, or strike the set and move on to the next set-up. For continuity, the Prop Master or Assistant will take photographs of each scene and where the props are placed, co-ordinating with the Script Supervisor for the purposes of pickup shots and editing. Photos are also kept to maintain inventory records and to identify quickly each piece assigned to the production.

Standby Props One and Two

Standby Number One stays with the camera crew, organizing any adjustments to the set dressing to the camera crew's requirements and checking the positioning of props on a monitor. They are also available to advise the performers on the use of any specific prop. Standby Number Two is his assistant and carries out any adjustments necessary.

Property or Production Buyer

If you enjoy rummaging around antique fairs and car boot sales, trying to find the unusual and obscure, then you might be just right for the job of Production or Props Buyer. This is the ideal job for a professional shopper – searching markets, arcades, rental houses, jumble sales and auction sites for the props and set dressings that transform a newly built set into a convincing and atmospheric environment. Working in the Property Department, the Production Buyer starts the job during pre-production, carefully reviewing the script with the Property Master and Set Decorator to identify all action and dressing props required.

During principal photography, the Production Buyer will spend most of his time in the Production Office, checking up on deliveries, confirming returns and hunting down last-minute additions. On a low-budget film, the Production Buyer might also stand in as the Assistant Set Decorator.

Graphics Artist

The Graphics Artist produces all the film props that contain graphic items, such as money, newspapers, magazines, handwritten or typed letters, musical scores, books, maps, shop signage, menus, credit cards and passports. The audience should be completely unaware that these items used by the characters on screen are not genuine articles but clever reproductions.

Working closely with the Production Designer, Property Master, Standby Props and the Art Director, the Graphics Artist manufactures printed props, carefully crafted to reflect the period and setting in which the story unfolds. Ensuring that these printed props appear as realistic as possible is a highly specialized job. The role is creative but work is sporadic and most Graphics Artists work not only on a wide range of films and television programmes, but also in the commercial world.

Concept Artist

Generally working on big-budget sci-fi, fantasy or historical films, the job of a Concept Artist (sometimes referred to as an Illustrator) is to take an abstract idea and turn it into a tangible image. Starting in the early stages of pre-production, the Concept Artist begins to work with the Director and Production Designer to produce a selection of sketches. These could be of building facades and interiors for the Designer, or the look of suggested alien faces for the Director and the Special Effects Make-up Artist, or fantasy creatures and imaginary landscapes for both the Special Physical Effects and Visual Effects Supervisors.

The Concept Artist, from suggestions by the Director and Production Designer or other creative Heads of Department, is able to focus in on the keywords of the idea and then produce multiple versions of the necessary drawing. He will experiment with different colour palettes and styles so that the Director and Production Designer can choose which they prefer and offer suggestions for revision. The Concept Artist will repeat this process until a final concept is agreed upon.

*Drapesmaster

Working with the Production Designer, Set Decorator and Property Master, the Drapesmaster is responsible for the production and installation of all soft furnishings on set, such as curtains, carpets, blinds, upholstered furniture, drapery and scenic backing (on which the Scenic Artists paint backgrounds), as well as the interiors of any cars, carriages and boats that feature in the film. These 'drapes' are either designed, produced or sourced by a team of highly skilled *Drapesmen, whose work is organized and overseen by the Drapesmaster, usually working out of a Drapes Shop situated within the studio complex for the duration of the production.

Miniatures Builder (UK) or Modeler (USA)

The Miniatures Builder works with all types of wood, metal and plastic, including fibreglass and other casting materials, to make three-dimensional scale models that can be anything from two-thirds life-size to tiny models for an animation set. The job spans the Art, Effects, Camera and Construction Departments, making model sets of venues that may be too expensive to hire for the shoot – say, a stately home or theatre, an ancient galleon or perhaps something that needs to be destroyed as part of the action.

The process for constructing models and miniatures begins long before the shoot is scheduled to take place. Instructions can be as simple as rough sketches, or as complex as specific designs and the Miniatures Builder has to work out not only how their models will look on film, but also to make sure that they are historically and culturally accurate.

Specialist Researcher

There is usually only one Specialist Researcher required on period films or fantasy productions. The role involves working closely with and providing research back-up to the entire Art Department. This may involve anything from finding a specific visual reference that will define a set, or sourcing intricate detailing that enables the Draughtsmen to produce accurate technical drawings, right through to researching a specific craft or skill that might be needed to make a prop. The Specialist

Researcher supports the Production Designer in ensuring that every detail on set – which can range from the interior of a spaceship to the contents of a country cottage – is as authentic and believable as possible. On fantasy films, although the sets are often part of an imagined world, the references used to inspire the Production Designer's and Concept Artist's ideas are usually researched and sourced from the real world. On historical epics or costume dramas, painstaking research into the smallest detail is crucial and it can often take long periods of time spent in libraries, museums and online.

Examples of card models built by the Art Department.

*Greensman

The Greensman supplies plants and natural scenery of all descriptions from all parts of the world (regardless of season) and a wide selection of all things horticultural. A Greensman is a horticultural expert – a Set Dresser with specialized skills. He uses that expertise to create landscapes from the ground up, to disguise and decorate interiors and exteriors with plants and flowers to suit the requirements of the Production Designer and the script.

CARD MODELS

Although there are very efficient modelling software packages available, the traditional method of creating three-dimensional card models is still widely used throughout the design process. See the images of card models for very fine and detailed examples of the skills and patience required.

Aspects of the interior of a finished card model.

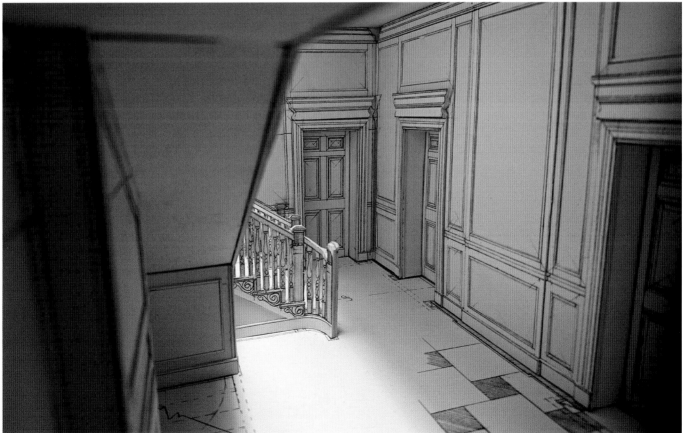

Aspects of the interior of a finished card model.

Aspects of the interior of a finished card model.

Sections of a card model under construction showing the perspectives that will be required for the set build.

TECHNOLOGY

During my career, the tools available to me, and which I used on all my films, were my pen and drawing board. The ethos behind starting Film Design International was to make sure that anyone entering the world of set design, whether for film, theatre or television, was fully conversant with the traditional methods. These methods allow the student to understand fully how everything works together and how the subsequent technology evolved. Once the traditional skills have been honed, then technology is a valuable tool that can really enhance the work of the Art Department. Computer-Aided Design (CAD) is now widely used by design teams on a daily basis in tandem with hand-draughting. The following article will discuss the current software programs used in the industry and how to select the best one to achieve the end product.

Section of a card model under construction showing the perspectives that will be required for the set build.

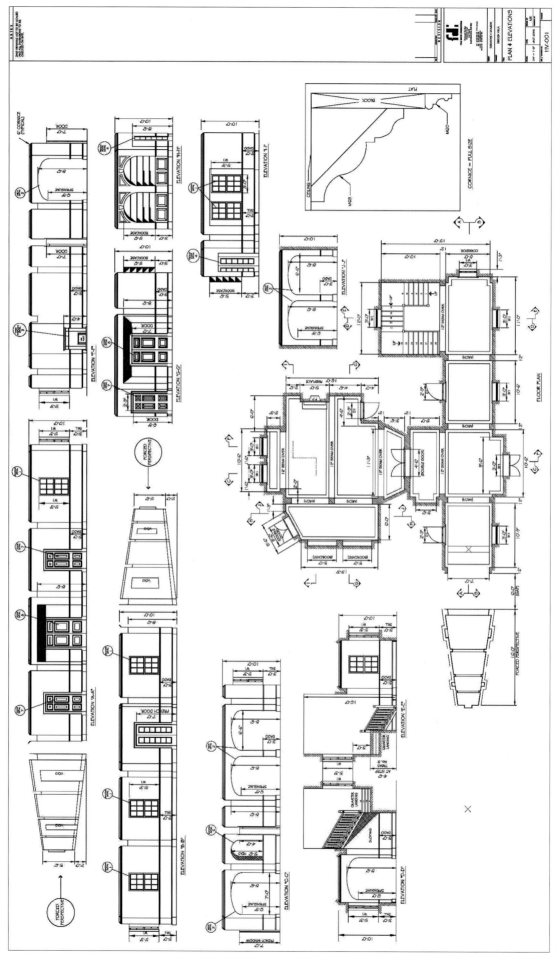

Plan and elevation drawings for office and corridor set in AutoCAD.

FILM: THE GOLDEN PALM   SET: WOODY FRED'S OFFICE

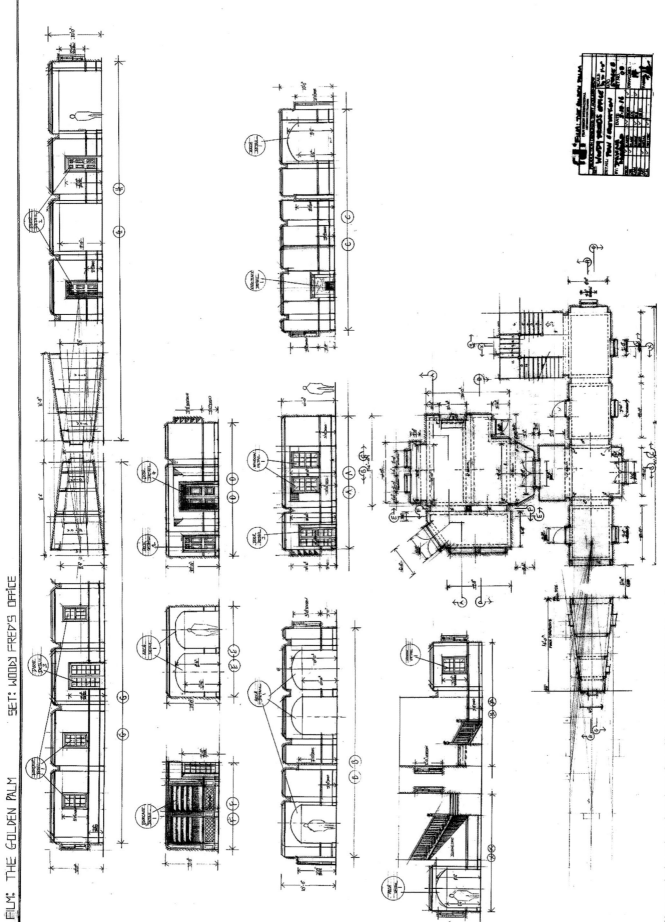

Plan and elevation drawings for office and corridor set hand-drawn.

PROFESSIONAL PERSPECTIVE: FDI GRADUATES

Film Design International graduates Andy Proctor, Dorrie Young, Tim Dutton, Liam Georgensen and Molly Sole have all worked extensively with the Visual Effects and Special Effects Departments on their films. Their combined credits since graduating include: *Rogue One: A Star Wars Story; Star Wars: The Force Awakens; Cinderella; The Edge of Tomorrow; Jack Ryan: Shadow Recruit; World War Z; Wrath of the Titans; Sherlock Holmes: A Game of Shadows; Prince of Persia: The Sands of Time; Robin Hood; Moon; Stardust; Charlie and the Chocolate Factory; Harry Potter series (The Sorcerer's Stone; The Prisoner of Azkaban; The Goblet of Fire; The Order of the Phoenix; The Half-Blood Prince; The Deathly Hallows Parts 1 and 2); Saving Private Ryan; Justice League; Fantastic Beasts and Where to Find Them; The Legend of Tarzan; The Man from U.N.C.L.E.; Prometheus; Snow White and the Huntsman; Wrath of the Titans; Robin Hood; The Imaginarium of Doctor Parnassus; Miss Pettigrew Lives for a Day; Fred Claus; The Da Vinci Code; Revolver; Separate Lies.*

A BASIC GUIDE TO USING CAD IN ART DEPARTMENTS

Whilst the audience might think that Computer-Aided Design (CAD), as used in film production, is the same as the Computer-Generated Imagery (CGI) that you see in the finished film, everyone working in the Art Department is fully aware that CAD is just another tool for the design team to use, helping to enhance the traditional methods of draughting and modelmaking. The traditional methods of set building are still the best way to create believable environments, with computer-generated elements added in post-production in order to enhance and extend the often stunning in-camera sets and action.

Over the past twenty years, the Visual Effects (VFX) and Art Departments have worked more and more closely, bridging the gap between real life and digital environments. Sets are now often built to incorporate green and blue screens so that they can be seamlessly extended in post-production.

To this end, a mixture of traditional and new methods is employed with each Art Department member, using a combination of hand-draughting on a drawing board together with digital draughting and 3D modelling on a computer. Most Supervising Art Directors are happy to leave it to the judgement of a Draughtsman or Art Director to choose when to work on the drawing board and when to turn to the computer. In fact, many Draughtsmen would choose to work in pencil wherever possible, although even when a pencil drawing is in progress, CAD can still be useful and a particularly complex drawing will often mean moving between computer and board. This can be when working out complex geometry, checking a dimension is accurate, or establishing a curve where the radius point lies off the drawing board, for example. Almost every member of the Art Department will use some form of CAD on a daily basis for efficiency.

The genre of the film very much dictates the best tools to use, be it pencil or digital. For example, organic sets such as jungle environments, which require dense foliage and crumbling ruins, or period films like Cinderella, featuring Baroque and Rococo architecture, lend themselves best to hand-drawn methods, which allow for a fluidity of style that most Art Department members prefer.

However, for science-fiction films or instances of repetitive, modular architecture, a computer-aided approach can prove to be the best choice. Furthermore, if the Art Department is working in conjunction with the Special Effects (SFX) Department, involving elements of engineering or companies providing 3D printing and Computer Numerical Control (CNC) cutting services, then easily sharable and compatible computer files help to keep the Art Department's creative vision intact.

There are many software programs in today's creative world and it can often be hard to know which ones you need to learn in order to remain useful. Like most technologies, computers and software are being developed and improved constantly. How best to keep up with this progress from the Art Department's point of view is a commonly asked question. As with most things, it largely comes down to personal preference.

First and foremost, it is very important to have a comprehensive understanding of more traditional methods. The fundamentals of hand-drawing, how to read scales and proportion, knowing what plans and elevations are and learning about classical architecture make up the foundation of Art Department knowledge. This means that you are not relying on a computer to draw and work out elements such as a traditional moulding, where the computer tools will not follow the subtle shapes and rules required.

There are so many types of CAD programs and it can be difficult to know which are worth learning. Most programs provide a range of techniques, but there are those that build 3D models using less memory from your computer, or produce better rendered images than others, whilst some are better for 2D drawings.

Firstly, think about what you want your end product to be. Are there only 2D architectural drawings required, or will you need 3D-rendered visuals and files for 3D printing and CNC manufacture? Because of the ever-changing nature of technology, the program suggestions I outline will change in time; however, the process to making the program selection will not. Below are some of the more popular programs currently used in the Art Department.

Vectorworks is an advanced draughting program used to produce highly detailed 2D drawings and 3D models. In the Art Department, a high proportion of computer draughting is done with Vectorworks because it is easy to click and draw with the mouse or drawing tablet, rather than inputting co-ordinate or dimension data. Many people use it simply as a 2D drawing package.

However, some people also like to model in Vectorworks and then section the model to create plans and elevations in what are called Viewports. Working in this way means that when you revise and update the model, the Viewports containing your plans and sections will update automatically as well. This method can cause the file to become very large because your complex 3D models, elevations and sections are all contained in one file. However, this can be prevented by using accurate and thorough modelling to keep the file size down.

AutoCAD was one of the original CAD draughting packages and is a very good software program for producing highly detailed 2D drawings and 3D models. Because it was one of the original CAD packages, it has generally been the standard used by industries outside of the film industry.

AutoCAD and Vectorworks are virtually interchangeable. While Vectorworks is currently the most commonly used program in the Art Department, a fair proportion of Draughtsmen use AutoCAD. Similar to Vectorworks, AutoCAD is an extremely effective 2D and 3D modelling program that can be used to produce 2D drawings from 3D models, or to create 2D drawings from scratch. It is also good for creating CNC files and other outsourced manufactured elements.

SketchUp is a simple but very effective 3D program, providing a good tool to create quick 3D models that can then be rendered and enhanced with Photoshop or by hand. Many Draughtsman and Art Directors find it extremely useful for quickly communicating ideas for stage layouts or minimal set builds for locations. It has a very readable, graphic look, which is important when conveying designs and ideas, particularly to other departments on a film. It is also cheaper than most other software packages. A very basic version is available for free, which is useful for learning the program. The full Pro version includes a feature called Layout, which is a quick and effective draughting tool.

Rhino is a 3D modelling program that has rapidly become more popular within the Art Department and many people are now using it. It offers a number of advanced modelling techniques and tools and Rhino files can be exported easily to other programs and also to 3D printers.

Maya is one of many programs used in the Visual and Special Physical Effects Departments. Although this program is aimed mainly at the gaming industry, some Art Department Draughtsmen and Art Directors use it as a 3D draughting tool too.

Some people prefer to switch between programs for modelling and draughting, such as importing line work from Rhino into Vectorworks. This again comes down to personal preference and which programs you find easier and more intuitive to use. In some tasks, a Vectorworks file can be exported as a DWG file (a proprietary binary file format used in design) and imported to AutoCAD (which tends to be the outside industry standard) and other 2D programs. In other cases, a watertight 3D model can be required for CNC-ing large set pieces or vehicle bodies, so Rhino would be useful for achieving this.

Another strength of computer draughting is the ability to produce multiple documents at different scales with the same format and to make alterations quickly. Stage plans often need updating at a moment's notice and CAD is ideal for achieving this. Being able to move plans of every set on every stage of a film and to quickly calculate greenscreen lengths or set finish areas is incredibly valuable to Art Directors. It would be wise for anyone getting into the industry to have experience with Vectorworks, even if they don't want to use it as a way of producing their drawings; it is often so ubiquitous and useful for sharing information with other departments.

Draughting on computers does offer up the possibility of extremely accurate and detailed models and drawings, but, just like draughting by hand, it is still extremely important to be mindful of your dimensioning and notes. With care and experience, it is possible to produce very complex and beautiful drawings, but it takes patience to mimic the variable line weights, shading and fluidity of traditional hand-draughting.

Outside of draughting, many Concept Artists work with a variety of specific programs. Some predominantly use Photoshop, although if modelling architecture or props they will tend to use a mixture of SketchUp, Cinema 4D, Modo or even ZBrush for sculpting with more organic textures.

The workflow varies depending on the speed at which the work needs to be completed and the level of accuracy or detail required to sell the visual or object. If time permits, a Concept Artist will model the object in 3D, possibly importing a 2D Vectorworks plan or other assets from an Art Director or Draughtsman. The end result will often be rendered in programs such as Keyshot or Podium for SketchUp, with Photoshop used for finishing touches.

You will never really stop learning any of the computer programs that you choose to use. The collective sharing of skills and knowledge throughout Art Departments means that as the software progresses, so do individuals. Learning one computer program is like learning a new language – once you master one, it becomes easier to pick up others. So initially it doesn't matter what software you learn, just learn it well and comprehensively.

The future will arrive fast in the CAD world, with more and more immersive visualization packages already available. The time will come when a Designer or Director can walk on to an empty sound stage and see a virtual set design within the space, or VFX extensions added on to a finished set, or location in real time.

CHAPTER 2

THE PRODUCTION OFFICE AND THE ART BUDGET

Every department in the film production process works under the watchful eye of the Producer and his or her team in the Production Office. The Producer 'owns' the film from the moment he obtains the script until it ceases to be shown in any format, anywhere in the world.

The Production Office controls every aspect of the production process from script to screen and beyond. Although the Director and his or her team are part of the Production Office and have creative responsibility for the film, the office itself contains financial and legal people who have the unenviable task of looking after the many millions of pounds or dollars that have been invested, as well as the good name of all concerned.

THE FOUR MAIN AREAS IN FEATURE FILM PRODUCTION

Pre-Production or Read-Through for Technicians

This is the time span between the Producer finding a script he likes, right through to the time that the Director walks on to the set and starts filming.

The pre-production process may take many months and will include meetings involving the Producer, Writer, Financial Controller, Director, Production Designer, Art Director, Cinematographer, Visual Effects Supervisor, Special Effects Supervisor, Post-Production Supervisor – and all other Heads of Department. The Storyboard Artist, who works alongside the Director but under the management of the Art Department, will be called in to illustrate scenes from the script so that the Director's desired style can be fully discussed. In the case of science fiction and fantasy films, the Graphic Artist will be asked to visualize certain fantastic characters. These characters may be produced as Animatronics filmed as live action, or as visual effects introduced into the film during the post-production process – whatever the Director decides is appropriate for the style of the film.

Also at this time a Casting Agent will be involved and the lead actors and actresses will be discussed and approaches made via their agents. The cost of the cast will have a significant impact on the budget, but selecting well-known stars will also encourage a higher level of financial investment. Well-seasoned filmmakers will also include the Music Supervisor, as the music track is a most important part of the final audience experience. At this time the Producer will have already made approaches to the Distributors, as having a prospective outlet for the production is key to raising the necessary finance.

Production

Although the Producer is still in charge of the overall project and in ultimate charge of the budget, the Director now takes over control of the production process. The Director of Photography (Cinematographer) will have selected his Camera Crew, Lighting Technicians (Sparks), Grips and Riggers, as well as equipment and suppliers. The Production Designer and Art Director will have recruited the Construction Manager, who, in turn, will select his Construction Heads of Department – Carpentry, Plastering and Painting.

The Costume Designer and the Hair and Make-up Designer will bring their own teams together. If the film includes any special physical effects for action sequences, then the Special Effects Supervisor will choose his crew. Depending on the method (film or digital), the laboratory will transfer the original footage into a format required by the Editor and Post-Production Department. All this has to be achieved within budget.

This is the period when all the physical filming occurs and, as such, there are many detailed schedules for each department to follow in order to keep the shooting on time and on track. There can be many sets and locations involved in one production, so planning a time-effective shooting schedule is essential.

Post-Production

The Director and the Film Editor, Supervising Sound Editor, Music Supervisor and Visual Effects Supervisor take control of this part of the process. In general, the material will have been digitized for post-production and the Director, with the Heads of Department, will have selected Picture and Sound Technicians and the preferred hardware, software and facilities companies. This is a critical process in producing the finished film involving many highly skilled creative people.

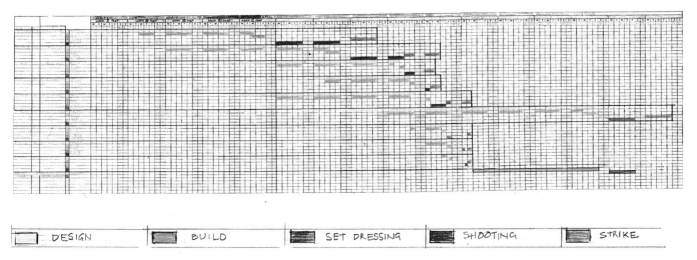

	DESIGN		BUILD		SET DRESSING		SHOOTING		STRIKE

Design and Build Schedule example.

STUDIO/LOC	SET N°	SET		MARCH WEEK ⑤ PREP							WEEK ④ PREP							WEEK ③ PREP							WEEK ② PREP					
				M 29	T 1	W 2	T 3	F 4	S 5	S 6	M 7	T 8	W 9	T 10	F 11	S 12	S 13	M 14	T 15	W 16	T 17	F 18	S 19	S 20	M 21	T 22	W 23	T 24	F 25	S 26	S 27	M 28
A STAGE	0.8	INT DAVIDS OFFICE	DESIGN																												
			BUILD																												
			DRESS																												
			STRIKE																												
			SHOOTING																												
B STAGE	0.6	INT CIARAS APPT	DESIGN																												
			BUILD																												
			DRESS																												
			STRIKE																												
			SHOOTING																												
C STAGE	10	INT HOTEL ROOM	DESIGN																												
			BUILD																												
			DRESS																												
			STRIKE																												
			SHOOTING																												
C STAGE	12	POLICE STATION RE	DESIGN																												
			BUILD																												
			DRESS																												
			STRIKE																												
			SHOOTING																												
D STAGE	14	INT LECTURE HALL	DESIGN																												
			BUILD																												
			DRESS																												
			STRIKE																												
			SHOOTING																												
A STAGE	16	INT RED LION PUB	DESIGN																												
			BUILD																												
			DRESS																												
			STRIKE																												
			SHOOTING																												
A STAGE	18	INT. PRISION CELL	DESIGN																												
			BUILD																												
			DRESS																												
			STRIKE																												
			SHOOTING																												
B STAGE	4	INT TRAIN TOILET	DESIGN																												
			BUILD																												
			DRESS																												
			STRIKE																												
			SHOOTING																												
B STAGE	20	DARK ROOM	DESIGN																												
			BUILD																												
			DRESS																												
			STRIKE																												
			SHOOTING																												
MOROCCO		LOCATION																													

Building Breakdown example.

END OF DAY 14 -- Wed, Sep 23 1998 -- 4 pgs
Shoot Day 15
Leave hotel TBA Travel to London, Wrap TBA

3	Kingston Court	E/I	Crown Court	DAY	3/8 pgs	8,9,14,15
			The Watkins arrive at Court	3		
6	Kingston Court	I/E	Crown Court	DAY	7/8 pgs	1,6,8,9,12,13,14
			All marvel at the collapse of the case	3		
5	Kingston Court	INT	Crown Court corridor	DAY	3/8 pgs	1,6,8,9,14,
			Watkins tahnks Kavanagh	3		
45	Kingston Court	INT	Solicitor's Office	NIGHT	1 pgs	12,13,20
			Kelso persuades Labone to identify Boxer's photo	9		

END OF DAY 15 -- Thu Sep 24, 1998 -- 2 5/8 pgs
Shoot Day 16 - Unit Call 0.800 to 19.00

1	Kingston Court	INT	Crown Court, Courtroom	DAY	3 5/8 pgs	1,6,8,9,11,12,13,
			The case against Watkins collapses when Boxer retracts his statement	3		14,16,17
2	Kingston Court	INT	Police Interview Room	NIGHT	7/8 pgs	11,12,13
			Phil Boxer Identifies Watkins	2		
28 Pt	TBC	INT	Hastings, Phyllis Labone's Sitting Room	DAY	4/8 pgs	20
			Labone recognises Watkins on TV	8		

END OF DAY 16 -- Fri Sep 25 1998 -- 5 pgs
Rest Day - Sat 26th Sep 1998
Shoot Day 17 - Unit Call 09.30/Wrap 20.30 approx.

14	Middle Temple	EXT	Middle Temple Gardens	DAY	7/8 pgs	1,6
			Kavanagh & Winslow discuss watkins	5		
12A	Middle Temple	EXT	River Court	DAY	1/8 pgs	8,9
			Barbra & Alex Watkins walk through river court	5		
16	Middle Temple	EXT	River Court	DAY	4/8 pgs	1,2
			Kavanagh & Foxcott discuss the case	7		
7	Westminster	EXT	Westminster	DAY	1/8 pgs	
			Cabinet reshuffle excitement	4		
8	Westminster	EXT	Westminster, Downing Street	DAY	1/8 pgs	18
			Cabinet members enter Downing Street	4		
9	Westminster	EXT	Westminster, Downing Street	DAY	1/8 pgs	
			Cabinet members leaving No. 10	4		
12	Palace Gardens	EXT	Thames Embankment	DAY	1 pgs	8,9
			Tense exchange between Barbra and Alex Watkins	4		
34 A Pt	Palace Gardens	EXT	Thames Embankment	NIGHT	1/8 pgs	8
			Barbra Watkins stares at river	3		

END OF DAY 17 -- Sun Sep 27, 1998 -- 3 pgs
Shoot Day 18 - Unit Call 08.00/Wrap 19.00 approx.

46	Stage 8	INT	River Court, Kavanagh's Room	DAY	5/8 pgs	1,3,23
	Elstree		Kavanagh chats with Mrs Aldmarten	10		
48	Stage 8	INT	River Court, Kavanagh's room	DAY	5/8 pgs	1,2,23
	Elstree		Mrs Aldermarten tells Kavanagh of her fears for Jeremy	10		
63	Stage 8	INT	River Court, Kavanagh's room	DAY	5/8 pgs	1,2
	Elstree		Kavanagh and Foxcott discuss shades of Grey	12		
66	Stage 8	INT	River Court, Kavanagh's room	NIGHT	5/8 pgs	1,2,3,
35	Elstree		Foxcott & Kavanagh discuss Watkin's child	8		

Shooting Schedule example.

— F I L M —

WEEK			DAY	STAGE 'B'	STAGE 'A'	STAGE 'C'	STAGE 'D'	LOT	LOCATION	BUDGET
1. BUILD	M A R C H	14	M	START BUILD INT PUB			START INT OFFICE BUILD COMPOSITE	START BUILD EXT STREET		
		15	TU	" "			"	"		
		16	W	" "			" "	" "		
		17	TH	" "			" "	" "		
		18	FR	" "		:	" "	" "		
			SAT							
			SUN							
2. BUILD	M A R C H	21	M	" "	START INT BALLRM BUILD	START CAFE AND BUILD SHOP	" "	" "		
		22	TU	" "	" "		" "	" "		
		23	W	" "	" "	" "	" "	" "		
		24	TH	" "	" "	" "	" "	" "		
		25	F	" "	" "	" "	" "	" "		
			SAT							
			SUN							
3. BUILD	M A R C H	28	M	" "	" "	" "	" "	" "		
		29	TU	" "	" "	" "	" "	" "		
		30	W	" "	" "	" "	" "	" "		
		31	TH	" "	" "	" "	" "	" "		
	APRIL	1	FR	" "	" "	" "	" "	" "		
			SAT							
			SUN							
4. BUILD	A P R I L	4	M	" "	" "	" "	" "	" "	PREPARE WOOD LOCATION	
		5	TU	" "	" "	" "	" "	" "		
		6	W	" "	" "	" "	" "	" "		
		7	TH	" "	" "	" "	" "	" "		
		8	FR	FINISH SET	" "	" "	" "	" "		£50 000
			SAT							
			SUN							

SHOOT WEEK				STAGE 'B'	STAGE 'A'	STAGE 'C'	STAGE 'D'	LOT	LOCATION	BUDGET
1 SHOOT	A P R I L	11	M	START SHOOTING	" "	" "	" "	" "	" "	
		12	TU	SHOOTING	" "	" "	" "	" "	" "	
		13	W	STRIKE	" "	SHOOT	" "	" "	" "	
		14	TH	STRIKE	" "	SHOOT	" "	" "	" "	BOTH SETS
		15	FR	STRIKE	" "	STRIKE	" "	" "	SHOOT	£100.000
			SAT							
			SUN							
2 SHOOT	A P R I L	18	M	START INT BUILD LIVING RM	" "	STRIKE	" "	" "	SHOOT	
		19	TU	" "	" "	START BUILD INT BASEMENT	" "	" "	REST DAY (FOR NIGHT)	
		20	W	" "	" "	" "	" "	" "	SHOOT (NIGHT)	
		21	TH	" "	" "	" "	" "	" "	SHOOT (NIGHT)	LOCATION
		22	F	" "	" "	" "	" "	" "	SHOOT (NIGHT)	£30.000
			SAT							
			SUN							
3 SHOOT	A P R I L	25	M	" "	" "	START SHOOTING INT BASEMENT	" "	" "		
		26	TU	" "	" "	STRIKE	" "	" "	SHOOT. DOCKS	
		27	W	" "	" "	START BUILD INT. POLICE CELL	" "	" "	SHOOT INT CHURCH	
		28	TH	" "	" "	" "	" "	" "	SHOOT INT CHURCH	LOCATION
		29	FR	" "	" "	" "	" "	" "	SHOOT EXT GRAVEYARD	£30.000
			SAT							
			SUN							
4 SHOOT	M A Y	2	M	" "	" "	SHOOT INT POLICE CELL	" "	" "	STRIKE	£20.000
		3	TU	" "	START INT SHOOTING BALLROOM	STRIKE	" "	" "		POLICE CELL
		4	W	" "	SHOOT	START INT BUILD COURT ROOM	" "	" "		
		5	TH	" "	SHOOT	" "	" "	" "		
		6	FR	" "	SHOOT	" "	" "	" "		
			SAT							
			SUN							

Sequential Monthly Shooting Schedule examples.

				STAGE 'B'	STAGE 'A'	STAGE 'C'	STAGE 'D'	LOT	LOCATION	
5 SHOOT	MAY	9	M	'' ''	SHOOT	'' ''	'' ''	'' ''		
		10	TU	'' ''	SHOOT	'' ''	'' ''	'' ''		
		11	W	'' ''	SHOOT	'' ''	'' ''	'' ''		
		12	TH	'' ''	SHOOT	'' ''	'' ''	'' ''		BALL ROOM
		13	FR	'' ''	SHOOT.	'' ''	'' ''	'' ''		£200.000
			SAT							
			SUN							
6 SHOOT	MAY	16	M	'' ''	STRIKE	'' ''	START INT OFFICE SHOOTING COMPOSITE	'' ''		
		17	TU	'' ''	STRIKE	'' ''	SHOOT	'' ''		
		18	W	'' ''	STRIKE	'' ''	SHOOT	'' ''		
		19	TH	'' ''	STRIKE	'' ''	SHOOT	'' ''		OFFICE COMPOSITE
		20	F	'' ''	STRIKE	'' ''	SHOOT.	'' ''		£80.000
			SAT							
			SUN							
7 SHOOT	MAY	23	M	START INT SHOOTING LIVING ROOM			STRIKE	'' ''		
		24	TU	SHOOT.			STRIKE	'' ''		
		25	W	SHOOT.			STRIKE	'' ''		
		26	TH	STRIKE		START COURT SHOOTING ROOM	STRIKE	'' ''		
		27	FR	STRIKE		SHOOT	STRIKE	'' ''		£50.000
			SAT							
			SUN							
8 SHOOT	MAY	30	M		STRIKE		START EXT SHOOTING STREET			
		31	TU		STRIKE		SHOOT			
	JUNE	1	W				SHOOT			
		2	TH				SHOOT			
		3	FR				SHOOT.			
			SAT							
			SUN							

				STAGE 'B'	STAGE 'A'	STAGE 'C'	STAGE 'D'	LOT	LOCATION	
9 SHOOT	JUNE	6	M					SHOOT		
		7	TU					SHOOT		
		8	W					SHOOT		
		9	TH					SHOOT		
		10	FR					SHOOT.		
			SAT							
			SUN							
10 SHOOT	JUNE	13	M					SHOOT		
		14	TU					SHOOT		
		15	W					SHOOT		
		16	TH					SHOOT		
		17	F					SHOOT		
			SAT							
			SUN							
11 SHOOT	JUNE	18	M	START BUILDING PICK-UPS				SHOOT		
		19	TU	BUILD				SHOOT		
		20	W	BUILD				SHOOT		
		21	TH	BUILD				SHOOT		
		22	FR	BUILD	W R A P			SHOOT	WRAP £600.000	STREET
			SAT							
			SUN							
12 2ND UNIT SHOOT	JUNE	23	M	2ND UNIT SHOOT				STRIKE	£20.000	
		24	TU	PICK-UPS				STRIKE	PICK-UP	
		25	W	STRIKE				STRIKE		
		26	TH	STRIKE				STRIKE		
		27	FR					STRIKE	TOTAL → £1,180,000	
			SAT							
			SUN							

Sequential Monthly Shooting Schedule examples.

Again, well-established Directors will make sure that the Director of Photography is involved in this process, as the quality, depth and colour of the image on the screen are paramount.

Display

The final process comes back to the Producer and the Distribution and Marketing Managers in the Production Office. By the time the film has reached its finished state, the Distributor should have prepared for a film's release on either a national or a global level. The Cinema Chain(s) involved are a vital part of the process. If the audience doesn't have the viewing experience that the Director and Producer visualized, then the time and money spent on a feature film's production can be wasted. At the centre of this is the Projectionist, whose training and experience are key to a perfect screening, with the images in focus and the sound exactly right.

UNDERSTANDING THE JOBS IN THE PRODUCTION OFFICE

Producer

The Producer is the first person to become involved in a film production and is the one who brings together the whole production team. Once the Producer takes possession of the script, the film belongs to them for the rest of its commercial life. This is why, in the main, they are extremely selective and only buy into scripts or concepts that they believe will give a good financial return. The Producer needs to have the personality, focus, contacts and determination to persuade others to commit to their commercial and creative vision.

The Producer's many responsibilities span all the phases of the production process. The Producer and the Financial Controller, with input from the Heads of Department, are responsible for setting the budget and schedule for the whole project.

PROFESSIONAL PERSPECTIVE: TERRY BAMBER

Terry Bamber.

Terry Bamber was born into a family with the film industry in its blood. His father, Dickie Bamber, started as a Prop Man and worked his way up to Producer; one of Terry's uncles was a Sparks and the other a Painter. Terry worked with his dad in the school holidays as a Runner, but, even with that level of family influence, in order to get into the business he still had to be a member of the ACTT union (now BECTU) and, in order to be in the union, had to have a job – a classic chicken and egg situation! However, Terry went on to become a very successful Director, Second Unit Director and Production Manager.

Terry Bamber's credits include: *Now You See Me 2; A Christmas Star; The Man From U.N.C.L.E.; Decline of an Empire; Hercules; World War Z; Skyfall; My Angel; Gulliver's Travels; Quantum of Solace; City of Ember; Casino Royale; The Hitchhiker's Guide to the Galaxy; The Phantom of the Opera; Tomb Raider: The Cradle of Life; Die Another Day; Lara Croft: Tomb Raider; 102 Dalmatians; The World is Not Enough; Tomorrow Never Dies; Carry On Columbus; The Adventures of Sherlock Holmes' Smarter Brother; The Man with the Golden Gun; Poirot; Dinotopia; Cadfael; Young Indiana Jones; Jeeves and Wooster; Paradise Club.*

PRODUCTION MANAGEMENT

One of the great pleasures of working in the film and television industry is the collaboration with the Production

Designer and Art Director. I have been privileged to work with wonderfully talented people who inspire and, in my experience, are all the top 'team players' when it comes to planning and solving problems.

As a Production Manager, one is always aware of the budgetary issues. The Production Designer or Art Director will encourage the hiring of a Location Manager who is familiar with his work and style. This is particularly important when there are a great many locations to find.

The Production Manager will be alerted to the amount of lead (prep) time each set and location will require, including construction, set dressing and the strike period once the set is completed. In a studio shoot, the Production Designer will always be mindful of the stage rental costs and where it is possible to recycle sets on the same stage.

As both a Production Manager and First Assistant Director, one must work with the most vital of ingredients – communication! The Production Designer/Art Director can provide sets as weather cover options during exterior location shooting and often saves potentially 'lost' days to inclement weather.

A good Production Designer/Production Manager relationship can save money from being wasted and ensure that it is spent wisely to create the vision and look that the film/television production requires.

I well remember wonderful Production Designers having to work against seemingly impossible schedules, but somehow, with good teamwork among the Production Office, Assistant Directors and the Art Department army, whether on a large feature film or a low-budget independent production, magic is created.

Assistant Producer

The Assistant Producer is a highly competent administrator who works with the Producer throughout the production process – from Script Development through to Marketing and Distribution. They must be well organized and highly flexible, with a comprehensive overview of film production. The Assistant Producer may be either freelance or a long-term employee of the production company. It is a privileged position and should never be confused with the job of a Production Assistant.

The work of the Assistant Producer may range from writing coverage on scripts, co-ordinating the fundraising process, assisting with duties on and off set, liaising between the Producer and the other departments and helping to prepare publicity materials. They might also oversee the job of securing clearances for copyright materials.

Associate Producer

Associate Producers in feature film production can come from several sources. They may be someone within the primary production company who has played a particularly significant role in the development of the script or screenplay, or have contributed important creative ideas. They may be another Producer, or a senior Script Editor who helped to shape the direction of the final drafts of the screenplay, without whose input the film may not have been financed, or the Producer's Assistant who supervised development or post-production for the Producer in their absence. They may also be a Producer from a smaller production company that is involved in co-producing the film and who has typically raised a small amount of funding for the project, but not enough to warrant Executive Producer or Co-Producer credit.

The Associate Producer can be involved throughout the production process and may assist in development, research, packaging and raising production finance. In fact, they could carry out any production work that the Producer is too busy to supervise personally and which is not covered by one of the other production roles such as Executive Producer, Co-Producer or Line Producer.

As an integral part of the Production Team, the Associate Producer should be able to plan, inspire, supervise, delegate – and act decisively and sensitively under pressure. It is essential to have a good understanding of feature film budgeting and scheduling, as well as a comprehensive knowledge of the different creative departments involved in feature film production.

The job of Associate Producer can be a good opportunity for promising young Producers with limited experience to learn on the job from a seasoned professional. It can be exhausting and require endless patience, but may be the best way to learn about this particular role and the career path ahead if the aim is eventually to become a fully fledged Producer. This is not an entry level position.

Line Producer

Where does the job title come from? They are called Line Producers because they cannot start work until they know what the 'Line' is. 'Above the line' relates to Writers, Producers, Directors and cast. 'Below the line' relates to development costs, crew salaries, set design and construction, equipment hire, locations, catering, travel and insurance.

During pre-production, the Line Producer works closely with the Director, Production Manager, Art Director and other Heads of Department to prepare the production schedule and budget in order to set the start date for shooting. Line Producers oversee all other pre-production activities, including hiring the production team, setting up the production office, location scouting, ensuring compliance with regulations and codes of practice, sourcing equipment and suppliers, selecting crew, engaging supporting artistes and monitoring the progress of the Art Department and other departments.

During production, the Line Producer hands over control of the final budget to the Production Accountant and delegates the day to day operation of the Production Office to the Production Manager and Production Co-ordinator. However, Line Producers are still ultimately responsible for making sure that the production keeps to schedule and budget. This requires setting up and implementing financial monitoring systems, controlling production expenditure, controlling production materials and monitoring and controlling the progress of productions. Line Producers are responsible for certain Health and Safety procedures and for sorting out any insurance claims. At the end of the shoot, the Line Producer oversees the 'wrap', or winding down, of the production.

No qualifications can prepare anyone completely for this hugely demanding job. Line Producers must have considerable industry experience, which can only be gained by working for a number of years in film, television and/or commercial production. The progression to Line Producer is by working through a variety of jobs such as Assistant Director, or working through the Production Office. A great deal of responsibility falls on the shoulders of the Line Producer, so this job isn't for the under-qualified or the faint-hearted.

Production Manager

The Production Manager is the pivotal role for any film production, combining the business skills involved in running a temporary company with the creative skills necessary to appreciate the vision of the Producer and Director. The Production Manager helps to determine the most efficient and economic way to schedule shoots, negotiate business deals for crews, locations, technical equipment and make day to day decisions to ensure that the production proceeds smoothly. Production Managers are dynamic and highly self-motivated individuals.

Production Management requires a set of skills that takes years of working in film production to perfect. The

Production Manager has budget control and is a procurement expert, legal expert, the interface between facilities, human resources, paymaster, accountant, logistics professional, mediator and is the Producer's right hand. Add to that the responsibility of being one of the first to be hired for a project and certainly one of the last to leave, combined with the need for a considerable knowledge of the technology involved in an ever-changing workplace, and this gives new significance to the expression 'multitasking'.

No qualifications can prepare anyone completely for this hugely demanding job. To qualify for this position, the Production Manager must be highly experienced in the film industry and have enhanced management skills.

Production Co-ordinator

The Production Co-ordinator is directly responsible to the Production Manager. There are many operational duties in film production, including office and studio space to be found, supplies and equipment to be purchased or rented and production team members to be hired. Whilst the Production Manager oversees and signs off on all of these activities, it is the responsibility of the Production Co-ordinator to ensure that they are executed without a hitch.

In addition to employee relations and operational duties, a Production Co-ordinator will perform many clerical duties. This may include drafting internal and external correspondence, creating cast and crew contact lists, as well as typing daily call sheets. Additionally, a Co-ordinator may type revised scripts, photocopy and distribute them.

Director

If the cast and crew of a film can be likened to a creative army going into battle, then the Director is the General in charge of that army and is the ultimate creative voice of the production. The Director leads and inspires his troops. He has the schedule and strategy pre-planned in order to achieve his goal – to make a financially and creatively successful film to satisfy the Producer, the financial backers and the eventual audience.

The Director, working with the Producer, will select the creative and technical Heads of Department, usually beginning with the Production Designer and the Director of Photography and, from there, start to create a detailed budget and production schedule.

The Director of Photography, a most important asset to the Director, will work with the Director on set. They will almost always have worked together on previous productions and so trust each other's judgement. The Director's own crew of Assistant Directors (and Second Unit Directors on a big budget feature) will also be trusted colleagues.

Whereas the Producer is in total control of the production, the Director is in charge of all the action on set. Along with the leading Heads of Department, the Director will establish a shooting schedule, determine locations, hire the crew and select the cast members. Decisions on costume and all other creative elements fall to the final approval of the Director and are determined during pre-production. From rehearsing the actors before principal photography begins, right through to sitting in on picture and sound post-production, the Director is in creative control.

Production Designer

As the Head of the Art Department, the Production Designer works very closely with the Director and other Heads of Department – Art Director, Construction Manager, Costume and Make-up Designers and the Director of Photography – and plays a crucial role in helping the Producer and Director with the visual requirements of the film.

A successful Production Designer will be artistically talented and resourceful, with the ability to turn ideas into something tangible. The look of a film set or location is vital in drawing the audience into the story and is essential in making a film convincing and evocative. Every story is intended to leave the audience with a particular emotion, so the design of the set and scenery is just as vital to that experience as an actor's portrayal of a character.

Location Manager

Supported by the Assistant Location Manager and the Location Scouts, the Location Manager uses investigative research with on-site photography and notes to document potential locations that are perfect for filming. A good Location Manager, Scout or Assistant Manager will usually have an extensive portfolio of locations to make initial suggestions to the Director, Producer and Production Designer, as they will already have travelled extensively during their career and worked in many overseas and local sites.

The primary duty is to find an environment best suited for a particular scene, or, in some cases, the entire movie. The search begins with the script, which indicates what kind of location is needed. The scouting of potential sites usually begins with a file search, leading to physical visits to actual sites, whether exterior or interior. The Scout is responsible for contacting property owners to gain permission to investigate their property, plus permissions must be obtained from the appropriate authorities to prevent the possibility of trespassing or other legal liabilities that may occur, as well as noting details about the logistical implications of the site.

The more details they can provide to the Director, Producer and other Heads of Department, the more complete picture of what to expect during the shoot can be obtained. Ambient lighting conditions, ambient sound, parking areas for the crew, sources of electricity and access to the site are just some of the most crucial details that should be scouted. Once the location is chosen, the legal issues have been worked out and the crew arrives on site, the Location Team photograph the site to ensure that any 'dressing of the location', in the form of props and furniture or actual structural changes, can be easily undone and the location returned to its original condition once filming is complete.

Assistant Directors

The First Assistant Director (1st AD) works as the Director's right hand, taking responsibility for a number of important tasks so that the Director is free to concentrate on the creative process. During pre-production, 1st ADs break down the script shot by shot, working with the Director and the Art Director to determine the shooting order and then drawing up the overall shooting schedule (a timetable for the filming period).

Once filming starts, the 1st AD is in charge of making sure that every aspect of the shoot keeps to this schedule. The main duties are to assist the Director and to co-ordinate all production activity on set – the 1st AD is the key link between the Director, the cast and crew and the Production Office.

The core responsibility of 1st ADs is to keep everything on schedule, so they are not always the most popular person on set! They frequently have to co-ordinate the cast and crew, control discipline, supervise the other Assistant Directors and oversee the preparation of the daily 'call sheet'. The 1st AD must be an authoritative team leader and motivator and must try to cultivate as pleasant an atmosphere on set as possible by remaining calm (hopefully!), whilst keeping everything running efficiently.

The Second Assistant Director (2nd AD) works directly under the 1st AD. The 2nd AD's main function is to ensure that all of the 1st AD's orders and directions are carried out. During production, 2nd ADs have two main responsibilities: the preparation of the 'call sheet' (the document that details the daily filming logistics for distribution to cast and crew) and overseeing all the movements of the cast, ensuring that the principal actors are in Make-up, Wardrobe, or standing by on the set at the correct times.

On smaller productions, where there may be no 3rd AD, the 2nd may also be responsible for finding and looking after background artistes. Most 2nds liaise between the set or location and the Production Office, updating key personnel on the timings and progress of the shoot.

The Third Assistant Director (3rd AD) is the next step up for someone who's been a Floor Runner for some time and has proven to be quick, efficient, reliable, pleasant, willing to work hard and able to absorb information – all the things necessary to progressing up the ladder to success. But even upon reaching these dizzy heights, I'm afraid that, as a junior member of the team, you are still likely to be 'tea-maker in chief' for the Cast, Director and Crew, so, instead of having to make three or four cups at a time, you'll be catering for thirty or more!

The 3rd AD supports the First and Second Assistant Directors in whatever ways are necessary, which can involve a wide variety of tasks, but mostly consists of working around the movement of the actors and background artistes involved in the action. The great thing is that every day is new and, because a 3rd doesn't have to worry about the grander things on set, you can use every moment to watch, listen and learn.

Production/Floor Runners and Assistants

These are likely to be people who answer the phone first in a Production Office when you ring looking for a job, and they are doing the one that you want – the Production Runner.

Runners either work in the Production Office or on set. The term 'Runner' comes from the time when the footage from the day's shoot (Rushes in the UK or Dailies in the USA) from either film sets or newsreels had to be carried as quickly as possible, back and forth between the set or the location and the laboratory for processing, so that the footage could be viewed by Director, Producer and Cinematographer early the next morning. Although this still happens to some extent when the Cinematographer is using film, the digital footage can now be transmitted electronically – but the title still lives on and describes the job perfectly.

The Runner is responsible for fetching, carrying and doing most of the odd jobs. They are the foot soldiers of the production team, whose duties are general office work, but mainly fetching and carrying for absolutely everyone and, oh yes, making gallons of tea and coffee with a smile! You are there to support anyone who needs help in a variety of ways, until such time as you have learnt enough to take on more responsibilities and begin to earn the title of a Production Assistant in the office, or a Trainee Third Assistant on set. There are no specific qualifications necessary for this job, but a good basic education is very necessary, combined with a passionate interest in all aspects of film – this passion will carry you through all the difficulties and disappointments, which are all part of working in this mainly freelance industry where you are constantly on the search for the next job.

Script and Development

Script and Development are at the core of every film. Each film begins as an idea; a script. Whose idea is it? Do they own it? Is it a marketable story? Development means extending an idea to the point where it becomes a film that the financiers might like – in other words, a 'package' (that is, bringing talent to a project, or finance when a project is packaged to include a pre-sale to a territory). It is during this stage that the crucial decisions are made in the creation of the project's 'value chain' (that is, a framework to identify all activities and analyse the costs and value for the financiers from production to display).

If all those decisions prove to be right, this chain may extend many years after the initial release of the film.

So, what's the process? The Producer selects a story – it may come from a book, a play, another film, a true story or an original idea. Once the story or script has been chosen, the Producer works with his writing team to prepare a synopsis, then a step by step outline, which breaks the story down into one-paragraph scenes concentrating on dramatic structure, with a description of the story, mood and characters, often with storyboard illustrations to help visualize key points. Next, the Screenwriter will prepare a screenplay, which may be rewritten several times and take several months. This screenplay will be pitched to potential financiers and, if successful, the film will be given a 'green light', that is, an offer of financial backing is secured.

However, this process is often shortened if the script/screenplay submitted to the Producer has already been assessed by either investors or a distributor as a potential financial success. Once all parties have settled the deal, the film will proceed into the pre-production stage. By this time, on a major feature film, there should be a clearly defined marketing strategy and target audience.

Casting Director

Good casting is the make or break ingredient between a box-office flop and a ratings hit. The Casting Director is the person who puts together that magic blend of performers who bring the story on the screen to life and the audience into the cinema. Although the headliners, the 'stars', rarely have to go through the full and extensive casting process that unknowns endure, the Casting Director is responsible for every role from the romantic lead, to the old lady on a bus, to a hundred background artistes.

This job involves working closely with the Director and Producer to understand what the story needs, suggesting ideal artists for each role, as well as arranging and conducting interviews and auditions. The Casting Director will negotiate fees and contracts and act as a liaison between the Production Office, the performers and their agents. The Casting Director must have an extensive knowledge of actors and their suitability for a particular role, with a massive contact list of agents, and will generally stay on board with a film through to the end of shooting in case a role has to be recast or additional characters added.

Product Placement Executive (aka Brand Integration)

If a scene in the film shows the star driving the latest model of fast car in a stunt-filled chase, or the leading lady's dress sparkles with a well-known brand of crystals, or the drunk at the bar is gazing fondly at a branded bottle of whisky, you can be sure that the Product Placement Executive has been doing their job!

Depending on the unique circumstances of each project, Product Placement may be answering calls or placing them. Whether a leading fashion house wants to dress the hero of the film, or a cosmetic company wants the heroine to use their lipstick and mascara in a scene, the Product Placement Executive representing the film production company takes proposals from specialists and agents concerning verbal, visual or hands-on embedding.

It is their responsibility to determine the most lucrative and positive brand-integration opportunities, whether that be carefully considering offers from advertisers, or identifying exceptional opportunities for placement and seeking out an agreement and securing the rights to use a trademarked brand. When the negotiations are complete to mutual satisfaction, the advertiser reaches its audience and the Producer receives the much-needed goods or financial support.

Executive Producer

An Executive Producer is typically someone who is either financing the film, representing a third party who is financing the film, or is involved with a property that has been optioned into a film but has no direct input into the creative process of the film itself. For example, authors of optioned books sometimes get an Executive Producer credit on films made from their work, even though they have no hand in the actual production process. Occasionally, a leading actor or actress, whose international audience appeal will assure financial backing and distribution, will be credited as an Executive Producer.

Most films have multiple backers and therefore more than one Executive Producer. They don't necessarily need to have any filmmaking experience at all, so their sole responsibility is to protect the investors' interests. The traditional role of the Executive Producer is to supervise the work of the Producer on behalf of the financiers or the distributor.

Co-Producer

The Co-Producer can be involved in a film's production from several angles. They may be a Line Producer who is also involved in the creative aspect of the film, or the lead Producer from a partner company that is co-producing the film, or a partner or corporate officer from the primary production company.

Occasionally the title of Co-Producer is accorded to a Producer who finds, options, develops or packages the project, but does not own the rights and who plays a less significant role in the physical production of the film. For example, they may be Producers who are relatively new to the job and need to work with, and gain experience from, a more senior Producer.

Alternatively, they may have raised a significant portion of the budget for the film, but have less creative input than the lead Producer and, in some cases, the individual may choose to be credited as Co-Producer rather than as Executive Producer, in order to indicate that they played an important part in the physical production of the film.

Financial Controller and Accounts Department

A large production company, or broadcaster, may employ an experienced and qualified Accountant as Financial Controller to ensure that proper controls and reporting procedures are in place across every aspect of the company's activities, including those of individual productions. On larger productions, a freelance Senior Production Accountant may function as a Financial Controller to oversee the work of the Accounts team. The role is very challenging and requires excellent analytical skills, a wide-ranging perspective and flexibility.

Financial Controllers are responsible for controlling accounting, taxation and financial analysis for all the company's areas of operation, which may encompass development, production and distribution. Financial Controllers may also be required to supervise the activities of one or more full-time Assistants. On individual productions, Financial Controllers will assist Producers and Executive Producers to prepare original budgets and to raise finance, taking into consideration any relevant tax incentive schemes that may be available at that time.

Publicity, Marketing, Distribution and Display

On major feature films, the Marketing and Publicity Department oversees the creation and planning of the film's marketing campaign, once the Distributor has identified the target audiences and potential revenue. The advice from most professionals is that you should research the Marketing and Distribution options before committing one penny of anyone's money into full production. Currently, filmmakers with a limited budget may use all the resources available through the social networks, using crowd-funding and other options.

Marketing campaigns should reach target audiences as efficiently and frequently as possible, both before and during the release. Feature films are amongst the most eagerly anticipated products available to consumers and, as every film is different, every marketing campaign must also be unique.

Big-budget films involving top stars usually spend more money on marketing and publicity because they have more production costs to recoup. Smaller niche, art house or 'indie' films have less to spend and must therefore use considerable ingenuity in order to be noticed. Work on a film's marketing campaign may begin over a year prior to its release, but, more usually, the lead time is several months, during which the Marketing and Publicity Managers must promote the film's visibility and stimulate public interest.

The aim is to enhance a film's visibility and to raise the public's awareness by convincing audiences that this is a 'must-see' movie and to ensure that the campaign peaks when the film opens, followed by further promotion to keep interest in the film after its theatrical (cinema) distribution into the television,

satellite and DVD marketplace. Tactical skills are vital because of the ongoing need to develop and enhance the promotional campaign, whilst keeping channels of communication open with all parties in order to achieve maximum revenue.

Press and publicity plays a vital role in the marketing of films. Press campaigns are carefully planned in advance and encompass both Unit Publicity, carried out during the film shoot, and Distribution Publicity, arranged to coincide with the film's release. These two areas require different specialist skills and usually involve two different experts or publicity companies.

Unit Publicists

Unit Publicists are hired by Producers, Distributors or Sales Agents and together they plan appropriate press strategies involving regional, national and global media. During filming, Unit Publicists work closely with the First and Second Assistant Directors to ensure that actors and selected crew members are available for interviews and arrange the schedules for journalists and EPK (Electronic Press Kit) to schedule and conduct the interviews.

The Unit Stills Photographer

The Unit Stills Photographer works closely with the Publicist, taking enough good quality photographic stills during the shoot. This is an important part of the Publicity process and can make the difference between a newspaper or magazine editor deciding whether or not to run a piece. EPK crews are hired by Studios, Distributors, Sales Agents, or sometimes Unit Publicists, to produce interviews and behind the scenes footage of feature films. These segments are edited and transferred on to suitable formats and supplied to broadcasters as a package.

Film Title and Poster (FTP) Designer

The FTP Designer works closely with the Director and the Marketing and Publicity Department. They are Graphic Designers with a talent for interpreting the ethos of the film into posters used for publicity and the ever-important title sequence of the film. The doyen of this art was Saul Bass, who started designing titles for Otto Preminger for the 1954 film *Carmen Jones*. For *The Man with the Golden Arm*, he created such an iconic opening sequence that Preminger sent instructions with every can of film telling the projectionists to 'pull the curtains back before rolling the titles'. Until that point the titles were so dull that the projectionists only revealed the screen once the titles were finished.

BUDGETING AND SCHEDULING

The Art Department budget, although part of the total budget of the film and therefore still under the final control of the Production Office, is a separate entity and is managed by the

Production Designer and the Art Director. This budget covers the entire design and construction procedure and will continue throughout the filming process until the final wrap. It will be constantly monitored and adjusted by the Art Director, working closely with the Production Manager.

Anyone involved in the accounting and budgeting process has to be conversant with every area of film production – if not a downright expert when it comes to predicting cost and time overruns. The rapidity of spending during the production of a feature film or television show is so high that it would be a nightmare for someone who hasn't been exposed to the system.

There are many downloadable budget and scheduling templates available, as well as professional software products, which are designed to make the job a little easier to manage. However, as with everything else involved with film, experience is the key. The Art Director will have had to deal with budgeting and scheduling issues throughout his or her progression through the department and so will be very used to the process.

Budget

Creating a draft budget for the Art Department happens within the first few weeks of the pre-production meetings. This is done in order to establish benchmarks, to create a sense of cost for materials and labour based on the Art Director's experience. The initial or draft budget is produced to see if a production works within the Producer's parameters and to ascertain if the production is actually worth doing, or if scenes are expendable. Once this is absorbed into the overall production budget, the Producer will have the ammunition needed to do their job and find the finance.

A carefully crafted budget provides the pivotal roadmap, not only for the entire film project, but for each department. Whether the film is expected to cost £5k or £5m, the budget must represent a spending plan for every penny needed for the production. The budget, in all its stages, serves as a proportional guide for each department. For example, if the performers are being paid millions, then the Art Department has to make sure that the 'look' of the film matches the amount of money spent.

The performers can also affect the budget in unexpected ways and it's wise to remember that, despite careful planning and design considerations, key factors can change rapidly. For example, there was a situation on *The Anniversary* in 1968 with Bette Davis, who was quite a difficult lady to deal with! She had just arrived on the *Queen Mary* and, on her first day, asked to have us all lined up on one of the stages, so that she could see who her crew was. She then disappeared off the stage with the Producer, who came back and promptly fired the Director, along with other members of the team. (Thankfully I was working for the Art Director, John Blezard, and was deemed

acceptable to stay!) She requested Roy Ward Baker as the replacement Director, as she had worked with him before and trusted him. On Miss Davis' instructions, he had to have the set completely reversed because she wanted to wear the eyepatch (an integral part of the film) on her left eye instead of the right and so the layout didn't suit her. This is a good demonstration of the types of characters you might have to work with and the need to be flexible.

The budget could, and generally does, alter as the film progresses depending on changes in action scenes, special and visual effects, locations and set alterations, both during and after principal photography. If a particular location must be used to tell the story, or a special effect defines the action, then that element has to be identified and included in the initial budget.

The whole process runs from the start of the project through to the completion of the film. The Art Department's budget, being a separate sector of the main production budget, has to take into consideration everything involved in set design and construction – right from the initial sketches to the finished set ready to take the performers and everyone involved in the shooting process.

The budget has a number of important internal and external purposes. It sets the framework for all the decisions regarding design and construction. For example, if an independent or short film is to be made on a minimal budget, then it can be filmed locally, or in places that can double for more exotic locations, because the finance cannot support transport, travel and other expenses. This is where the 'don't worry, we can fix it in post' attitude cannot be part of the thinking process, as post-production is many times more expensive than trying to get over the problem whilst planning and shooting the film or programme.

The available production budget sets the tone of the picture and the parameters to which the Art Department can work. Small or large, each has its restrictions. Small budgets mean that you have to use your ingenuity and skill to get over the problems, while large-feature budgets mean that you have to be on top of your game as everyone will expect you to perform miracles!

The budget is effectively a planning tool that may fluctuate during the planning, production and post-production stages of the project. For a low-budget film there may be a variety of options. The Art Director compiling a budget for an independent or short film, for example, might not be able to include a trip to the Acropolis in Athens, but may be able to 'trick' the audience with the clever use of a model or a miniature.

Ultimately, the budget plays a pivotal role in identifying the costs of every element of the production. Once the final commitment has been made, there can be few significant changes without approval from the Producer and Production Accountant. No matter how artistically compelling, an

Construction Budget --- V6 --- 17/02/16

BASED ON REQUIREMENTS 17th Feb 2016

	SET NO.	I/E	SET NAME (ADAPTED FOR CONFIDENTIALITY)	LOCS	SPEND LOCALE	£ LABOUR	MATERIAL	TOTAL	VAR -V5	$$$ TOTAL	NOTES
UK											
	101	EXT	SHOP	LOC	UK	5,500	2,000	7,500		$11,625	
	102	INT	SHOP	STAGE	UK			0	---8,000	$0	
	106	EXT	CHASE	LOC	UK	20,000	8,000	28,000	15,500	$43,400	
	108	EXT	CHASE	LOC	UK			0	---12,500	$0	
	109	EXT	CHASE	LOC	UK	18,000	6,500	24,500	12,500	$37,975	
	115	INT	RENDEVOUS	STAGE	UK	66,000	32,000	98,000	8,000	$151,900	
	116	INT	TUNNEL	STAGE	UK	10,000	5,000	15,000		$23,250	
	117	EXT	STREETS	LOC	UK	2,000	1,000	3,000		$4,650	
	120	EXT	HOUSE	LOC	UK	2,000	1,000	3,000		$4,650	
Y	121	INT	HOUSE·	STAGE	UK	111,000	45,000	156,000	11,000	$241,800	SIGNED OFF
Y	122	INT	HOUSE	STAGE	UK			0		$0	SIGNED OFF --- moved into 121
	125	EXT	EXT FLAT	LOC	UK	1,500	500	2,000		$3,100	
Y	126	INT	INT FLAT	STAGE	UK	26,000	8,000	34,000	---11,000	$52,700	SIGNED OFF
N	130	EXT	STATELY HOME	LOC	UK			0		$0	
Y	131	INT	OFFICE	STAGE	UK	37,000	17,000	54,000		$83,700	SIGNED OFF
Y	132	INT	DINING ROOM	STAGE	UK	50,000	20,000	70,000		$108,500	SIGNED OFF
	133	INT	APARTMENT	STAGE	UK	30,000	15,000	45,000	45,000	$69,750	
	134	INT	EXPLOSION	LOC	UK	7,000	3,000	10,000		$15,500	
	136	EXT	STREET	BL	UK	60,000	35,000	95,000	---5,000	$147,250	READY FOR SIGN OFF
	137	EXT	SHOP	LOC	UK	5,000	3,000	8,000		$12,400	
	147	INT	ROOM	LOC	UK	14,000	4,000	18,000	5,500	$27,900	READY FOR SIGN OFF
	150	EXT	CHURCH	LOC	UK	6,000	2,000	8,000	8,000	$12,400	
	152	INT	BEDROOM	LOC	UK	1,500	500	2,000	2,000		
	160	EXT	GARDENS	LOC	UK	18,000	7,000	25,000		$38,750	
	161	INT	TENT	STAGE	UK	28,000	12,000	40,000		$62,000	
	162	INT	TENT	STAGE	UK	22,000	8,000	30,000		$46,500	
USA											
	170	EXT	DIST.	LOC	USA	3,500	1,500	5,000		$7,750	
	171	INT	DIST.	LOC	USA	3,500	1,500	5,000		$7,750	
	172	INT	HALLWAY	LOC	UK	8,000	4,000	12,000		$18,600	
	173	INT	VAULT	LOC	UK	50,000	20,000	70,000		$108,500	
	174	INT	ELEVATOR	STAGE	UK	20,000	10,000	30,000		$46,500	
	178	INT	BOARDROOM	STAGE	UK	35,000	15,000	50,000	---40,000	$77,500	
	180	INT	ROOM	STAGE	UK	25,000	10,000	35,000		$54,250	
Y	181	INT	ROOM	STAGE	UK	42,000	23,000	65,000		$100,750	
	185	INT	OFFICE	STAGE	UK	85,000	40,000	125,000		$193,750	
	186	INT	STREET	STAGE	UK	45,000	20,000	65,000	10,000	$100,750	
	190	INT	TEST	STAGE	USA	19,000	6,000	25,000		$38,750	
	193	INT	BAR	STAGE	UK	50,000	25,000	75,000	---24,500	$116,250	READY FOR SIGN OFF
	196	INT	ROOM	STAGE	UK	100,000	50,000	150,000		$232,500	
	197	INT	ROOM	STAGE	UK	20,000	10,000	30,000		$46,500	
Y	220	INT	OFFICE	STAGE	UK	70,000	30,000	100,000		$155,000	SIGNED OFF
	221	EXT	AVE	LOC	UK	10,000	4,000	14,000		$21,700	
SWEDEN											
	234	INT	WARDROBE	STAGE	UK	19,000	6,000	25,000		$38,750	
	236	INT	CATHEDRAL	LOC	UK	4,000	1,000	5,000		$7,750	
POPPY'S											
	240	EXT	DINER	STAGE	UK	1,275,000	550,000	1,825,000		$2,828,750	
	242	INT	SALON	STAGE	UK	54,000	26,000	80,000		$124,000	
	250	INT	ALLEY	LOC	UK	58,000	27,000	85,000	25,000	$131,750	
	251	INT	THEATRE	STAGE	UK	20,000	10,000	30,000	---45,000	$46,500	
	255	INT	LAB	STAGE	UK	45,000	20,000	65,000		$100,750	
	257	EXT	FIELD	LOC	UK	18,000	7,000	25,000		$38,750	
ITALY											
	261	I/E	LODGE	LOC	UK	5,000	3,000	8,000		$12,400	
	262	INT	ROOM	STAGE	UK	10,000	5,000	15,000		$23,250	
	263	EXT	STATION	LOC	UK	10,000	4,000	14,000		$21,700	
	264	INT	LABORATORY	STAGE	UK	65,000	30,000	95,000		$147,250	
	270	EXT	SLOPE	LOC	UK	12,000	6,000	18,000		$27,900	
	275	I/E	CORRIDOR	S/L	UK	4,000	2,000	6,000		$9,300	
	276	I/E	STAIRCASE	S/L	UK	4,000	2,000	6,000		$9,300	
	277	I/E	TANK	S/L	UK	20,000	15,000	35,000		$54,250	
	278	I/E	DEPOT	S/L	UK			0	---85,000	$0	
	279	I/E	HOUSE	S/L	UK	60,000	25,000	85,000	85,000	$131,750	
HONG KONG											
	281	EXT	SHOP	LOC	HK	1,500	500	2,000		$3,100	
	282	INT	SHOP	LOC	HK				---35,000	$0	
	283	EXT	DEALER	LOC	HK	5,000	3,000	8,000		$12,400	
	284	INT	DEALER	LOC	HK	19,000	6,000	25,000		$38,750	
	286	INT	ROOM	LOC	HK			0	---8,000	$0	
	287	INT	BOAT	LOC	UK	60,000	35,000	95,000	95,000	$147,250	
MONTAGE											
	290	EXT	MONTAGE	TBD	UK	750	250	1,000		$1,550	
	290	INT	EXCHANGE	TBD	UK	750	250	1,000		$1,550	
	290	NT/EX	PARTIES	TBD	UK	750	250	1,000		$1,550	
	290	EXT	MAYHEM	TBD	UK	750	250	1,000		$1,550	
	290	INT	ASSEMBLY	TBD	UK	750	250	1,000		$1,550	
	290	INT	A&E	TBD	UK	750	250	1,000		$1,550	
	290	INT	READER	TBD	UK	750	250	1,000		$1,550	
	290	EXT	CRASH	TBD	UK	750	250	1,000		$1,550	
	290	INT	CONTAINERS	TBD	UK	750	250	1,000		$1,550	
	290	EXT	STREET	TBD	UK	750	250	1,000		$1,550	
CODE TO SET TOTAL						2,902,500	1,291,500	4,194,000	48,500	$6,500,700	

Construction Budget example.

Art Director may not decide unilaterally to change a location or an aspect of a set once the production process has started. In fact, it would show a distinct lack of professionalism to do so.

Above the Line Costs

The fees include the Producer, Director, leading cast members and script. These set the pricing tone of the film and are described as the 'above the line' costs. All the other costs are considered 'below the line'. The Art Department falls into this category.

The production budget is generally comprised of the summary page, known as the top sheet, with a series of department by department sectors. Absolutely everything must be budgeted, receipted and credited to its particular account. The numbers may get large but the attention to detail is paramount. Throughout the course of the production, the actual expenses are constantly compared to the original in order to maintain the production's accuracy in planning and to make any necessary adjustments.

For major films, the project must be protected with a completion bond. The completion bond company agrees to pay those fees in excess of the built-in 10 per cent contingency. The cost for this insurance is expensive in both financial and practical terms. The completion bond company can veto cast and crew and can take over the production if either the shoot begins to fall dramatically behind schedule, or too many reshoots are necessary. However, this is all in the Producer's domain and should not affect the Art Department unless something goes drastically wrong.

PROFESSIONAL PERSPECTIVE: PETER YOUNG

Peter Young.

Peter Young has worked in the film industry since the late 1960s, decorating sets for countless films and television programmes. On *The Dark Crystal* he was responsible for the ornate and alien settings, such as the Skeksis Castle, and went on to win several awards including two Oscars for Best Set Direction on *Batman* and *Sleepy Hollow*. He worked again for Brian Henson on *Jack and the Beanstalk: The Real Story* and continues to stamp his unique style on such films as *Charlie and the Chocolate Factory, Troy* and *Alice in Wonderland*.

Peter Young's credits include: *Alice in Wonderland; Stardust; Charlie and the Chocolate Factory; Troy; Shanghai Knights; Planet of the Apes; The Mummy Returns; Sleepy Hollow; Judge Dredd; The Rainbow Thief; Batman; Supergirl; Electric Dreams; Superman III; The Dark Crystal; Moonlighting; Superman II; The Tempest; Dracula; Father, Dear Father; Lock Up Your Daughters; Jack and The Beanstalk: The Real Story; Doomsday Gun; Inspector Morse.*

SET DECORATING AND THE BUDGET

The title Set Decorator – or even Art Director – is not to be confused with Interior Decorator! The Art Department on a film is responsible for selecting and/or building locations and sets that are suitable for the requirements of the Director and the script – subject to costs (always costs!).

Once a Designer has offered a Set Decorator a position within his crew, it is the Set Decorator's responsibility to read and break down the script into interiors and exteriors, compile a list of specific prop requirements that are referred to in the script and which require either sourcing or making, as well as attempting to assess and compile a budget in order to achieve what the Designer and Director require.

On larger films there will be many concept sketches of the Designer's and Director's visions and it is the Set Decorator's responsibility to manifest these concepts; to interpret them and to offer discussions and compromises with the help of the Prop Master and Prop Makers. These visions have to be produced on time and always within budget.

The first job for the Set Decorator on any film is to read and absorb the script – to discuss with the Designer and the Director their requirements – then break it down to exterior and interior sets and attempt to produce a provisional budget for the intended script. The provisional budget is always too great!

Whether it be a TV drama or a big Hollywood blockbuster, the process is the same – the script dictates the style: upper class, lower class, futuristic, mediaeval, present day, good taste and bad taste – and whether to use made props or hired props.

The Set Decorator's knowledge is vital in assessing how to achieve the Designer's, Director's and script's requirements. The industry is a collaborative medium – nobody stands alone and everyone is dependent on each other. In a way, the Production Designer is the eyes of the Director and the Set Decorator is the eyes of the Designer – providing they all agree.

As the days and weeks go by and the problems present themselves – and they always do – finally a submitted budget is provisionally accepted and the Set Decorator is given a Buyer and an Assistant (if lucky and if no more meetings over budget and concepts are needed).

Now it is time to go around prop hire companies to explore what is available and what might be of use on the film. Subject to the experience of the Designer, the Director and, indeed, the Set Decorator, mood boards of props and fabrics available will be assembled for approval by all concerned, so that everyone is fully aware of what is intended for each set and there are no surprises.

At the same time, a schedule of filming is released by the Production Office and the Set Decorator can now start reserving furniture and props from the hire companies for the named sets. Personal taste and the style of individual Set Decorators does indeed come into play. It would be interesting to see a comparison between three different Set Decorators given the same script and set to interpret. All would have their own style and taste and the results would be completely different, yet totally acceptable – providing they work within budget!

A few days before the intended set is filmed, the selected props and furniture are collected from the prop hire companies, brought to the set and then assembled (dressed) by the Set Decorator and the Props Department and presented to the Designer and the Director for approval – fingers crossed!

CHAPTER 3

CONSTRUCTION AND SET DRESSING

The Construction Crew on a feature film can have as many as 200 to 300 people working at any one time, all under the control of the Construction Manager, who is directly responsible to the Art Department. Each section of the crew has its own Head of Department to supervise that particular facet of the build – Carpenters, Plasterers, Painters, Riggers, Stage Hands and Sculptors. Each member of the Construction Crew is a talented craftsman with skills well beyond those of a domestic or commercial builder.

The build on set, constructed of scaffolding, wood and plaster, not only has to look like the real thing, but also has to conform to rigorous Health and Safety standards, as well as being able to support whatever action is necessary – people, equipment, vehicles and so on.

UNDERSTANDING THE JOBS IN THE CONSTRUCTION DEPARTMENT

Construction Manager

The Construction Manager (or Construction Coordinator in the USA) is the Head of Department and is responsible for interpreting the Art Department's plans and designs to establish the number of sets required, their size, design, colour and texture in order to turn those blueprints into fully functional film sets.

Hired by the Production Designer to oversee the entire process of set building, from initial planning through to the final coat of paint on the finished sets, they will employ Heads of Department for Carpentry, Scenic Painting, Ornamental Plastering and Rigging. These are usually people who will have worked with them on many films and for many years, trusting them implicitly to do the best job. The Heads of Department, in turn, will employ their own crews.

The Construction Manager will have worked on many films as part of the Construction Crew – perhaps as a Carpenter. They need to understand complex drawings and specifications, so a good understanding of physics and mathematics is essential, as many aspects of film sets have to function as 'real' buildings with all the inherent load-bearing and safety aspects in place.

Assistant Construction Manager

Working directly for the Construction Manager, the Assistant has to have comprehensive construction experience with a full understanding of the complexities of working in film and pulling together a crew of highly skilled individuals.

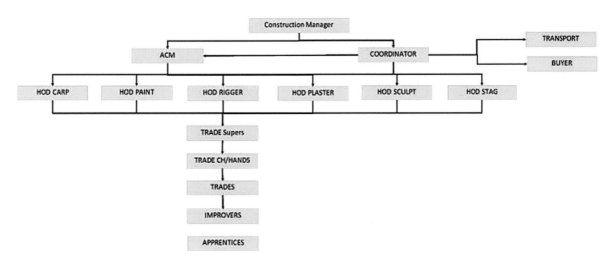

Construction Department flow chart.

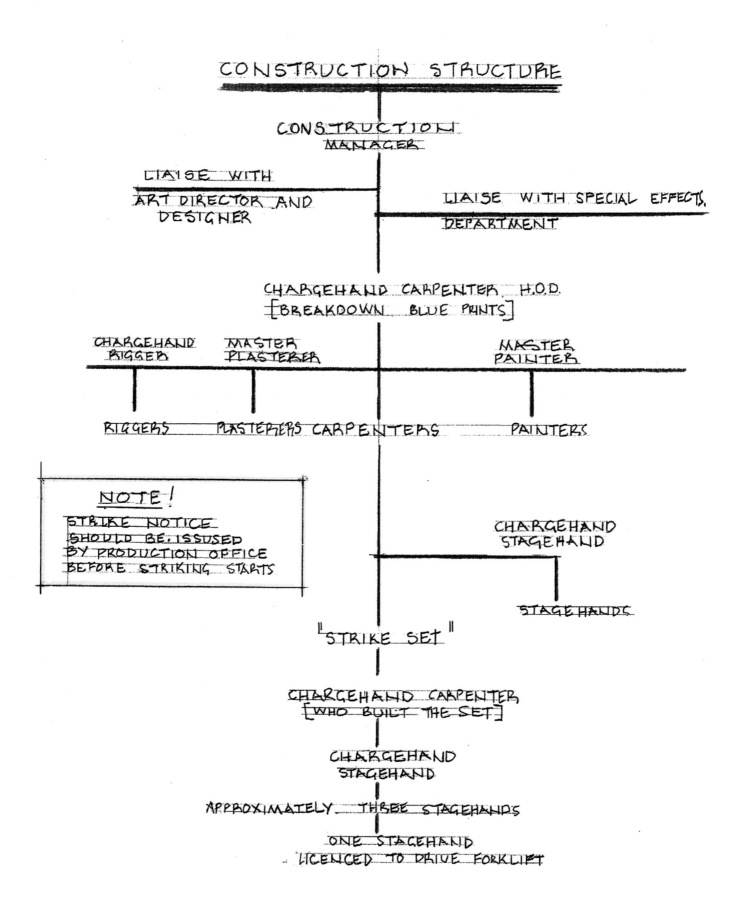

Construction Department flow chart.

On a daily basis there will be problems on set such as an unforeseen alteration, or a delay in delivery of materials, which the Assistant Construction Manager will have to solve. They are responsible for the management of the crew, sorting out differences and making sure that everything is working efficiently.

Heads of Department

The Heads of Department work directly for the Construction Manager and control their individual crews of Scenic Carpenters, Ornamental Plasterers, Scenic Painters, Riggers and Stagehands. Under their leadership, the Construction Crew will bring the designs of the Production Designer to life, working to the models, sketches and blueprints produced by the Art Department, building all interior and exterior sets and physical scenery for the production.

Chargehand

The work of the Construction Department can cover builds on several stages within a studio complex, as well as any required locations. It would be impossible in these circumstances for the Heads of Department to be on hand to supervise all the work on each of the sets, so this responsibility is handed on to the Chargehand. The Chargehand will be allocated a specific build and will oversee all activity on set and in the workshop under the direction of their Head of Department.

The Chargehand is responsible for their own crew of Carpenters, Painters, Plasterers or Riggers on specific projects during production and will be a fully qualified craftsman with the ability and temperament to bring out the best in their crew.

Standby

The Standbys in the Construction Crew are highly experienced practitioners who are available on set or location during shooting and are responsible for dealing with any changes or improvements to the set that may be required during a film shoot. If any problems arise with the structures, fittings, props or scenic equipment on the set, it is the job of the Standbys to organize the repair, refit or reassembly.

Scenic Carpenter

The Scenic Carpenter makes the basic flats, rostrums, ceilings, floors and walls of the set. They will also make staircases, tables, benches, chairs – in short, everything on set that is made of wood! They are all skilled carpenters and joiners. The Scenic Carpenter is probably the bedrock of the Construction Crew. After the Riggers have finished constructing the basis for the set, the Carpenters move in to 'flesh out' the physical elements – both interior and exterior.

Working both on the sound stage and in the studio-based carpentry workshop, they translate the models, sketches and blueprints to create set pieces, which are then assembled on set or location. Scenery can include anything from a few flat walls and doors to highly involved construction projects such as an entire castle, a ship captain's cabin, or the interior of a spaceship. For productions that demand on-location filming where is it not logistically feasible to transport sets, carpenters set up shop wherever space can be found. Again, the production industry can be unpredictable, so those who intend to make a career must be flexible and able to adapt.

Ornamental Plasterer

These craftsmen make the cladding of the sets. They can create brick-wall surfaces of any style and age, stone walls and models, from Egyptian artefacts to gnarled prehistoric forests. They are adept at working with all manner of materials – plaster, clay, fibreglass, plastics, latex and vermiculite.

The 'Plaster' element of set construction is crucial and the job is considered to be a craft rather than a trade because of the wide range of skills used. Fibrous plastering, with a full understanding of the chemicals involved, is the essential basis of the job, combined with a good eye for shape, form and texture. It is necessary to be able to understand complex drawings and basic sketches and have the skills to convert them into a wide range of structures, from moulds for the interior and exterior of buildings such as castles, entire city centres or extra-terrestrial landscapes, to tree trunks and boulders to create the necessary illusion.

Scenic Painter

Scenery absorbs the audience and cast into a particular setting, into the time and place where the story on screen is unfolding. The Carpenters, Plasterers and Riggers build these sets, but they are not complete until the crew of Scenic Painters have taken up their brushes and worked their magic.

The Scenic Painter has to have a good eye for colour and texture. The range of expertise needed to put the finishing touches to a film set takes the word 'painter' to an entirely different level. The job is to trick the camera lens and convince the cinema audience that what they are looking at is a real street of shops, a castle with its baronial hall, a theatre with stage and dressing rooms, or a cosy farmhouse kitchen.

Scenic Artist

The number of Scenic Artists will depend on the size of the production. They are highly skilled craftsmen who paint the backings, create special portraits, murals, paintings, glass painting and posters. Many of these artists will have trained in the theatre and will have an extensive knowledge of painting media, perspective, period styles and architectural subjects.

Sculptor

When you look at a film on screen, not everything you see is necessarily real. Think about a mediaeval battle scene where the set is littered with the bodies of men and horses. The people aren't such a problem, as most actors can lie still for a while, but the animals and other bits and pieces you see on screen are most likely the work of the Sculptors. The Sculptors work primarily with the Props, Construction and Physical Effects Departments on sculptures ranging from larger than life to miniature items. They can produce a huge range of work, from animals and concept models (for science fiction and fantasy sequences), to creature development for animatronics or moulded body suits for actors.

Sculptors are employed by the Art Department of a feature film, but usually work within the Construction Crew. They work from detailed drawings, using their skills to create any number of special features, from giant rocks and trees in a landscape, to statues of all types and proportions; from ornate panelling to more specialized pieces for fantasy films. The material often used for large objects is polystyrene as it is lightweight and can be carved easily. Polystyrene can also be used to sculpt mid-sized items that are difficult to build in wood and too large for clay, such as a moulded chair, which can then be cast with plaster and reproduced in fibreglass. Clay modelling is still preferable for any item needing detail and is always used for smaller and finer work.

Rigger

The Rigger is essentially a scaffolder with extended skills. Not only do Riggers work within the Construction Crew, erecting the essential structural skeletons on which the set is supported, ready for the Carpenters, Painters and Plasterers to turn into camera-ready facades, but they also construct heavy 'mobile' sets, hang the lighting rails and complete any construction needed to support equipment, such as independent and birdcage, tower, cantilever, pavement and roof scaffolds. They are responsible for installing the lifting and suspension apparatus, such as wire and fibre ropes, chains and slings, winches and pulley blocks, as well as any platforms required by the Plasterers, Painters and Scenic Artists. These constructions have to be completely safe and able to carry considerable weight, very often needing to support any given number of people and vehicles.

Stagehand

A Stagehand's work, whether in film, theatre or television, is very similar. Working alongside the Construction Crew, the Props and Set Dressing teams, they assist with everything from hanging backdrops and moving heavy props to taking care of transport – including location vehicles, storage and general 'housekeeping' on set. In fact, the Stagehand is a very essential 'Mr Fixit'. On large feature films Stagehands have their own Head of Department, Supervisors, Chargehands and Standbys and may work either in the studio or on location.

Trainee/Apprentice

This is the entry-level role for anyone wanting to work in the Construction Department. There's a very good reason why you will have to start here as, no matter what your expertise or age, the work you'll be asked to do will be varied, complex and very different from anything tackled previously. Anyone wanting to be taken on as an Apprentice will need to have basic qualifications in their chosen skill, preferably with experience of working on commercial construction sites for a while before researching industry-based training schemes. Even for an experienced craftsman, progress through the department will depend very much on attitude and the ease with which you work as part of the team, as well as technical ability.

STUDIO PROCEDURE

The procedure followed by the Designer, Art Director and Construction Manager from script to the build will depend almost entirely on the type of production and the Director's initial concept. Thumbnail sketches, storyboard (continuity) sketches, finished set sketches, white card models, mattes and miniatures may all have to be produced, although some Directors will only need a limited amount of information. For example, there were no storyboards on *A Clockwork Orange* (Kubrick) or *Frenzy* (Hitchcock), as these Directors were themselves able to visualize each set-up.

There is a difference in this procedure among studios in different countries. In the UK, most of the studios are independent 'four-wallers' and will rent out their stages or backlot for a contracted amount of time, therefore the production company has to introduce everything it needs on to the set. Obvious economies can be made by individual production companies by using sets or parts of sets that have been built for their own films or television programmes that are part of a series where there is a continuity of, say, an office or living accommodation used throughout the series – for example, Bond, Downton Abbey and Harry Potter. The elements of these sets can be stored until they are needed for the next production.

In the USA, many of the studios are owned entirely by major production companies or distributors and therefore, when they make their own films within their own studio complexes, they may use and reuse many of the set builds and props.

BUILDING FLEXIBLE SETS

Very often, the Designer will have to work within a restricted area, perhaps if studio space is limited or there are budget restrictions. In these cases, the Designer might be required to produce drawings of multiple sets within a stage area. Or perhaps a Floater Wall (or Wild Wall) within the build will be used, where a piece of scenery in a set is designed to be moved, removed and replaced as needed to allow the set to be

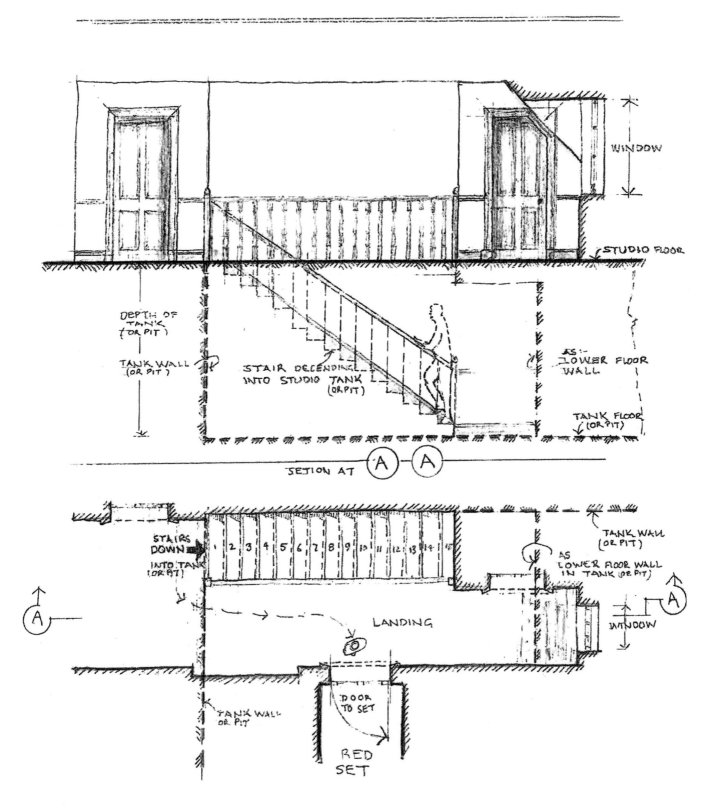

PLAN AND SECTION
SHOWING STAIR DECENDING INTO STUDIO TANK
READ WITH STAGE LAYOUT ▤ RED SET

A plan of a descending staircase using the tank inside the studio.

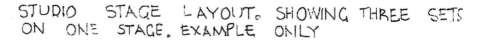

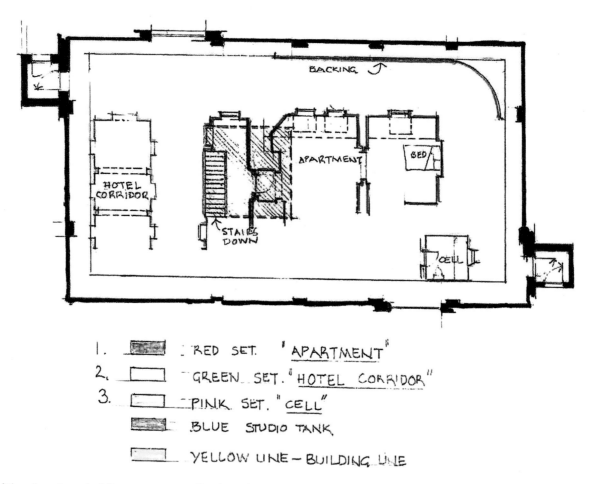

Plan of the stage layout of the same scene. See how the apartment, staircase and hotel corridor fit into the set.

lit and shot from a different angle in order to give the appearance of being larger than the actual area used.

REALITY AND FANTASY

The contribution of a Designer to a set often reflects his own character as a creative artist and each Designer will differ tremendously in their approach to the script. Although most Designers will be more than capable of creating modern, period or fantasy sets, an experienced Director who has worked with a number of Designers will know instinctively which one will be best able to fulfil his idea of the finished production.

Fantasy and science fiction films may require the control of a studio setting, where the impact of the scene often depends on superbly finished sets, which are convincing representations of future design. However, the increase in digital effects and technologies such as motion capture and green screen in production, as well as computer-generated effects in post-production, has taken this genre to another and exciting level.

WORKING FROM PHOTOGRAPHS

Locations that are to be reconstructed in the studio require a great deal of careful research to ensure accuracy and, if the Draughtsmen in the Art Department are to reproduce the set accurately, several photographs of the location will be taken. Often the Draughtsman will just be given an image and may have to rebuild what is in the photograph without there being any indication of measurements and no indication of the camera angle, or, indeed, the camera height. The photograph may be of an architectural feature with a figure standing somewhere, therefore the Draughtsman will hazard a guess at the height of that figure – or there may be some brickwork visible and the Draughtsman will know that, as a rule, there are four bricks to the foot. This kind of dilemma outlines the absolute need for the Art Director and Draughtsmen to have a good working knowledge not only of architecture but of building practices.

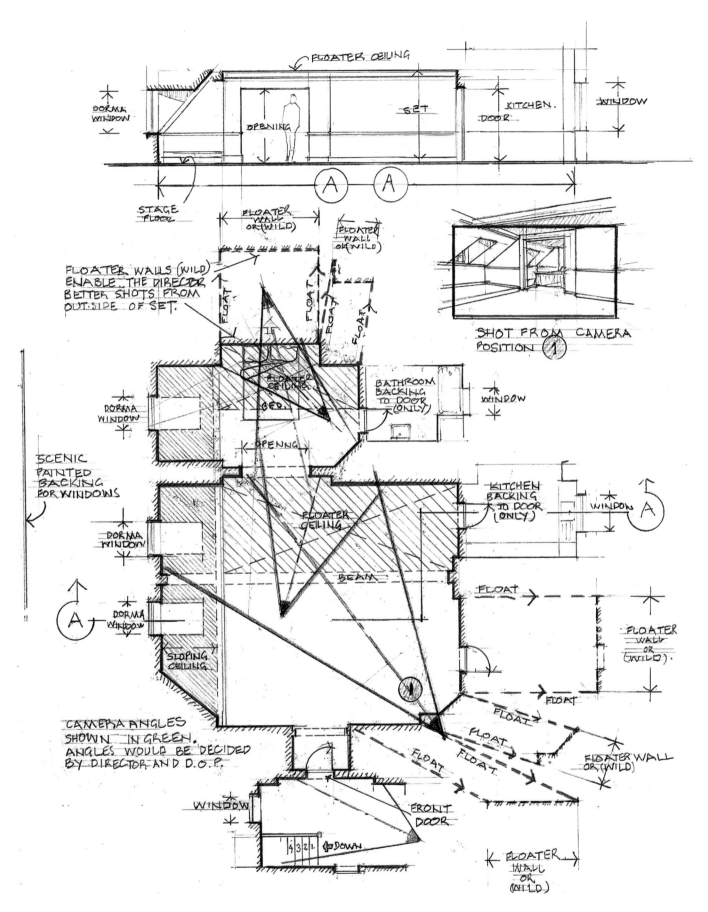

An example of Floater or Wild Walls in a set. This type of construction enables the Director to obtain shots from outside the set.

PROFESSIONAL PERSPECTIVE: TERRY APSEY

Terry Apsey.

Terry Apsey's credits include: *The Phantom of the Opera; Sleepy Hollow; Saving Private Ryan; Band of Brothers; Michael Collins; Braveheart; Interview with a Vampire; Patriot Games; Batman; Superman IV; Greystoke; Pink Floyd: The Wall; Superman II; Force 10 from Navarone; Stardust; Murphy's War; The Italian Job; Help!*

The back view of an aeroplane on the runway as constructed.

CONSTRUCTION MANAGEMENT

Building a set can be a juggling act for the Construction Manager – trying to keep on budget for the Producer whilst giving the Designer as much as you can. Sometimes you have to tell the Designer that he can't have the changes or alterations he wants as there isn't the money in the budget. If he really wants it, then it's up to him to approach the Producer directly.

On some films we have to reinforce parts of the set to accommodate the action. For instance on *The Phantom of the Opera* (designed by Tony Pratt), we constructed a metal structure to support the balconies in the auditorium, which had to hold several hundred people in the theatre audience.

Another example of reinforcement was for a bridge in *Saving Private Ryan*, which was set in World War II (designed by Tom Sanders). The set was all built on the site of a former British Aerospace factory in Hatfield (now Warner Bros Leavesden Studios). We had to dig the 'river' first and then construct the bridge, which had to take the weight of German Tiger tanks driving across – then the bridge was stone-clad to represent the period.

The side view of an aeroplane on the runway as constructed.

The front view of an aeroplane showing the painted and finished look.

The back view of an aircraft hangar showing the construction of scaffolding and wood.

A full shot of the hangar and plane as the camera and the audience would see it.

First stage of constructing a bridge designed to carry heavy vehicles with a reinforced structure.

Second stage with partial stone cladding for period effect.

Third stage, set almost complete with riverside buildings.

PROFESSIONAL PERSPECTIVE: KEN BARLEY

Ken Barley's credits include: *Kingsman II; Cinderella; Maleficent; Snow White and the Huntsman; Mirror Mirror; Hugo; Prince of Persia: Sands of Time; Green Zone; The Other Boleyn Girl; Sweeney Todd: The Demon Barber of Fleet Street; Stardust; Sunshine; Basic Instinct II; Star Wars: The Phantom Menace; Attack of the Clones; Return of the Jedi; Revenge of the Sith; Michael Collins; Braveheart; Interview with a Vampire; Castaway; Indiana Jones and the Temple of Doom; Tommy; Alien.*

Ken Barley.

TEXTURE AND PLASTERWORK

I started off as an apprentice at Shepperton Studios in 1962 and stayed on working for British Lion Films for nine years before going freelance in 1971, eventually starting work with Terry Apsey's company, working on *Pink Panther* and *Tommy*. I remember moulding those big boots for Elton John!

Plaster, being both economical and flexible in its use, is an extremely valuable set-building material. When people think of plastering they don't always realize how many different disciplines are involved. Ornamental and Fibrous Plasterers work with at least eight or ten different types of plaster and aggregates, plus various vermiculites, in order to achieve the many different textures required. This takes a great deal of experience and the crew, like all the other disciplines, have to keep abreast of any and all improvements in technology and technique. For one of the 'Bond' films, an ice set was built entirely by Plasterers – I know because I cast the bar in the ice hotel!

When deciding on the materials to use, the Head of Department takes into account the kind of textures that will be required. Traditional materials like plaster are useful because they can be formed into any texture. Again, lighting is the key to bringing out the full value of the texture of a surface, though oblique lighting should be avoided on hard and rough textures. Flat-on light can destroy a surface texture very easily and, if the Designer wishes to give emphasis to a texture, he will involve the Cinematographer and Lighting Gaffer to ensure the best lighting angles.

There are 'keys' to texture in every set. The Head of Department has to know if the set is to be silky-soft and feminine, or deliberately vulgar, or with hard and rough textures using stone, brick and earth. The setting of the story determines the texture, but beyond the overall character of the story smaller contrasts can be created within the individual settings.

Example of plasterwork for a gothic fireplace in Stardust.

Example of plasterwork on a set depicting eastern grandeur in Prince of Persia: Sands of Time.

Example of plasterwork for a sixteenth-century house in The Other Boleyn Girl.

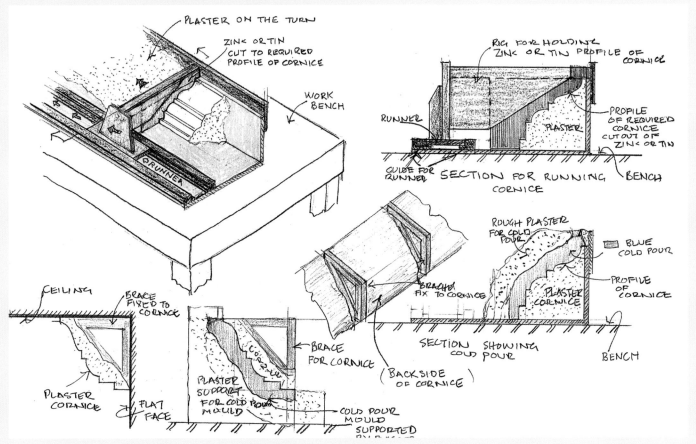

Examples of the basic structures involved in construction.

PROFESSIONAL PERSPECTIVE: KEN BARLEY (continued)

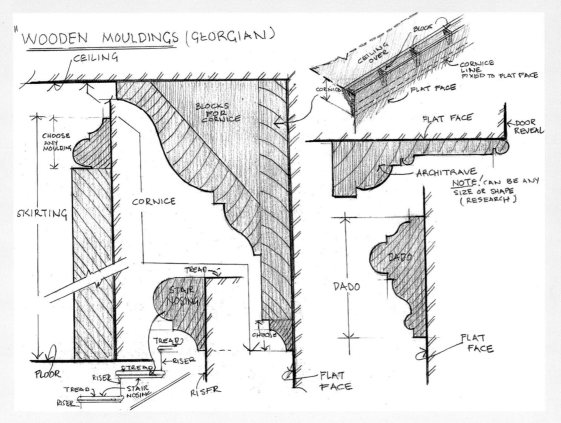

LEFT: *Examples of constructing wooden mouldings.*

BELOW: *Examples of how to make a brick wall.*

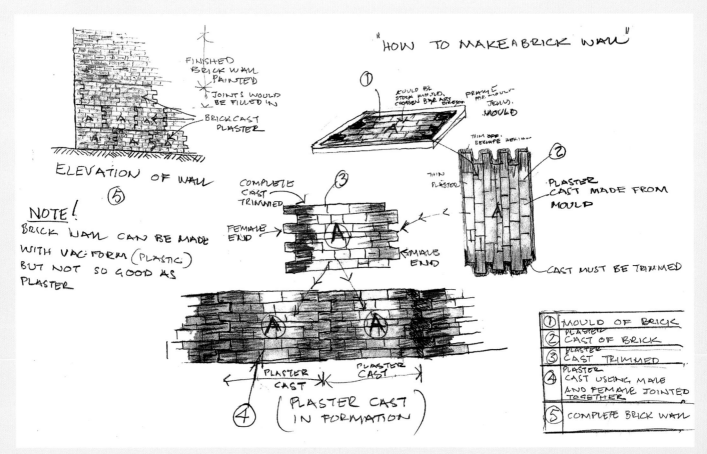

PROFESSIONAL PERSPECTIVE: ADRIAN START

Adrian Start.

Adrian Start's credits include: *Game of Thrones; Your Highness; Prince of Persia: Sands of Time; Green Zone; National Treasure: Book of Secrets; Sweeney Todd: The Demon Barber of Fleet Street; The Queen; V for Vendetta; Batman Begins; The Phantom of the Opera; Finding Neverland; Sky Captain and the World of Tomorrow; Vanity Fair; Neverland; Gosford Park; Sleepy Hollow; Saving Private Ryan; Band of Brothers; In Love and War; Michael Collins; Braveheart; Interview with the Vampire; Patriot Games; Batman; Empire of the Sun; The Company of Wolves; The Bounty; The Dark Crystal; The Elephant Man; Quadrophenia.*

A sample of the finish on an aged brick wall.

SCENIC PAINTING

The Paint Crew are extremely talented artists who bring to life the work of the Plasterers and Carpenters. Their skill and expertise turn the bare construction into believable brickwork, woodwork, wood-graining, rock and stone finishes, gilding and marbling (both tank-dipped and hand-finished); in fact any kind of paint effect necessary to create the atmosphere for the set using a level of technical as well as creative talent that can only be gained from experience on set.

The job is very different to painting and decorating houses! It's really hard to see four or five weeks' worth of work being thrown into a skip as soon as filming finishes, but you get used to it. Sometimes a whole set will be binned without ever being used because the Director or production company have a change of mind.

The job of Head or Master Painter is an important one – what we paint is what you see on the screen. It doesn't matter how good a job the Carpenters or Plasterers have done before us, we can either mess it up, or, hopefully, make a good job of it.

The Head of Department Painter involves close collaboration with the Designer and the Art Department as a whole, to try to translate their ideas into practicable finishes on the set. After that, we have to work closely with the Construction Manager, who has the huge task of co-ordinating all the set builds. In the images accompanying this section, you can see the types of finishes that we deal with.

An example of 'dipped' marble balustrade.

An example of marbling on a floor.

Hand-painted marbling on a staircase.

PROPS, SET DRESSING AND DECORATING

The Set Dresser, Props Master and Drapes Master are involved early on in the process and so, when the set is built, they are ready to do their job. They have to be very familiar with the proposed action on set, so this means that they will be present at rehearsals in order to research and make up a ground plan from which they will work.

Props and Dressing are an integral part of the story-telling process. The process isn't used simply to fill up screen space in a decorative way – it has to have its origins within the characters, the period of the production and the action. It can tell the audience a great deal about the character's circumstances – is a man wealthy or poor, is he a family man or does he live alone? Dressing and Props are related to and fully integrated into the action, so a chair has to be for sitting on, a table has to be able to be walked around, a curtain has to open and close, a gas stove has to work and so on.

"CONSTRUCTION"

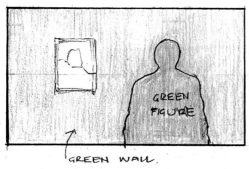 

GREEN WALL.

GREEN FIGURE AGAINST GREEN WALL
BACKGROUND COLOUR GREEN WALL
"NOT GOOD"

RED WALL

GREEN FIGURE AGAINST RED WALL
BACKGROUND COLOUR RED
MAKE CONTRAST COLOUR, FROM FIG
AND BACKGROUND THIS IS GOOD

LEFT: *Examples of the wrong and the right way to co-ordinate the décor of a set with the performer's costumes. It is an illustration of the essential co-operation between all departments.*

BELOW: *A further example of co-ordinating set dressing with the action on set.*

"SET DRESSING"

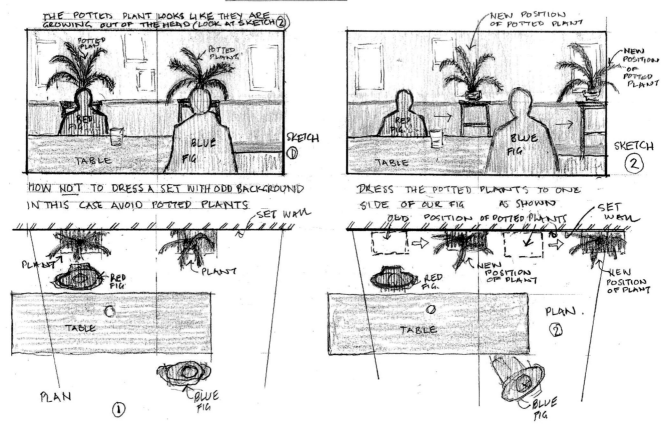

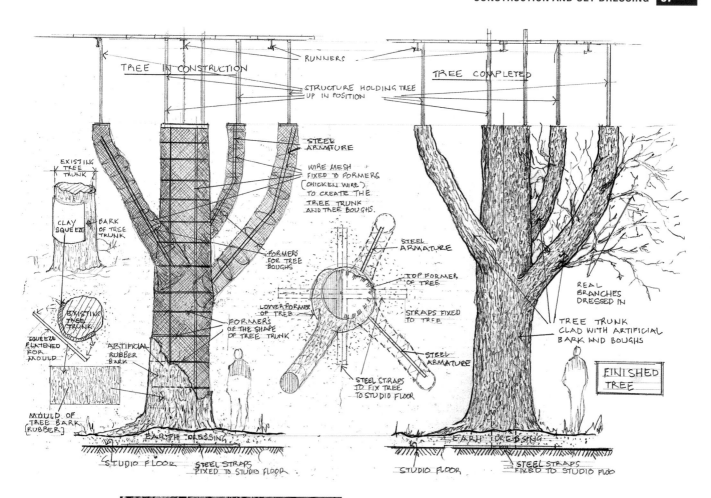

TREE IN CONSTRUCTION

TREE COMPLETED

RUNNERS

STRUCTURE HOLDING TREE UP IN POSITION

STEEL ARMATURE

WIRE MESH FIXED TO FORMERS (CHICKEN WIRE) TO CREATE THE TREE TRUNK AND TREE BOUGHS.

EXISTING TREE TRUNK

CLAY SQUEEZE

BARK OF TREE TRUNK

FORMERS FOR TREE BOUGHS

STEEL ARMATURE

TOP FORMER OF TREE

REAL BRANCHES DRESSED IN

EXISTING TREE TRUNK

LOWER FORMER OF TREE

STRAPS FIXED TO TREE

TREE TRUNK CLAD WITH ARTIFICIAL BARK AND BOUGHS

SQUEEZE FLATTENED FOR MOULD

FORMERS OF THE SHAPE OF TREE TRUNK

ARTIFICIAL RUBBER BARK

STEEL ARMATURE

FINISHED TREE

MOULD OF TREE BARK (RUBBER)

STEEL STRAPS TO FIX TREE TO STUDIO FLOOR

EARTH DRESSING

EARTH DRESSING

STUDIO FLOOR

STEEL STRAPS FIXED TO STUDIO FLOOR

STUDIO FLOOR

STEEL STRAPS FIXED TO STUDIO FLOOR

ABOVE: A typical example of the construction of a tree using armature, wire mesh, artificial rubber bark and finishing off dressed with real branches.

An example of a similar tree built on set.

It is imperative that, at an early stage, the Designer and the Director agree about the characterization and the action. Both may change and develop as the film proceeds, but it is better to be continually adjusting ideas about points of dressing than to present the Director with something at rehearsals that has little to do with the characters or the action. Sometimes the situation and characters are fairly clearly defined at the outset and, after examining the initial sketches or models, the Director may leave the Designer to get on with the set, working with the Dresser and Buyer. However, other Directors may be less clear about how certain characters will develop and it is important to be in constant communication to ensure that the design is as relevant as possible at any particular stage. The importance of the set to the dramatic structure of the film means that whatever the Director wishes to say in the scene will be said within the set before any action takes place. Changes in the accent given to certain scenes may lead to drastic changes in the dressing of a set and this can cause practical problems.

If you have to project the idea of great age in the dressing, it is often useful to use objects that are authentically old. Experienced Props Masters and Set Dressers will have a multitude of sources for furniture, household items, soft furnishings, vehicles, armaments and boats – even down to period door knobs and letter-boxes!

Batman

In the late 1980s I was approached to be the Art Director, alongside Nigel Phelps and Les Tomkins, on the 1989 Tim Burton film, *Batman*. The Production Designer was Anton Furst and we filmed in Pinewood Studios and various UK locations. Hatfield House in Hertfordshire doubled as Wayne Manor, with both Acton and Little Barfield Power Stations standing in as Axis Chemical Works. It turned into an iconic film and grossed $413m worldwide, winning an Oscar for Art Direction along the way.

We had quite a few obstacles to overcome in the Art Department, not least of which was the Batmobile! First, we contacted a major motor manufacturer in Detroit, but were told that it would take them around three years to custom-build a vehicle, so we had to take a different direction. We sourced a couple of Impala drophead cars (one pink and one yellow) and used the frames as a base. Part of the job was finding larger than life petrol caps on a London Routemaster bus and basing the rear lights on those of a Ferrari. We completed the whole build in four months!

Whilst we were building the Batmobile and working on the carving of the distinctive body features in polystyrene, Tim Burton came in and said, 'Great, it's very good Terry, but how do they get in, there aren't any doors …' I hadn't thought of that! However, I'd recently been in a Harrier Jump Jet which had a hood that slid forward, so it gave me an idea. I asked the Special Effects Supervisor John Evans if he could have the hood built and he custom-built a tricky hydraulic mechanism to make it work properly.

Batman, played by Michael Keaton, had to sit in the car, so we had Rocaro seats fitted. Unfortunately, when Michael was fully dressed in hood complete with ears, the ears hit the roof and were bent forward just a little – so Tim asked if I could lower the seat down. However, we were almost at the limit of how low the seat could go, as there was very little clearance on the car. Eventually we solved the problem by Bob Ringwood, the Costume Designer, making a 'Batmobile' hood for the costume with slightly shorter ears. Both of these incidents highlight the occasions on film sets that no one ever notices – all the small problems that have to be overcome. This demonstrates exactly how a good film crew should work together, each department making sure that the finished product is the best it can be.

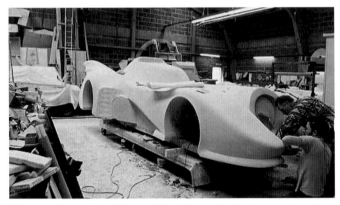

The polystyrene sculpture of the Batmobile being prepared for a model cast for the actual body. The construction was done in a UK factory that specializes in Formula One car bodies.

The finished Batmobile in all its glory!

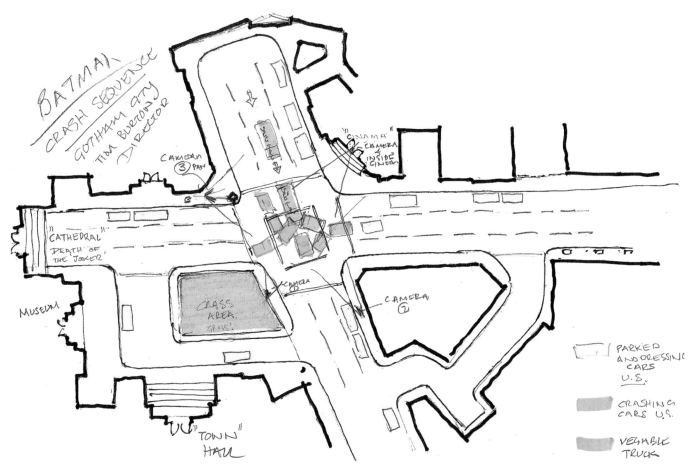

The draft plan of Gotham City streets as they would be built on the back lot at Pinewood Studios, showing the outline of the approximate collision of vehicles. It also shows camera positions.

A close-up of some of the intricate build details.

An aerial shot of the Gotham City streets constructed at Pinewood, adjacent to the 007 Stage.

A photograph of the streets under construction.

PROFESSIONAL PERSPECTIVE: DARCEY CROWNSHAW

Darcey Crownshaw.

Over thirty years ago, Darcey Crownshaw founded Snow Business, which is now known as a world leader in artificial snow and winter effects. Snow Business' film credits to date include: *A Very Muppet Christmas; Alice in Wonderland; Avengers: Age of Ultron; Batman Begins; The Bourne Trilogy; Brotherhood of the Wolf; Cadfael; Charlie and the Chocolate Factory; The Chronicles of Narnia: The Lion, the Witch and the Wardrobe; Chronicles of Riddick; Cold Mountain; Company of Wolves; The Day After Tomorrow; Enemy at the Gate; Enigma; Far from The Madding Crowd; Frankenstein: The Real Story; Gangs of New York; The Girl with the Dragon Tattoo; The Golden Compass; Harry Potter and the Chamber of Secrets/The Philosopher's Stone/The Prisoner of Azkaban; Hellboy; The Hitchhiker's Guide to the Galaxy; Killing me Softly; King Arthur; Kingdom Come; Kingdom of Heaven; Last Days of Pompeii; Love Actually; The Madness of King George; The Magnificent Ambersons; Maleficent; Mary Shelley's Frankenstein; Memoirs of a Geisha; Merlin; Muppet Treasure Island; Nanny McPhee; Notting Hill; Paddington; The Phantom of the Opera; Shackleton; Shadowlands; Skyfall; Sleepy Hollow; Snow White and The Huntsman; Stardust; Star Trek; The Tenth Kingdom; Tomb Raider 1 and 2; Troy; True Grit; Vanilla Sky; Wind in the Willows; Wonder Boys.*

SET DRESSING

In 1920, D.W. Griffith made what some people class as the greatest movie of all time – *Way Down East* starring Lillian Gish. Griffith wanted realism at any cost; he wanted nothing to do with the white-painted cornflakes that were regularly used as studio snow at that time. For the climax of the movie, Gish's character was to be driven out into the blizzard and to stumble on to the river's moving ice. After the event, Lillian Gish wrote:

Our house was near the studio and I was to report to work at any hour that snow started to fall, as we had both day and night scenes to film. I slept with one eye open, waiting for the blizzard. Winter dragged on and was almost over and still those important scenes hadn't been filmed. The blizzard finally struck in March. Drifts eight feet high swallowed the studio. Mr Griffith, Billy, the staff and assistant directors stood with their backs to the gale, bundled up in coats, mufflers, hats and gloves. To hold the camera upright, three men lay on the ground, gripping the tripod legs. A small fire burned directly beneath the camera to keep the oil from freezing.

Again and again, I struggled through the storm. Once I fainted – and it wasn't in the script. I was hauled to the studio on a sled, thawed out with hot tea and then brought back to the blizzard, where the others were waiting. We filmed all day and all night, stopping only to eat, standing near a bonfire. We never went inside, even for a short warm-up. The torture of returning to the cold wasn't worth the temporary warmth. The blizzard never slackened. At one point, the camera froze. There was an excruciating delay as the men, huddled against the wind, tried to get another fire started. At one time my face was caked with a crust of ice and snow and icicles like little spikes formed on my eyelashes, making it difficult to keep my eyes open.

Above the storm, Mr Griffith shouted: 'Billy, move! Get that face! That face – get that face!' … 'I will,' Billy shouted, 'if the oil doesn't freeze in the camera!' Although he worked with his back to the wind whenever possible, Mr Griffith's face froze. A trained nurse was at his side for the rest of the blizzard and the winter scenes. We lost several members of our crew to pneumonia as the result of exposure …

Falling snow technology has moved forward tremendously in recent years. Modern ground-based machinery can deliver vast amounts of snow into the air almost silently to fill acres with realistic, slow-falling, self-clearing falling snow. Gone are the plastic flakes or the polystyrene beads that seem to last forever, haunting old movie locations for many years whenever the wind changes. On any modern movie snow set you can expect to see a combination of seven or eight types of snow dressing in use at any one time: SnowMembrane to protect the location; SnowCel Full Size paper to give depth; SnowCel Half Size paper to give refinement; and SnowSparkle top dressing to add that 'twinkle'. Polymer top dressing is used for improved tracks and pickup on costume; PowderFrost or SnowEx to fill in background; BioFlake for use as falling snow; and IceWax white to simulate that frozen mountain 'crust' to break realistically under footfall.

Toxic materials that damaged locations are thankfully a thing of the past. By selecting the right material and processes and correct preparation, any location can be dressed realistically and can be left undamaged. Work is completed regularly on the most sensitive of sites. Modern materials are eco-friendly, biodegradable and incorporate low-embodied energy. The paper used is chlorine-free and the cellulose is from managed, renewable sources.

Stage two of set dressing – prepared with SnowMembrane.

Stage one of set dressing – original location.

Stage three of set dressing – finished with SnowCel.

Exterior set dressed with snow.

Interior set dressed with snow.

CHAPTER 4

WORKING ON LOCATION

THE SCRIPT AND LOCATION SHOOTING

The script is the starting point in the Designer's search for suitable locations. After discussions with the Director, the Designer considers the type of action involved and what kind of location will be required. After reading the script, the Designer will have an impression of the location he would like and he may go on a recce, on his own or with the Art Director, in order to substantiate his ideas.

Whether locations are needed or not depends on the script, the budget and the design concept. If they are a necessary part of the plot, and once the Director and Production Designer have decided on exactly how and where they want the action to take place, then the Location Manager is brought into the team.

FINDING LOCATIONS/RECCE

Almost without exception, a feature film will use the services of a Location Manager and his Location Scouts. This department is skilled in sourcing both national and international locations to the exact requirements of the Art Department. The experienced Location Manager will have already sourced many sites during his career and so will be able to advise immediately on the suitability of various options, as well as local bureaucracy.

If it is to be an overseas location, then a local Scout might be used, as they have a wider knowledge of the local landscape. Then it is the Location Manager's job, having taken on board the suggestions of the Designer and the Director, to find a selection of suitable sites with accompanying photographs and approximate measurements for the Art Director and the Designer to select. If, for example, a pub was required, then the Location Manager would look at perhaps twelve pubs with his Scout, then would narrow the options down to six when presenting to the Designer and Art Director, who together would select a final three out of the six, which would then be shown to the Director for the final decision. It is the Location Team's job to research thoroughly the surrounding areas in order to see what facilities are available, and also to ensure that the proper clearances can be obtained from the local police and municipal authorities and, very importantly, to check the local weather statistics.

Once this is done, the Designer and Art Director will visit each one in turn, taking more precise measurements and photographs, discussing what extra dressing is required and how much construction. The Art Director will advise the Director on the location he thinks fits all the required parameters.

EXAMPLE OF SCRIPT PAGE BREAKDOWN TO GO WITH INTERIOR & EXTERIOR SET BREAKDOWN EXAMPLES

SABINA - (matter of fact)

It's Death, he wants a drink. Here you are, Death.

She pours champagne into the leaking cup, it dribbles away onto the wooden floorboards.

SABINA - (Cont'd)

He's thirsty!

JUNG

The skull should really have a proper burial.

SABINA

They start to make love, knocking over the champagne bottle, spilling its contents, along with the skull goblet, which dribbles champagne out onto the floor of the room.

We move in close on the overturned blackened skull cup until all goes black.

FADE TO BLACK:

FADE IN:

88. SCENE CUT.

89. EXT TEMPLE, DREAM VISION. DAY - CONTINUOUS

From out of a thick, misty fog, we see JUNG and SABINA emerge, dressed in hooded ceremonial robes. Before them appears an image of a circular classical temple atop a little hill, framed against an unnaturally tempestuous sky.

SOUND: Mocking laughter.

On the steps of the temple sits WOLFGANG GOETHE, dressed in classical wig and finery.

JUNG - (To himself)

Goeth!

GOETHE - (Smoothly)

Ah, Doctor Faustus, and that must be little Gretchen

PINK - ACTION PROPS

BLUE - SPECIAL EFFECTS

Example of a page of script that will be broken down page by page into interior or exterior sets with specific scene numbers.

No.	Interior Sets		Scene Number	Script Pages
1	Screen Titles		1	1
2	Opening Titles		2	1
3	Int. Sleeper Compartment Train		5N,8N	4
4	Int. Train Toilet		7N	3
5	Int. Bleuler's apartment		13D	5
6	Int. Chapel Entance		14D,19D	5,8
7	Int. Corridor Burgholzli		15D,16D,22N,29D,45D,62D,65D,71D,78	6,7,9,16,34,49,51,60,71,77
8	Int. Jungs Apartment Burgholzli		12D,31D,53N,81D	4,17,43,71
9	Int. Mixed Ward		18D,66D	8,52
10	Int. Single Ward		21D,23D,24D,25D,34N,35N,37N	8,10,20,21,23
11	Int. Jungs Office		26D,28D,33D,36D,39D,44D,47D,54D,63D	14,16,18,21,24,30,36,44,50,69,72,76
12	Int. Sabina's beating Fantasy		3D,27,41	1,15,27
13	Int. Photographers Darkroom		30D	17
14	Int. Freud's Study (Vienna)		43D,46D,75D	30,35
15	Int Hotel Suit		49D,58D	38,47,65
16	Int. Sabina's Lodgings + bathroom		51N,52N,55D,60D,61D,69D,70D,73D,76N	43,45,49,55,57,61,65,75
17	Int. Lecture Hall Vienna		68D,99N	54,86
18	Int. Lecture Hall Zurich		64D,74D	51,64
19	Int. Library (Zurich University)		83D	73
20	Int. Examination Hall		88D	77
21	Int. Corridor (Zurich University)		90D,92D	77,79
22	Int. Restaurant Zurich		96N	82
23	Int. Corridor Vienna		100N	89

■ RED INDICATES TWO OF THE MAJOR SETS IF REQUIRED AT THE SAME TIME (GENERALLY FEATURING THE MOVIE STARS). BEST TO GO TO THE PAGE NUMBERS RATHER THAN THE SCENE NUMBERS

Breakdown of interior sets marked red to indicate sets that might be required at the same time. 'D' refers to day and 'N' refers to night.

No.	Exterior Sets		Scene Number	Script Pages
1	Ext. Snowy Street		4D	2
2	Ext. Train		6D,9D	3,4
3	Ext. Desert (Dream Vision)		10D,103D	4,91
4	Ext. Burholzli Institute		11D,80D	4,71
5	Ext. Grounds Burholzli		40D,42D	27
6	Ext. Stream	■	32D,38N,56D,97N	18,24,46,84
7	Ext. Hotel		48D,57	38,47
8	Ext. River	■	50D	41
9	Ext. Sabina's Lodgings		51N	43
10	Ext. Jerusalem		59D,91D	49,79
11	Ext. Park Zurich		67D	53
12	Ext. Leafy Path	■	84D	73
13	Ext. Sparse Wood	■	85D	74
14	Ext. Entrance Gates		93D	79
15	Ext. Grave	■	94N,95N	81
16	Ext Jungs House		98N	84
17	Ext. Snowy Landscape		101D,102D	89,91

■ BLUE INDICATES POSSIBLE SETS COULD BE AT THE SAME LOCATION IE. WOODS (COPY MUST BE GIVEN TO LOCATION MANAGER)

Breakdown of exterior sets marked with 'blue' to indicate using the same location.

CALL SHEET NO: 65　　　　　　**THURSDAY 3RD AUGUST 2000**

Producer:

UNIT CALL: 11.30AM ON SET
ESTIMATED WRAP: 23.30PM
Director:　　James Hawes　　　　**BRUNCH FROM:　　10.45AM**
Associate Producer:　Peter Hider
UNIT MOBILES
2nd AD:　　　Lisa Jones
Loc Manager:　Rufus Andrews　　　　Sunrise: 05.26
Unit Manager:　Mally Chung
Co-ordinator:　Sue Young　　　　　Sunset:　20.47

WEATHER:　Remaining unsettled and breezy with further showers 23ºC max.

PLEASE NOTE EXTENDED DAY & CHANGE TO UNIT HOURS

LOCATION　　　　　　　　　　　　　**UNIT BASE**
1) **105 HICKS AVENUE** (Mowbray's House)　**PERIVAL PARK**
Greenford, Middx　　　　　　　　　　off Cowgate Road
Contact: Mally Chung　　　　　　　　South Greenford, Middx
2) **THE OLDFIELD TAVERN** (King's Arms and Car Park)　Contact:
Oldfield Lane North, Greenford, Middx
Contact: Paula Portsmouth

SC/EP	I/E	SET/SYNOPSIS	D/N	PG'S	CAST NO
22/4	INT	Mowbray House - Hall/Living Room Sally describes car sharing	N17	1 1/8	1,2,9,46
47/5	INT	Mowbray House - Kitchen Sally knows of Mowbray's affair	D25	6/8	1,2
60/5	INT	Mowbray House - Hall/Kitchen Mowbray is welcomed by Fred	D26	2/8	1
61/5	INT	Mowbray House - Bedroom Sally has moved out	D26	2/8	1
47/4	INT	Kings Arms Farewell to the departing detectives	N19	1 6/8	1,4,7,14
44/4	INT	Kings Arms Mowbray offers Walkinshaw a lift	N19	4/8	1,7
30/5	INT	Pub Car Park Middle of nowhere, two cars parked	N24	2/8	1,7

TOTAL PAGES　　　4 7/8

NO	ARTISTE	CHARACTER	P/up	M/up	W/D	ON SET
1	Terry Snow	JACK MOWBRAY	1000	11000	a/Reh	1130
2	Davina Poulter	SALLY MOWBRAY	0920	1045	1030	1130
3	Ciara Sheridan	PAULA MOWBRAY	1030	1115	1100	1130
46	Lucy Williams	GWEN	0920	1045	1030	1130
4	Charlie Harb	JIM BOULTER	1530	1645	1700	1800
7	Valentine Rogers	MARGARET WALKINSHAW	1500	1630	1700	1800
14	Astrid Guiness	LINDA HARRISK	1515	1615	1700	1800

CHARACTER	Scene	M/up & W/D	ON SET
1 x Rachel, Gwen's Friend	Sc 22/4	1100	1130
1 x Barmaid	Sc 443/4	1530	1800
1 x Barman	Sc 43/4	1530	1800
4 x CID (Male)	Sc 43/4	1530	1800
4 x CID (Female)	Sc 43/4	1530	1800
1 x 'NEW' CID (Male)	Sc 43/4	1530	1800
1 x 'NEW' CID (Female)	Sc 43/4	1530	1800
1 x PC	Sc 43/4	1530	1800
1 x WPC	Sc 43/4	1530	1800
1 x Cab Driver	Sc 44/4	1830	1930

Example of a Unit Call Sheet with Artist, Crew and Props requirements.

MOVEMENT ORDER NO: 33

DATE:	**THURSDAY 3 AUGUST**

UNIT BASE:	**PERIVALE PARK, SOUTH GREENFORD** **MIDDLESEX** <u>**OFF COWGATE ROAD**</u>
Contact:	MIKE LIDDALL

LOCATION 1: (for Set 1)	**105 HICKS AVENUE, SOUTH GREENFORD** **SOUTH GREENFORD, MIDDLESEX**
Contact:	Via Location Department
LOCATION 2: (for Sets 2 & 3)	**THE OLDFIELD TAVERN, OLDFIELD LANE N,** **GREENFORD, MIDDLESEX**
Contact:	Paula Portsmouth

SETS:	1. **INT. MOWBRAY HOUSE** 2. **INT/EXT KING'S ARMS** 3. **EXT. PUB CAR PARK**

POLICE:	**GREENFORD POLICE STATION** **21 OLDFIELD LANE, GREENFORD, MIDDX** **(T) 020 8575 1212**
HOSPITAL:	**EALING HOSPITAL** **UXBRIDGE ROAD, SOUTHALL, MIDDX** **(T) 020 8967 5613**
LOCAL COUNCIL:	**LONDON BOROUGH OF EALING** **Contact: MIKE LIDDALL**

Example of a Unit Movement Order with specific information for locations, routes and parking.

Travel Time from Studio: 5 mins   Mileage: 1.4 miles

>>>

PLEASE FOLLOW BLACK AND WHITE UNIT SIGNS

1. **From Production Office join WESTERN AVENUE at B&Q (A40 Eastbound)**
2. **Stay in Left Hand Lane and take the First Exit (signposted GREENFORD A4127/HARROW A404)**
3. **Move into Right Hand Lane and take the Third Exit (under flyover) signposted GREENFORD a4127/SOUTHALL A4020 (GREENFORD ROAD)**
4. **Move into Left Hand Lane and take the First Left into COWGATE ROAD immediately past the SHELL STATION**
5. **Continue along COWGATE ROAD, follow the road to the end. Entrance to UNIT BASE is <u>STRAIGHT AHEAD</u>**

ROUTE FROM PERIVALE PARK TO LOCATION - 105 HICKS AVE

Travel Time: 1 minute   Mileage: 0.1 mile

>>>

1. **Turn RIGHT out of UNIT BASE onto COWGATE ROAD and take the next RIGHT into HICKS AVENUE**
2. **Continue along HICKS AVENUE passing ANTHONY ROAD. Location is on the left.**

PLEASE PARK AS DIRECTED
ROUTE FROM LOCATION 1 TO LOCATION 2 - THE OLDFIELD TAVERN

Travel Time: 5 mins   Mileage: 2 miles

>>

1. **Turn LEFT out of location and continue up HICKS AVENUE**
2. **Turn LEFT and follow the road parallel to A40 WESTERN AVENUE**
3. **Join WESTERN AVENUE onto GREENFORD ROAD**
4. **Continue under RAILWAY BRIDGES, past GLAXO WELLCOME on LEFT**
5. **Continue across traffic lights. Location is on your LEFT - just before TEXACO STATION**

<u>UNIT NOTES</u>

NO SMOKING IN THE HOUSE
PLEASE DISPOSE OF CIGARETTE BUTTS IN ASH CANS PROVIDED
DO NOT BLOCK ANY DRIVEWAYS UNLESS SPECIFICALLY TOLD TO DO SO BY LOCATION DEPARTMENT
UNDER NO CIRCUMSTANCES MUST PRIVATE CARS BE TAKEN TO HICKS/DAVID AVENUE OR ANTHONY ROAD.

Rufus Andrews   Location Manager

Example of a Unit Movement Order with specific information for locations, routes and parking.

Barry Lyndon

Barry Lyndon was released in 1975 and won four Oscars in total and two BAFTAs. The Art Department won one Oscar and was nominated for a BAFTA. My experience of location scouting for this film was a memorable occasion and is a good example of how a Location Manager needs to expect the unexpected. We were asked to find a castle, so the options were narrowed down and we went to see Huntingdon Castle in Ireland. We didn't have specific directions for the castle, so we went into an old-fashioned hardware shop in the village of Clonegal to ask where the castle was located. Everyone who was in the shop went absolutely quiet! Eventually the shopkeeper told us it was 400yd down on the right, so I drove there with Bert from the Construction Department, who was a bit wary of the look of the place. We introduced ourselves to a man at the castle, who invited us inside to have a look around.

He escorted us to an oak-panelled room, which had a big roaring fire in the hearth and suits of armour, tapestries and such like, with many cobwebs hanging around. Eventually he called us out of the room to meet his sister, who looked a bit like Bette Davis in *What Ever Happened to Baby Jane?*, dressed in

Mr Durdin Robertson in his robes. He and his sister created the 'black magic' myth that still attracts visitors to the 'Temple of Isis' to this day.

Surveying the location windows for Barry Lyndon, *as they will have to be replaced by Gothic-style ones to suit the film.*

a big black cloak. She showed us upstairs and we went along a corridor that had all the doors painted black, each with a small flame-coloured symbol on them. When I entered one of the rooms, everything was black, including the big four-poster bed. She said that it was their initiation room and part of their 'black magic' practices. You can imagine that we got out of the room as fast as we could!

Our strange hostess then asked if we would like to see some of their Victorian collection of doll-houses and prams in the loft, so we obediently went up with her to look. However, while we were there she suddenly declared she could hear someone crying, which she suspected was the maid who had been murdered in the basement. By this time, Bert was hanging on to me like his life depended on it! She took us all the way down to the basement, which had a vaulted ceiling with a hook in it – apparently where the maid had been hanged – and then asked us to stay for lunch. That was, of course, the last thing we wanted to do, but I'd been told by the Location Manager to be polite, so we went back upstairs and into the dining room, which had been set with pewter goblets. The fireplace slid to

Diagram connecting the built film set in the studio with the location.

the left, opening up into the kitchen from where the servant pushed the food trolley, and the fireplace then slid back into position.

I mentioned that the way they lived was a little odd, at which point our hosts laughed and broke cover, showing us the brochure they had produced to encourage American tourists. If anyone could spend more than two nights in the place they could get their money back! So, actually the whole set-up wasn't a spooky ghost story, but a clever marketing ploy. We found out afterwards that the 'black magic' was, in fact, a Temple of Isis that they had put together and is apparently still a tourist attraction to this day.

When I got back to base I told Stanley Kubrick and the Designer, Roy Walker, and they had to go and see it for themselves, so we did actually shoot there in the end.

LOCATION INTERIORS AND STUDIO RECONSTRUCTION OF LOCATION EXTERIORS

Sometimes, for reasons of authenticity or economy, it might be viable to use location interiors – but generally interiors are built on stage sets in the 'home' studio.

Occasionally, and for practical reasons, it may be necessary to reconstruct a location exterior in the studio. In order for the construction to be a success, a great deal of painstaking recording of the original location has to be done. These sets are built because the shooting may take place over several days and might include destruction of walls, rain on windows, or shooting night and day shots – all these things have to be taken into consideration. Another advantage of building the set in a studio environment is to give the Director and Cinematographer greater freedom with camera angles and action.

MATCHING LOCATION EXTERIOR AND STUDIO INTERIOR

Location exteriors are often used to give greater reality to a scene that is mainly filmed within the studio. The exterior of a building, although only briefly used, can set the mood of the action and can say a great deal about the characters. To construct the exterior of a building within the studio would be expensive and so it is often much easier to find an actual house, office block or factory that fits the action and then match the interior and exterior shots convincingly, complete with matching dressing. The same applies in reverse – matching a studio set with a previously filmed exterior.

Locations are seldom exactly what the Director is looking for, so hard work is necessary by the Construction Crew to

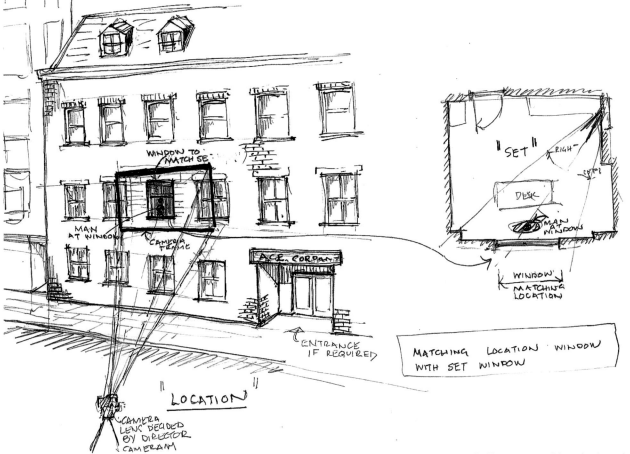

Sketch of a similar built film set matching the location.

change the character of the location to fit the script. Also, the script might call for seasonal changes to be taken into consideration, such as snow, floodwater and other elements.

In period dramas, everyday objects such as power cables and television aerials have to be masked, screened or removed entirely. If farmland is used and altered, then the production might have to buy a season's worth of crops, as well as restoring everything back to normal before leaving the area. All this might seem to be irrelevant since the advent of digital visual effects in post-production, but many Directors have come to regret not paying close attention to these details in production, as the much overused 'we can fix it in post' is a very costly experience!

LOCATION PROPS

When props are made especially for location interiors, it is essential that their dimensions will allow them access to the room or building. For example, for a scene where narrow access is necessary, using authentic local furniture and smaller props is preferable to using imitation.

On one occasion, many years ago, someone instructed a Junior Assistant to set a haystack alight, with disastrous results – he set fire to an actual haystack and not the carefully constructed prop that had been prepared for the job! This kind of situation must be handled by the Special Physical Effects crew, so that any blaze or explosion can be fully controlled and the current Health and Safety rules are observed.

The Deep

The 1977 film, *The Deep*, was filmed on location using an existing shipwreck in the Virgin Islands, as well as with matched sets in a purpose-built tank. The wreck had broken into five sections and were designated Wrecks A, B C, D and E. The boat – the 'Mobie' – from which the diving action took place

Underwater recce.

Underwater recce.

The Deep *in 1977. From left to right: Underwater Stills Photographer Peter Lake; Underwater Art Director Terry Ackland-Snow; First Assistant Derek Cracknell; Production Designer Tony Masters; Director Peter Yates.*

was not moved under its own power, but winched to the relevant area by cables attached to buoys located above each section of wreck. This allowed the divers – both actors and stunt performers – to dive directly on to each area, thereby enabling the underwater camera crew to get the best shots.

Jacqueline Bisset was the female lead and, in one scene, we needed to lower her down about 60ft at the bottom of a section of wreck. There was a hole there and the idea was that she would poke her probe stick into this hole and it would be grabbed by a moray eel. Al Giddings, the Underwater Cinematographer, would be on the other side of the hole and would grab the stick, pulling it as hard as he could so that she would bang against the

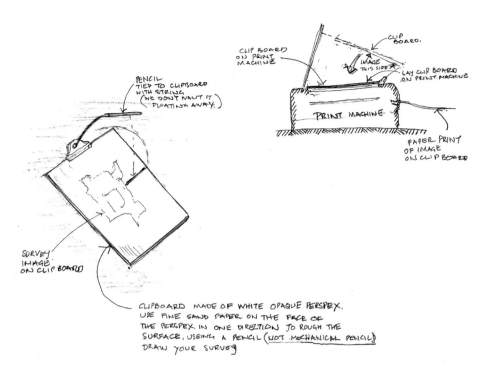

Solving how to sketch underwater!

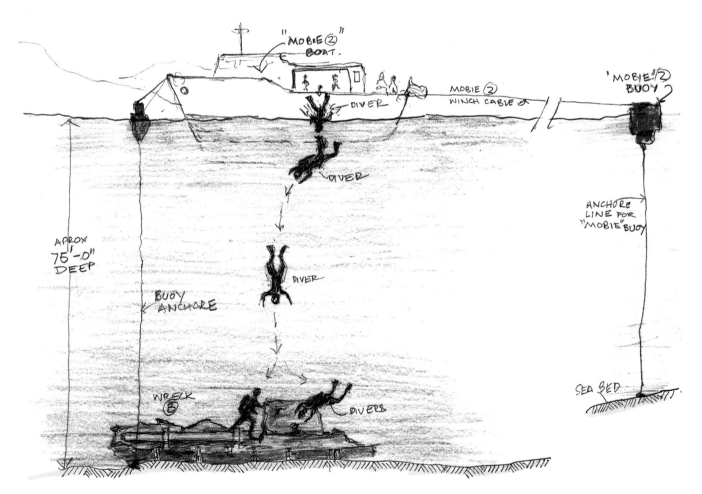

The dive boat 'Mobie' anchored over the location, allowing the divers to descend vertically.

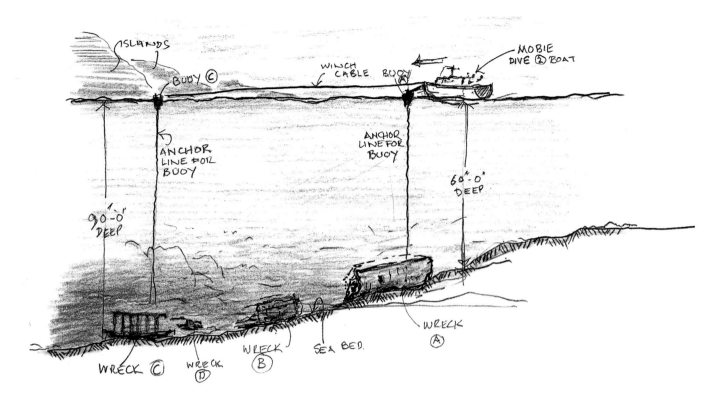

Section showing the sea and seabed with wrecks A, B, C and D. The dive boat was winched to the site and anchored.

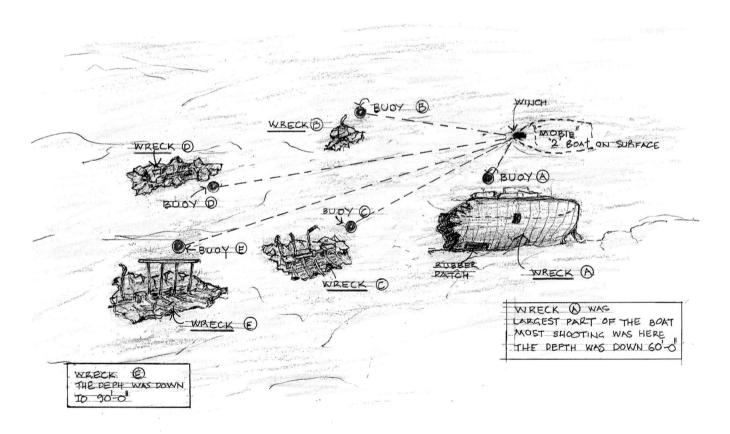

Existing shipwreck in the Virgin Islands. This is a plan of the wreck on the seabed, broken into sections. The winch cable would be fixed to the bow of the boat 'Mobie' (2). The other end of the cable would be fixed to Buoy 'B', situated over Wreck 'B', where the action was to take place.

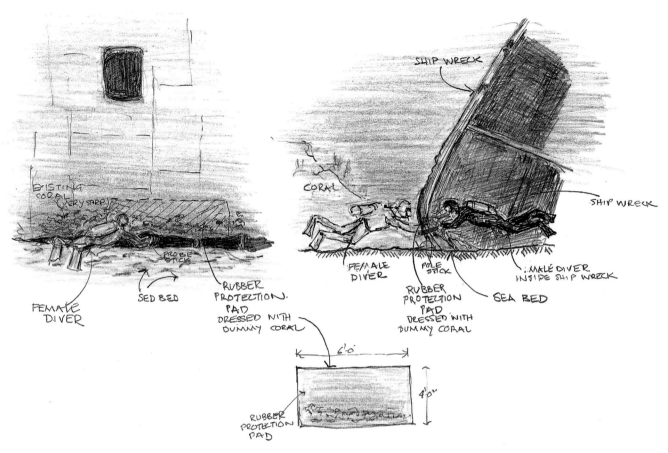

Showing the female diver searching for treasure with the stunt man inside the wreck to grab her probe stick as if by a moray eel.
Note the placement of the rubber shielding dressed to match the seabed.

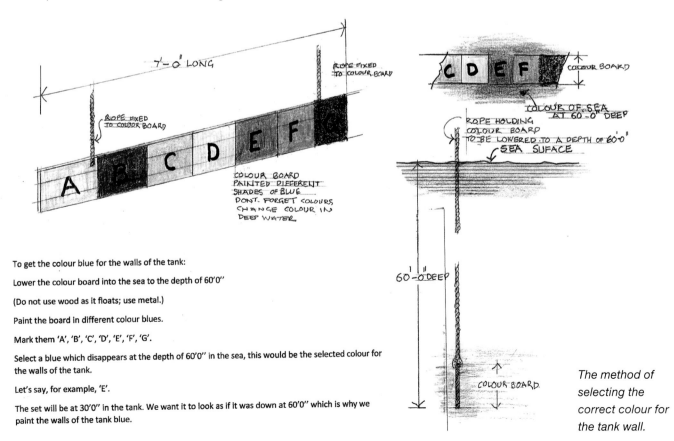

To get the colour blue for the walls of the tank:

Lower the colour board into the sea to the depth of 60'0''

(Do not use wood as it floats; use metal.)

Paint the board in different colour blues.

Mark them 'A', 'B', 'C', 'D', 'E', 'F', 'G'.

Select a blue which disappears at the depth of 60'0'' in the sea, this would be the selected colour for the walls of the tank.

Let's say, for example, 'E'.

The set will be at 30'0'' in the tank. We want it to look as if it was down at 60'0'' which is why we paint the walls of the tank blue.

The method of selecting the correct colour for the tank wall.

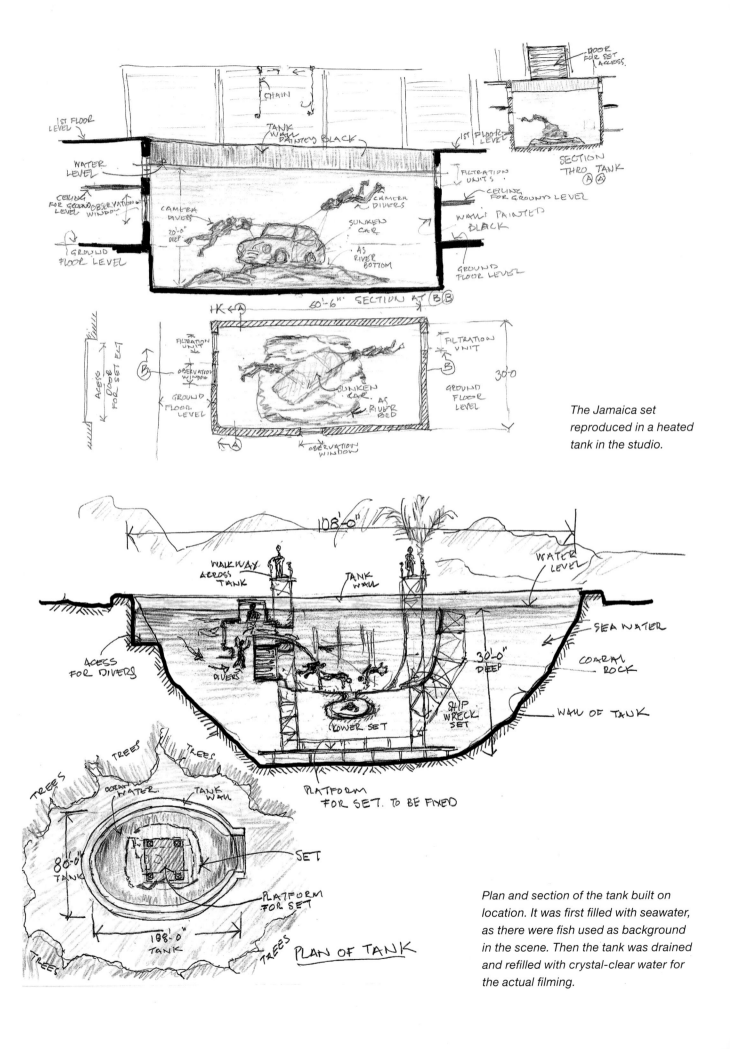

1ST FLOOR LEVEL

WATER LEVEL

CEILING FOR GROUND LEVEL OBSERVATION WINDOW

30'-0" DEEP

GROUND FLOOR LEVEL

CAMERA DIVERS

CHAIN

TANK WALL PAINTED BLACK

CAMERA DIVERS

SUNKEN CAR

AS RIVER BOTTOM

FILTRATION UNITS

1ST FLOOR LEVEL

CEILING FOR GROUND LEVEL

WALLS PAINTED BLACK

GROUND FLOOR LEVEL

DOOR FOR SET ACCESS.

SECTION THRO TANK A A

60'-6" SECTION AT B B

ACCESS DOOR FOR SET

FILTRATION UNIT

OBSERVATION WINDOW

GROUND FLOOR LEVEL

SUNKEN CAR AS RIVER BED

OBSERVATION WINDOW

FILTRATION UNIT

GROUND FLOOR LEVEL

30'-0

The Jamaica set reproduced in a heated tank in the studio.

108'-0"

WALKWAY ACROSS TANK

TANK WALL

WATER LEVEL

ACCESS FOR DIVERS

DIVERS

30'-0" DEEP

SHIP WRECK SET

LOWER SET

SEA WATER

CORAL ROCK

WALL OF TANK

PLATFORM FOR SET. TO BE FIXED

TREES

TREES

TREES

OCEAN WATER

TANK WALL

80'-0" TANK

SET

PLATFORM FOR SET

108'-0" TANK

TREES

TREES

PLAN OF TANK

Plan and section of the tank built on location. It was first filled with seawater, as there were fish used as background in the scene. Then the tank was drained and refilled with crystal-clear water for the actual filming.

side of the wreck, as if the stick had been grabbed by the eel. The problem we found was that the barnacles and the coral on the wreck were razor sharp, so we decided to make a big protective rubber sheet, dressed with coral to cover that part of the wreck – that took some doing! Once we got it down there we released it to place it carefully in position, but the pressure of the water 60ft down sucked it so hard against the hull that we couldn't move it. Fortunately, it landed in the right place so that during the action Jacqueline didn't damage herself.

We also built a tank that was 108ft long, 80ft wide and 30ft deep. It had to be sprayed with polyurethane, which unfortunately was honey-coloured and didn't represent the sea at 60ft down, so we had to paint it the blue of the sea. However, as you go deeper into the ocean the colour changes – big problem! I decided to get a wooden board and paint it various shades of blue in sections (A, B, C, D and so on), so that we could see which colour 'disappeared' at the required depth – but we only got it to about 3ft down, then it popped up to the surface as the wood was so buoyant that we couldn't keep it down, so we remade it with a strip of metal and the problem was solved.

Death on the Nile

For the 1978 film *Death on the Nile*, I was Art Director, alongside my brother Brian, for Designer Peter Murton, with John Guillermin directing.

My first job was to survey the boat we were going to use, which was the historic ship SS *Memnon* (renamed the SS *Karnak* for the film). I carried out a ten-day survey, measuring

The frontage of the hotel, which we redressed to suit the style of the film.

everything, because the cladding we were going to attach to the boat had to be built back in Pinewood. In order to be able to transport the cladding in one piece, we had to build a mock-up aircraft with a cargo door in the studio, so that we were sure that the cladding would fit. Fortunately, it fitted well.

We also had to build a large head to replicate the Sphinx in Ghiza, which was 30ft high and 40ft wide. *See* the photograph of the black and white banner showing the size in order for me to position the head.

I had already worked with a lot of the cast on previous productions, such as Peter Ustinov, Maggie Smith, David Niven, George Kennedy, Mia Farrow, Angela Lansbury and the formidable Bette Davis. It was really quite a team, both crew

On location for Death on the Nile. *Looking out from the hotel over the gardens, which we had to furnish with 'greens'.*

The SS Memnon *before being redressed and renamed the SS* Karnak.

Location for the Sphinx, measuring the size of the head for positioning.

and cast – though not without its turbulent moments! During filming one day, Peter was sketching when the phone rang and the message came through that Bette Davis wanted to speak to Peter in the studio. After what had happened on *The Anniversary*, he was understandably wary, so sent me down instead! She was filming the scene in the bedroom where the maid was combing her hair ready for their holiday. I inquired in an extremely polite tone, 'Miss Davis, do you have a problem?' She asked if I was Peter Murton and I replied that he was currently unavailable as he was out on a recce. Her unexpected reply was, 'Well, I just wanted to tell him what a wonderful set this is, probably the best set I've ever filmed on!' Which, coming from Bette Davis, was a huge compliment. Of course, I didn't tell Peter the good news straight away, but enjoyed going back to his office and watching his face turn pale as I said 'Dear, oh dear …', shaking my head. One of those memorable moments on a film production.

Spies Like Us

In the 1985 Warner Bros. spoof, *Spies Like Us*, starring Dan Aykroyd and Chevy Chase, with John Landis directing, I was joint Production Designer with Peter Murton.

One of my projects was to design a missile carrier. I remembered seeing a rocket launcher in the annual Russian military parade in Red Square on television, so I decided to base my design on that. I found a company in Bradford, UK, which serviced cranes, so I flew there with Brian Johnson, the Special Effects Supervisor. We found a sixteen-axle mobile crane that was missing the lifting cab and jib, so we hired it and designed the missile launcher around that. The missile was made in aluminium and so was lightweight.

Transporter with missile launcher up in the firing position.

The Spies Like Us *crew with the missile in the freezing Austrian Alps.*

CHAPTER 5

CAMERA ANGLES, LIGHTING AND PERSPECTIVE

Filmmaking is essentially the art of creating illusions. The Art Department builds magnificent sets in the studio and creates the same illusion on a location set whilst making it look untouched. Most feature films combine the two, although there are exceptions with films such as *The Phantom of the Opera*, which was made entirely in the studio on stages and the back lot of Pinewood Studios. However, the key to extending this illusion on to the cinema screen is the work of the Camera Crew and it is essential for the Art Department to have a good working knowledge of this process.

Every Junior Draughtsman, from the beginning of their training in the Art Department, will start to assimilate information about camera angles and perspective. The camera lens is the medium through which the audience sees the finished movie, so the Designer effectively has to imagine the scene as if 'through the lens' and all the drawings and blueprints have to reflect this. Given this fact, the experienced Production Designer and Art Director need to have a good working knowledge of cameras and lenses, both film and digital, and have to keep abreast of changes and innovations in camera technology and techniques. The Art Director will also be involved in any lens tests with the Director and Cinematographer, so a working knowledge of apertures, F-stops, T-stops, focal lengths, aspect ratios and perspectives should all be in their mental bag of tricks.

UNDERSTANDING THE JOBS IN THE CAMERA DEPARTMENT, INCLUDING GRIPS AND LIGHTING

* *Please note that the following titles marked with an asterisk are generic terms and are used to describe both male and female practitioners. All roles can be filled by either a man or a woman and references to 'he' are for convenience only.*

Director of Photography (DoP) or Cinematographer

The Director of Photography is in control of the Camera Department on set, orchestrating the Camera Crew, Grip and Lighting teams, who use their skills and expertise to film the action on set in order to capture exactly the images that the Director wants. Liaising closely with the Art Department throughout the shooting process, the DoP is key to maintaining the consistent 'look and feel' of the film. The input of the DoP also extends into the post-production phase. Once the edited sequences have been completed by the Director and the post-production team, the DoP must be involved with the final colour grading in order to ensure that the Director's desired 'look and feel' of the film is maintained prior to final release or screening.

Camera Operator

The Camera Operator is the right hand of the DoP during filming. Responsible for the physical operation of the camera, this entails the Operator working closely with the Director, the DoP and the individual members of the cast to line up and plan a sequence. When filming, the Operator must ensure that the desired photographic composition is both technically accurate and is maintained throughout the individual take.

The Camera Operator is in control of the Camera Crew and is the person who actually looks through the lens at the action. He will have spent many years perfecting the skills needed to maintain composition and camera angles throughout a given scene or shot. The seamless ease with which the camera captures the images is key to the narrative flow of every feature film.

*First Assistant Cameraman or Focus Puller

The First Assistant Cameraman (1st AC) is the technician who effectively controls the day to day running of the Camera Department. On set, it is the responsibility of the 1st AC to maintain the required focus on the individual actors, either from a fixed position or when the camera is being tracked on a dolly, and also to ensure that the set lights are suitably flagged in order to minimize the problems of any flares that might potentially degrade the image. Behind the scenes the 1st AC is responsible for the preparation and field maintenance of the camera equipment and for ensuring that any specialized equipment required for a particular shot is delivered, tested where necessary and available at the required time.

*Second Assistant Cameraman or Clapper Loader

The Second Assistant Cameraman (2nd AC) is the junior member of the Camera Department. On set, it is the 2nd AC's job to assist the 1st AC in ensuring that the camera equipment is placed on the set and is ready in good time for the filming of an individual sequence. The 2nd AC's more specific on-set duties include loading any camera magazines with the appropriate film stock, marking the actors' positions during line-ups/rehearsals and slating the individual takes as required. Behind the scenes, the 2nd AC is responsible for ensuring that adequate supplies of film stock are maintained at all times and for the unloading of any exposed film. They will also prepare the necessary camera data sheets for the laboratory (when using film stock), Production Office and Editors, liaising as required with the Script Supervisor to confirm the printed or selected takes. The 2nd AC is also responsible for safeguarding the exposed film until the end of the day, when it is then sent to the film laboratory for processing. On a digital shoot, the 2nd AC will liaise with the Digital Imaging Technician (DIT) to ensure that the necessary memory cards are handed over for transfer in a co-ordinated and appropriate manner.

Camera Trainee/Apprentice/Runner

This is the entry-level job in the Camera Crew. Camera Trainees will work with every member of the Camera Crew, but in particular will assist the 2nd Assistant Camera. On set, it is generally the Trainee who is responsible for ensuring that the required monitors or 'video village' for the Director and other departments are set up and positioned on the set as required. He/she also makes the tea!

Script Supervisor or Continuity

The Script Supervisor provides an invaluable link between the Director, the Cinematographer and the Editor. They have an in-depth knowledge of shot descriptions, lens sizes, screen direction, slating, as well as set-ups with single and multiple cameras – keeping track of sound and camera rolls when there are multiple units shooting. The Supervisor has to have an essential understanding of breaking down a script, back- and cross-matching the story, logging all pertinent information for each department, detecting overlooked coverage, stage direction, action and dialogue. For a musical film they will have to understand bar counting and overall timing and on live television productions they will have control of absolute timing. They are responsible for overall timing for a daily update. As well as this, they must have knowledge of post-production techniques, editing and dubbing, as well as CGI information for feature films.

On top of all the above, the Script Supervisor will make sure, with the help of the Standby Props, that anything used in the previous take is exactly the same in the next take.

For example, if a cigarette is partially smoked, the cigarette in the next take has to be smoked down to the same length and the wine in the glass on the table has to be filled to the exact same level. The actor would be reminded which hand holds the cigarette and how the hand is placed to start the next take.

The Director will generally ask the Script Supervisor before a take, 'Are the details OK with you?' This is a huge job – so never overlook the quiet person sitting behind a monitor on set. They are so very important to the finished product!

Specialist Cinematographers

An Aerial Cinematographer and Unit usually consists of a First or Second Unit DoP capable of aerial-mounted operation, as well as lighting and staging complex action scenes. Films often start with a sweeping bird's-eye view of the location – a city skyline, a rural scene or a snow-covered mountain range. Similarly, at some point in most car-chase sequences, a shot from the air illustrates all the action for a dramatic and exciting perspective. Creating these powerful images is the responsibility of the Aerial Cinematographer.

The Steadicam Operator is a highly skilled Cinematographer or Camera Operator who works with the Camera Crew as and when needed. The Steadicam is a stabilizing device invented by Cinematographer Garrett Brown, which mechanically isolates the camera from the Operator's movements, allowing for a smooth shot even when moving quickly over uneven surfaces. The Operator wears the Steadicam harness and armature, which has a counter-balance weight at one end and the camera on the other. There is a monitor that takes the place of the viewfinder, as the range of movements makes it impossible to look through the eyepiece in the conventional way.

The Underwater or Marine Cinematographer has to be an accomplished diver as well as being an experienced DoP. The Marine Crew are responsible for creating suspense and drama in the underwater world. They may work on location at sea, or in specially built tanks in a studio.

The Underwater Cinematographer works with a crew including a Diving Supervisor, who is responsible for assessing the risks of underwater scenes, and Camera Assistants, who often work on dry land, pulling focus and checking the camera by remote control.

Video Playback Technician

The Video Playback Technician is not a member of the Camera Crew as such, but nevertheless it is the task of the Playback Technician to liaise as required with the 1st AC to ensure that he/she is able to receive and record the individual takes for immediate playback when requested by the Director.

Digital Imaging Technician

The Digital Imaging Technician (DIT) works very much in the background on a digital shoot, but must liaise very closely with the Director of Photography to ensure that the required LUTs (look-up tables) are properly implemented, ensuring that the desired look of the resulting image is accurately maintained. The DIT is also responsible for the on-set back-up of any digital image files and for an adequate library management of that material if required.

GRIPS CREW

Along with the safe operation of camera cranes, everything from the camera head downwards generally falls within the domain of the Grip Department.

Key Grip

The Key Grip is Head of the Grip Department. There is very little that happens on the studio floor or on location that the Key Grip isn't aware of. He or she is a consummate professional, a master of engineering and mechanical skills, whose job it is to make sure that the Camera Crew can film each scene with ease and comfort. The Key Grip has responsibility for anything associated with the movement of all cameras on set and location.

Not only is the Key Grip a mechanical genius, with the management skills to oversee the department, but is also a highly creative individual. There are demands from the Director and Camera Crew throughout a production that need to be dealt with by an instinctive technician who can construct whatever is needed to get the job done.

*Best Boy Grip or Key Grip's Assistant

The Assistant to the Key Grip is usually called the Best Boy. The term probably predates the film business, as, in early apprenticeships, the 'Best Boy' was the master craftsman's most experienced apprentice, with more responsibilities than the other apprentices. In effect, he was the master's first assistant, as indeed the Best Boy Grip is on modern film sets.

The Best Boy organizes equipment rental, buying expendables, hiring crew and, during principal photography, works closely with the Key Grip to decide on the set-up and equipment necessary for each shot, assisting in organizing the crew in the placement and operation of camera dollies and cranes.

Grip

Every scene in a feature film is shot using one or more cameras, each mounted on highly complex equipment, which can be anything from a tripod to a 100ft crane. The Grips assemble this equipment and use it to push, pull or hang the cameras in a variety of settings. This job is very specialized – working under the direction of the Key Grip, they make the positioning and smooth movement of the cameras possible.

During shooting days, the Grips (which may include Remote Head Technicians, Crane Operators or Tracking Vehicle Drivers) arrive on set early and prepare everything for the day's filming. On set, you can anticipate a hectic pace and long hours. You have to be creative and flexible and have a strong work ethic. If you see someone carrying something heavy, you had better be following them carrying something heavier!

Dolly Grip

This is a specialist whose job it is to move the 'dolly' – a wheeled vehicle that is capable of carrying the camera and the Camera Operator for moving and tracking shots along a pre-laid track. The Dolly Grip plays a very important role when safely establishing fixed camera positions on a film set and they are also responsible for the laying of any camera tracks or tracking boards to assist in the smooth movement of the camera during a take. The Dolly Grip must work very closely with the Operator when tracking to ensure that any camera moves are made at the correct time and with the necessary control to ensure that the desired 'feel' of the shot is maintained throughout.

Crane Operator

Negotiating a crane carrying a heavy camera and a Camera Operator around a feature film set, or steering a remote head 100ft above a location on a hi-tech crane, is a highly skilled job. Operating these potentially hazardous pieces of heavy machinery in difficult locations, often under the pressure of hectic shooting schedules, isn't easy.

Crane Operators are responsible for setting up and operating all cranes on film productions. This can involve working with a variety of equipment, ranging from a small jib arm, used to make slight camera movements up and down, to a massive crane for shooting huge crowd or action sequences. Because the equipment is heavy and potentially dangerous, Crane Operators carry a great deal of responsibility for Health and Safety, as this is one of the few jobs on set that involves real-life risks for all cast and crew.

Trainee Grip/Apprentice

This is the entry-level job for the Grip Department. As it's the responsibility of the Grips to work with specialist companies and suppliers to produce tailor-made pieces of equipment to enable tricky camera movements, the Grip has to know what equipment is available – both new and old – so, instead of 'resting' in-between films, the Trainee Grip needs to visit the equipment rental companies and manufacturers in order to keep up with the latest developments.

LIGHTING CREW

Lighting Gaffer

The Head of the Lighting Department, aka the Gaffer, working with the Director of Photography, designs the lighting plot and chooses the right equipment for each shot, based on environment, camera angles, desired effect and available ambient lighting. The Gaffer is a fully qualified electrician with many years of experience in lighting film sets on studio stages and on a wide variety of locations in many countries. They must be creative and knowledgeable enough to be able to suggest solutions to the DoP, as well as having the ability to interpret the Director and DoP's ideas with ease.

As well as technical and creative abilities, the Gaffer, as Head of Department, has to have all the management skills necessary to control the budgeting and scheduling for the Lighting Department.

*Best Boy Lighting

The 'Best Boy' is the Assistant to the Lighting Gaffer – a supervisory role, liaising with the Assistant Director, Special Effects Supervisor and Art Director, and is responsible for ensuring that all required lighting equipment and appropriate crew are on set for each shot. Their most important piece of personal gear is a phone or a walkie-talkie, as they have to be in contact with the Gaffer at all times. For example, if the crew are shooting an office scene and are then moving on to another set, it's the Best Boy's job to make sure that all the lighting for the next scene is in place so that, once the Director wraps the shot, the crew can move seamlessly to the next set where everything is ready. Once the crew moves on, it's the Best Boy's job to make sure that the equipment on the finished set is de-rigged or 'struck'.

The Best Boy orders kit, arranges gear rentals and is involved in any hiring and firing of the crew. He or she oversees all lighting work on set, the loading and unloading of vehicles and organizing which lights, cables and accessories are needed for every scene. On set, the Gaffer and the Director of Photography will decide how a scene should be lit – it is then the Best Boy's job to lead the crew through pre-rigging, selecting the right equipment and ensuring that there is enough available power.

Lighting Technician/Sparks

The Lighting Technician or 'Sparks' does more on set than flip a switch. Part of the job is just like an electrician wiring a house – film and television sets can include practical wiring to sets, scenery and props – but mostly the Sparks operate the hundreds of lights and run the miles of cable necessary to illuminate the action and set the scene.

Skills will include concepts of electrical engineering, high-voltage safety, set construction and production lighting. This position demands that the Sparks have an expert-level understanding of electricity and proper wiring standards, as well as a familiarity with power distribution systems and generators. Often the Sparks is expected to devise ingenious, crafty solutions to impossible problems on a short deadline, so clever problem-solvers who thrive in hectic situations are a perfect fit.

Trainee Sparks/Apprentice

This is the entry-level job for the Lighting Department. The Trainee is learning to become a fully qualified specialist and must become familiar with all the lighting equipment, how it works and how it is used and maintained. As a Trainee, it may be a good idea to start working with a specialist film lighting equipment company, where you will be moved from one section or department to another, getting to know all about the equipment.

What is absolutely necessary is hands-on experience with theatrical and/or film lighting equipment and a thorough understanding of electricity. This involves not only knowledge of operating and maintaining the kit, but also an understanding of the theoretical principles behind set lighting and the quality of illumination produced by each piece of equipment. So study well before you find yourself staring blankly at the Gaffer on your first day on set when he asks you to fetch a blonde, a top hat or a brute!

Generator Operator

The Generator or Genny Operator is a specialist role within the Lighting Department and a job that an electrician may choose after initial training and some film experience. Most electrical current used on a film set – either on a stage in a studio, on a backlot or on location – is provided by electricity generators. Genny Operators are amongst the first to arrive on set, as no one can start work until they have provided power with feeds to numerous trailers used by Performers, Wardrobe and Make-up. Once this is done, the rest of the production day is spent waiting for something to go wrong!

To be a Genny Operator, you need to be a fully qualified electrician with a wide knowledge of the various types of generators that are used for different purposes, as you have to balance the load of distributed power amongst all output lines and feeder cables to electrical service points as needed, making sure that the power consumption does not exceed the generators' safe operating limits – which essentially amounts to watching paint dry!

CAMERA ANGLES

At the very beginning of the process of planning a set, the Designer will supply the Director with a number of usable camera angles. This will help the Director at an early stage to estimate what he will get from the various sketches he has been given. You can work backwards from the plan and

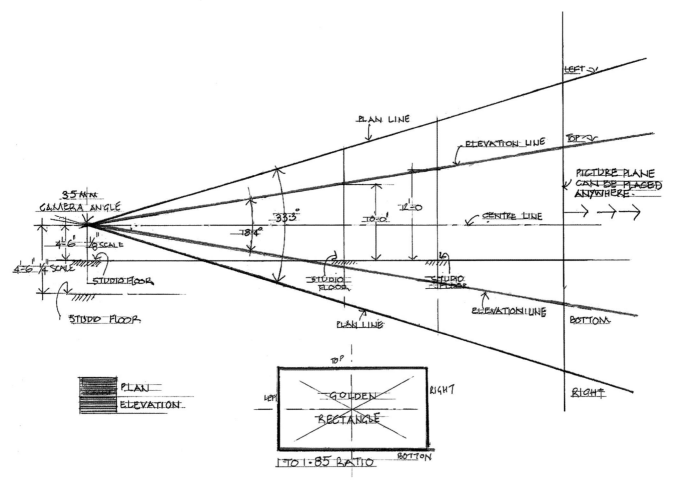

ABOVE: The Golden Rectangle is the frame in which the scene is shot. This shows the 35mm camera angle with plan and elevation using the Golden Rectangle reference.

RIGHT: Showing the effects of different camera angles, from 20mm (wide angle) to 100mm (acute angle), which are selected at the discretion of the Cinematographer and Director.

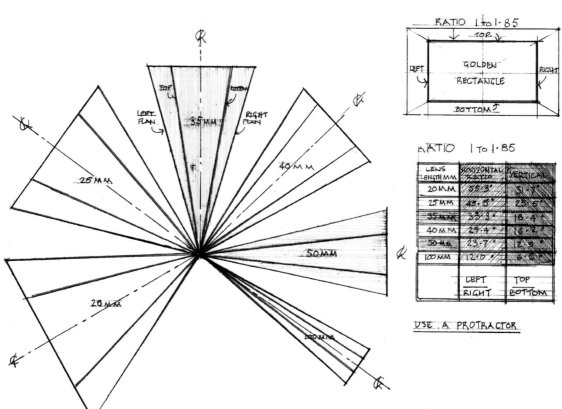

RATIO 1 TO 1·85

LENS LENGTH MM	HORIZONTAL RATIO	VERTICAL
20MM	55·3°	31·7°
25MM	45·5°	25·5°
35MM	33·3°	18·4°
40MM	29·4°	16·2°
50MM	23·7°	12·9°
100MM	12·0°	6·5°
	LEFT RIGHT	TOP BOTTOM

USE A PROTRACTOR

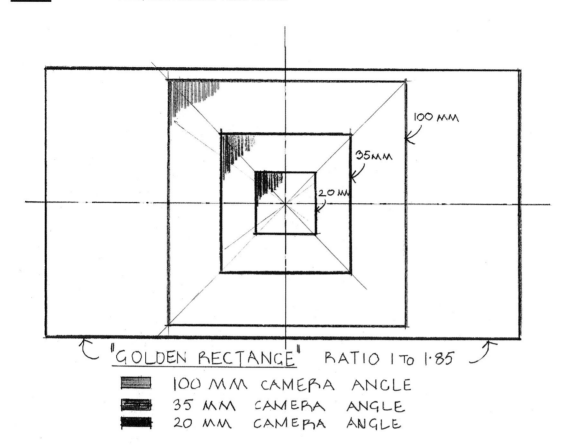

Showing the ratios and effect on the camera angles in the Golden Rectangle when using different lens sizes, as shown by the coloured lines.

100 MM

35MM

20 MM

"GOLDEN RECTANGE" RATIO 1 TO 1·85

100 MM CAMERA ANGLE
35 MM CAMERA ANGLE
20 MM CAMERA ANGLE

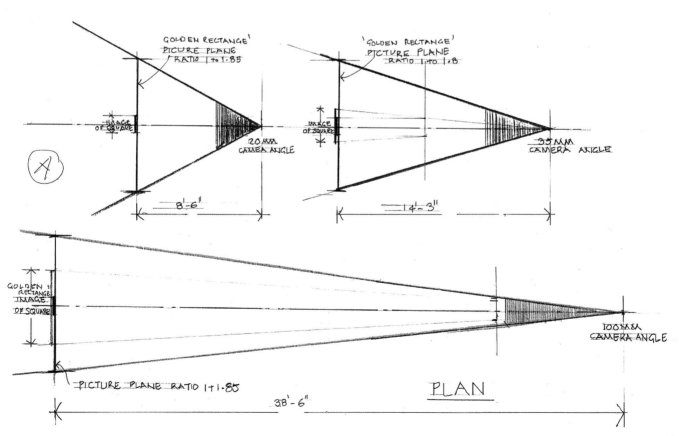

Side view of the Golden Rectangle.

PLAN

elevation of a sketch using a particular lens and can work out very precisely what will appear on screen after shooting with that particular lens. This process of layout of angle is done in co-operation with the Director and the Cinematographer.

THE SET AND LIGHTING

For practical purposes, the set is a collection of shapes, colours and textures. The way in which they are revealed on screen is of vital importance. Therefore, at a very early stage in set planning, the type of lighting will have to be decided upon. Lighting can be used effectively to convey a feeling. For example, lighting a period piece would be entirely different from lighting a dramatic set with emphatic textures, which can portray moods of sombreness, sadness, or fear. The Lighting Gaffer, in combination with the Cinematographer, will plan the lighting of the whole set according to the requirements of the action and design.

THE LENS ANGLE AND PERSPECTIVE

The lens angle is the factor determining what will be recorded in the camera. If you are considering a 25mm lens you will have a wide field of view, whereas if you are using a 50mm lens you will get a narrow field of view, making any room appear very flat on the screen. This 'flatness' can be counteracted by careful set design. For example, the Cinematographer may be shooting a close-up with a 50mm lens and, by bringing the top of the set down, he will achieve a more dramatic composition. However, you cannot 'perspectivize' the furniture or the floor – which cannot be 'cheated up' because the actors have to use it. When sketching, you should sketch the angle that you can actually see – the cone of vision that is about 60 degrees.

If you want to use a 35mm lens, having an angle view of, say, 90 degrees, then lines are going to enter the picture area at a sharper angle and the set automatically assumes a diamond shape in plan. You may not want this to happen and therefore, by dropping ceiling lines, you can counter the distorting effect of the lens.

PERSPECTIVE AND ARCHITECTURAL DETAIL

Modern sets with clean and simple lines may not present too much of a problem to construct in perspective if the camera angles are projected correctly. However, period sets can

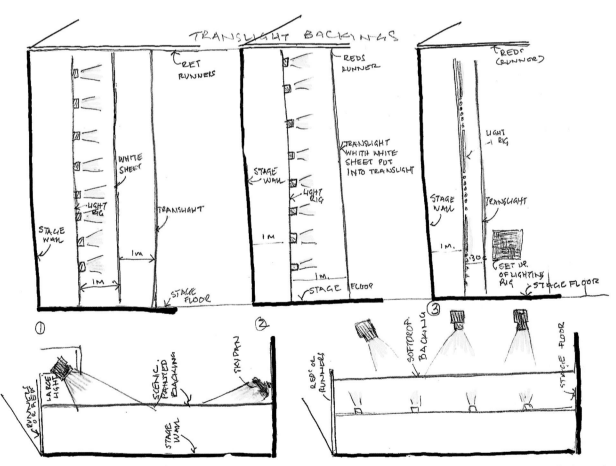

Translight Backings, as described in the text. The Lighting Gaffer and Cinematographer will plan the lighting to suit the action and design.

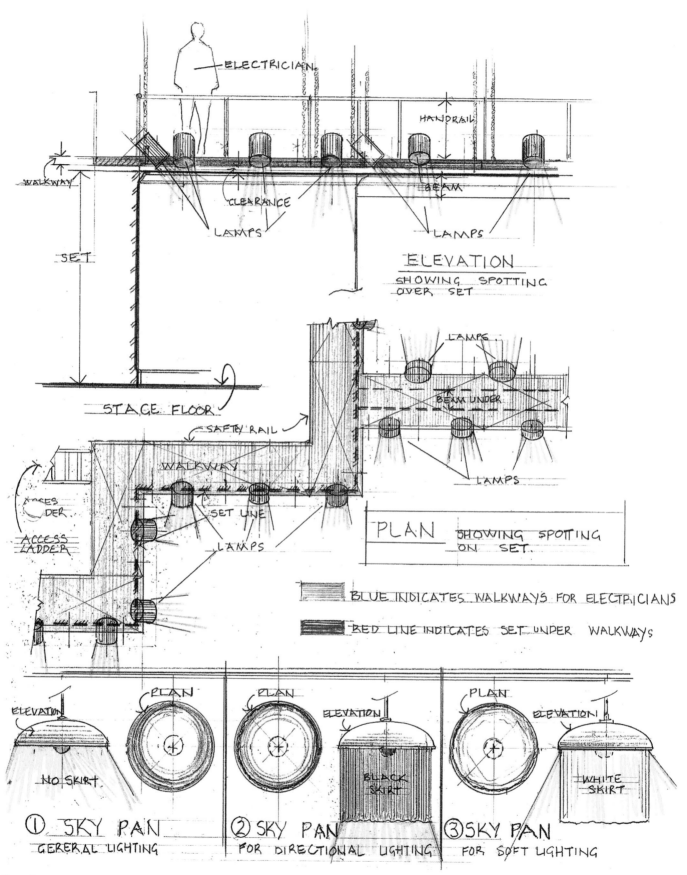

ELECTRICIAN

HANDRAIL

WALKWAY

CLEARANCE

LAMPS

BEAM

LAMPS

SET

ELEVATION
SHOWING SPOTTING OVER SET

LAMPS

STAGE FLOOR

BEAM UNDER

SAFETY RAIL

WALKWAY

ACCESS LADDER

ACCESS LADDER

SET LINE

LAMPS

LAMPS

PLAN SHOWING SPOTTING ON SET.

BLUE INDICATES WALKWAYS FOR ELECTRICIANS

RED LINE INDICATES SET UNDER WALKWAYS

ELEVATION   PLAN
NO SKIRT
① SKY PAN
GENERAL LIGHTING

PLAN   ELEVATION
BLACK SKIRT
② SKY PAN
FOR DIRECTIONAL LIGHTING

PLAN   ELEVATION
WHITE SKIRT
③ SKY PAN
FOR SOFT LIGHTING

Spotting on set. At a very early stage in set planning, the type of lighting will have to be decided upon, usually by the Cinematographer.

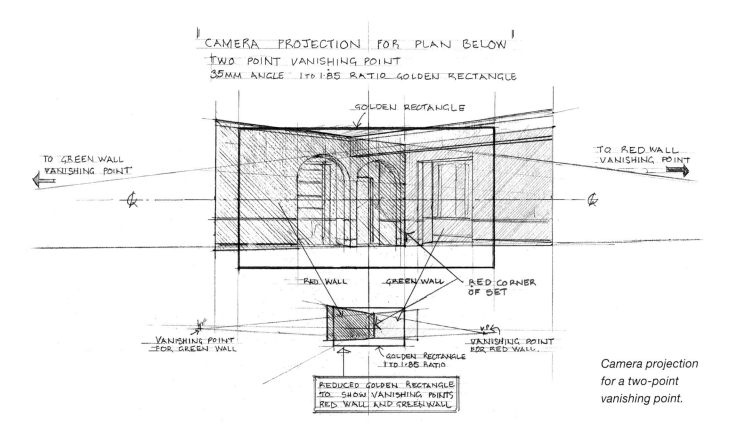

Camera projection for a two-point vanishing point.

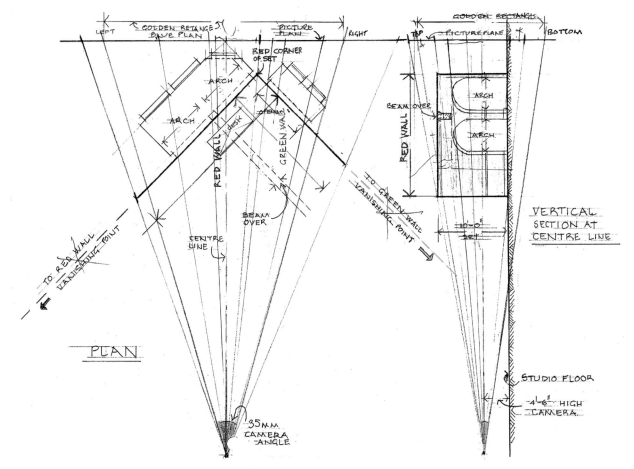

Vertical section at centre line. Two-point vanishing point.

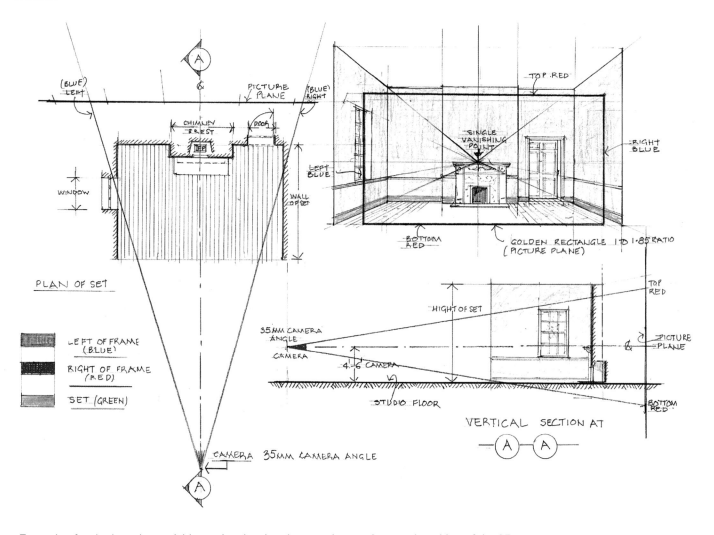

Example of a single-point vanishing point showing the set, picture plane and position of the 35mm camera.

PROJECTING A SET-UP FROM A PLAN AND ELEVATION

1. Having drawn up the plan and elevation of the set to scale, place the elevation of the set above the plan and lay the selected lens angle on to the drawing. Sketch in the action figure of one of the characters in the script. At any suitable point, draw the picture plane line.

2. Draw a line A at 45 degrees up to the elevation line. The next step is to form a picture plane frame. The frame area is drawn in the proportion of 1:1.33. Draw lines from the centre of the lens through the drawing of the plan and elevation and carry them through into the picture frame. Where the lines cut across each other is the beginning of the projected picture.

3. Draw the centre line CL through the picture frame and form the vanishing point where the lines intersect. Continue to project lines through from the plan

and elevation and form more projected images on the picture frame.

4. Project the figure in the elevation and plan (established at 6ft in height). Of course, if you know the exact dimensions of the actor in question it will make the projected sketch more authentic. Begin to add tone to the sketch and fill in more details.

5. Complete the set-up sketch and fill in details of dressing, colour and tone as necessary. From this sketch, you can get a very clear idea of what the camera will photograph from that angle. It will also show what area the set and camera will be when planning stage or location layouts. The broken lines show the 1:1.85 screen ratio and the area of cut-off, which will not be seen if the finished film is projected with this screen ratio.

present problems because the lines are not usually so clean – a baroque banqueting hall may have much embellishment built on to the basic structure. Unless you are careful, you may find that you are having to create perspective running in more than one direction.

Shooting Against Perspective

Since a 'perspectivized' set has been built from the viewpoint of one camera position, you might imagine that shooting within that set would be restricted to that single camera position. In fact, there is a great deal of freedom in the choice

MAKING A PLAN AND ELEVATION FROM A SKETCH

1. Set up the chosen lens in plan and elevation and take any point in the sketch that you know has a dimension. In this instance, you can use the man who is 6ft tall and the lines are run back to the picture plane until they scale at 6ft in the elevation plane. Draw the ground line and establish the scale of the man.

2. Continue to return the lines back to the plan and elevation and establish the lines AB and CD.

3. Continue to mark up lines X, Y and Z.

4. Having established the key points on the plan and elevation, the remaining windows, doors and steps can be quickly sketched on to the drawing. You will now know exactly what sort of set to build from the sketch as seen from the one camera position.

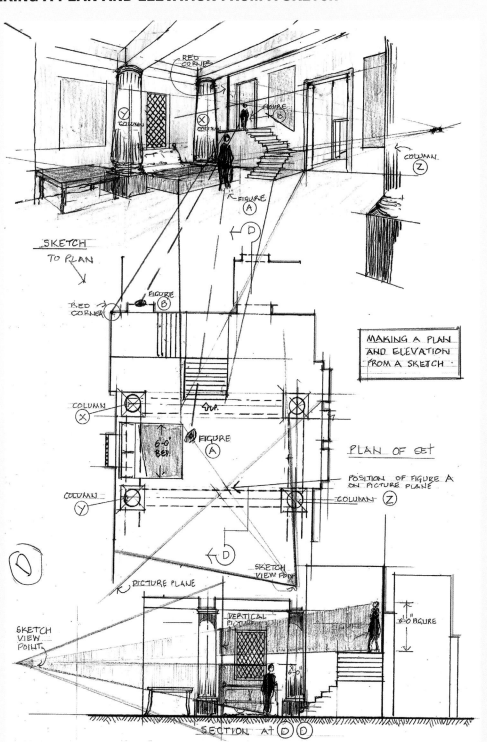

Making a plan from a sketch and a sketch from a plan.

of set-ups, as long as the perspective is always taken into consideration.

Forced Perspective

Forced perspective is a technique used not only for filming miniatures, but when shooting a scene in a studio that has less space than needed, maybe because of a schedule change, or perhaps additional shots are needed after the crew has left the location. This technique allows for a forced perspective set to be used in a smaller space. The forcing of the linear perspective causes the distance to be compressed. For example, in a street scene the buildings will start to condense towards the

FORCING THE PERSPECTIVE

1. Having decided on the length of corridor to be built, draw an imaginary extension of the corridor at any length necessary (Section B). Decide on the section into which you will 'force' the imaginary corridor. Establish the camera height and then draw the centre line (CL). Draw a line from point E and point D back to the camera lens point and mark its intersection with Plane F. Draw lines from point G through points F and where each line hits the centre line of the camera – which is the vanishing point.

2. The forced perspective area and the vanishing point of the perspective have now been established. Draw lines back to the camera lens point from the furthest door on the plan and elevation of the imaginary corridor. Where these lines hit the forced perspective section, we establish the first 'perspectivized' door.

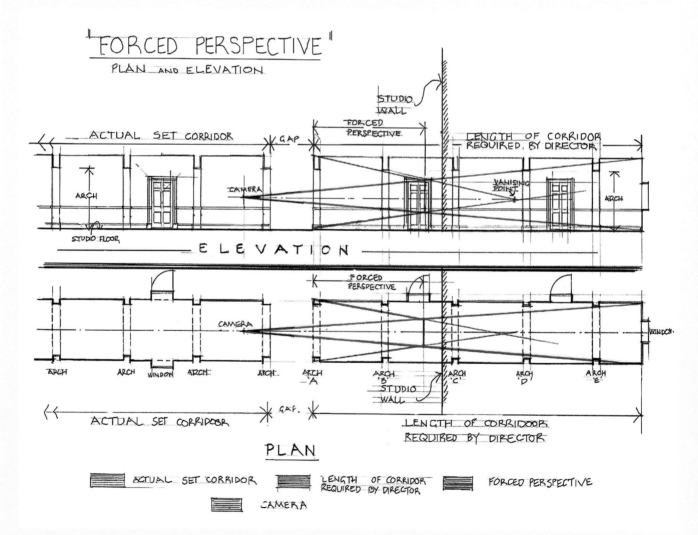

Forced perspective elevation.

end of the road and perhaps a ramp will be used to create a false horizon.

Tricks of lighting and careful placement of props add to the illusion, which was originally copied from theatre sets. Creating this illusion calls for very careful planning and a lot of experience. If you wish to give the impression of a long corridor but are restricted in stage space, it is often necessary to 'force the perspective' of the set by means of building a forced perspective section. At the end of the section you can carry on the illusion of depth by using a painted backing in the correct position, or create it in post-production with CGI, although this is a much more expensive method.

3. Having established the one perspective item on the plan and elevation, continue the process until all the doors are drawn up. You will find that, by connecting the tops of the doors with the vanishing point, all the lines will automatically follow towards the vanishing point and the forced perspective will be perfect.

4. It should be noted that the only perfect angle on the set will be from the camera position lined up with the vanishing point height and plan position. The camera can track and pan within these limitations. Once the Director and the Cinematographer understand these positions, the result on the screen will look right.

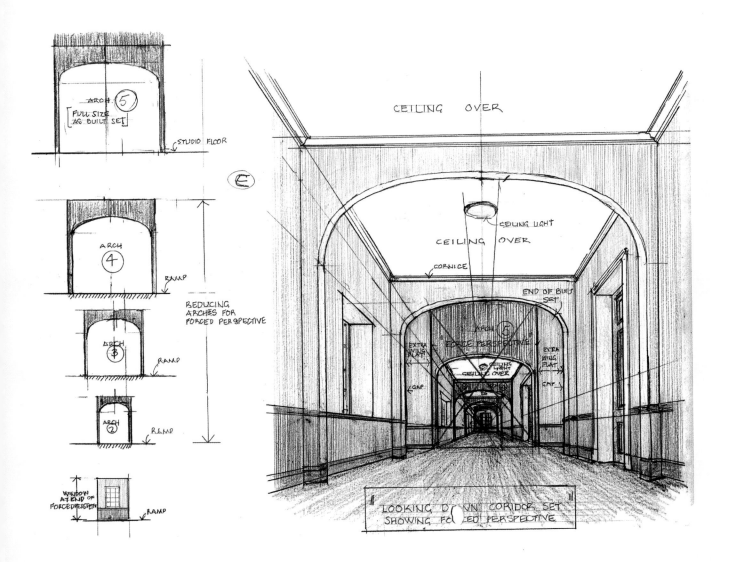

Front view of forced perspective.

(continued overleaf)

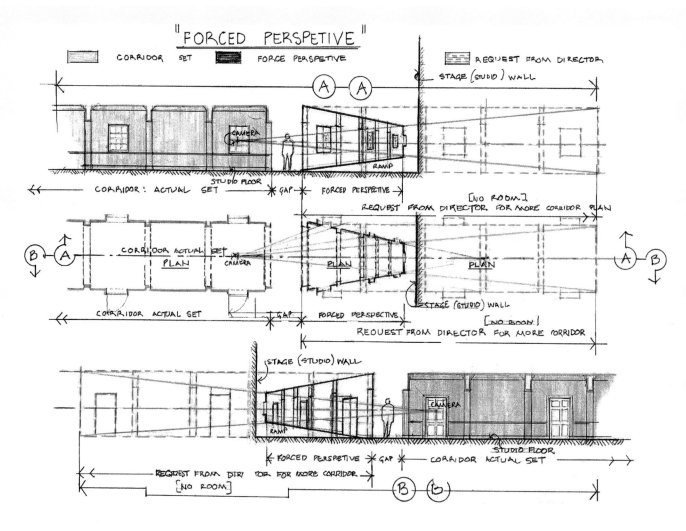

"FORCED PERSPETIVE"

CORRIDOR SET — FORCE PERSPETIVE — REQUEST FROM DIRECTOR

STAGE (STUDIO) WALL

CORRIDOR : ACTUAL SET — STUDIO FLOOR — GAP — FORCED PERSPECTIVE

CORRIDOR ACTUAL SET PLAN — CAMERA — PLAN — PLAN

CORRIDOR ACTUAL SET — GAP — FORCED PERSPECTIVE — STAGE (STUDIO) WALL

[NO ROOM] REQUEST FROM DIRECTOR FOR MORE CORRIDOR

[NO ROOM] REQUEST FROM DIRECTOR FOR MORE CORRIDOR

STAGE (STUDIO) WALL

RAMP — FORCED PERSPETIVE — GAP — CORRIDOR ACTUAL SET — STUDIO FLOOR

REQUEST FROM DIR TOR FOR MORE CORRIDOR [NO ROOM]

ABOVE: Plan and section of the forced perspective.

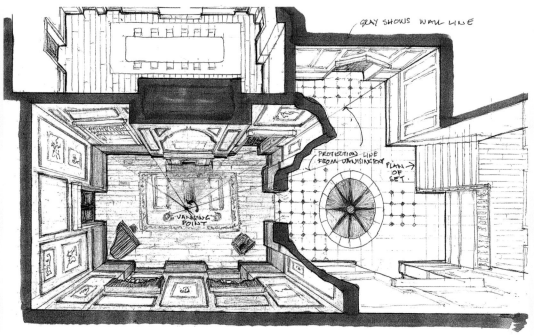

GRAY SHOWS WALL LINE

PROTECTION LINE FROM VANISHING POINT

PLAN OF SET

VANISHING POINT

"Birds Eye View of Set Sketch"

RED INDICATES PLAN OF SET

Bird's-eye view. This form of sketch helps some Directors to work out the action with cameras and actors. Draw a plan of your set (shown in red), then project from a vanishing point the set as shown.

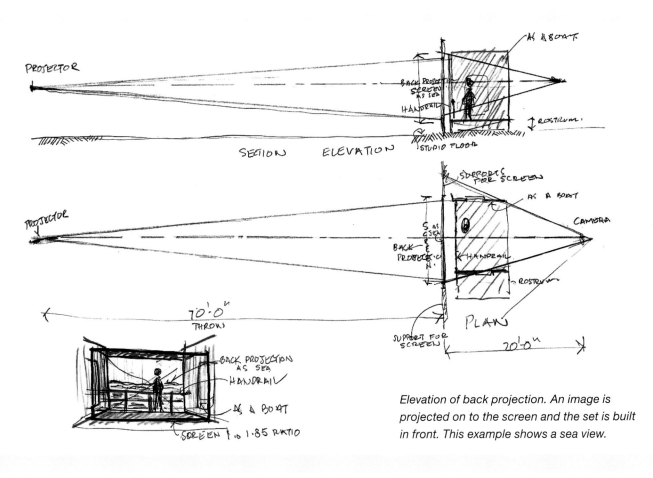

Elevation of back projection. An image is projected on to the screen and the set is built in front. This example shows a sea view.

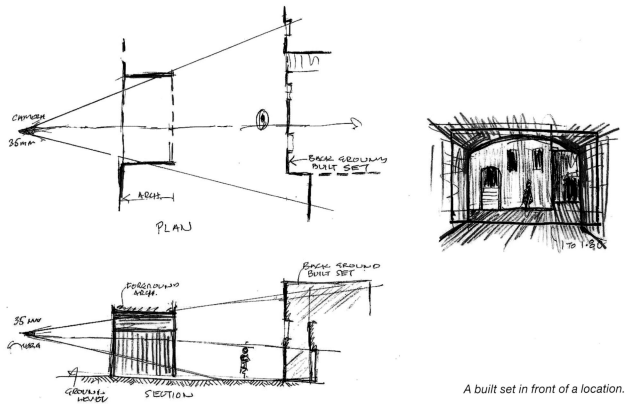

A built set in front of a location.

The Actor in a 'Perspectivized' Set

Putting actors into a 'perspectivized' set shouldn't create any problems as long as the obvious mistakes are avoided. If you were able to see somebody in one shot walk the full distance from the foreground to background, you might easily spot that something was wrong. Just as it is difficult to analyse the perspective line of a corner, a dado (a type of moulding fitted horizontally to a wall around the perimeter of a room) and a floor with your eye, then it is just as difficult to analyse perspective in the relationship between the actor and the set. You could work it out on paper, but the audience is dependent on what the effect is visually, so the Director has a large measure of freedom.

There may be occasions when you wish to put an actor into an obviously distorted set. The reason may be to heighten tension, as in a horror sequence, or it may be done in a television commercial to attract attention to the product being advertised.

Labyrinth

On the film *Labyrinth* in 1986, building the 'Labyrinth' itself involved the use of a lot of perspective, which was very effective when Sarah (the lead actress) first enters the set and tries to make her way to the castle where her baby brother has been kidnapped by the Goblin King. It was effectively a maze built to look like a normal path.

However, the biggest design and build problem we had was the staircase sequence with David Bowie, who played the Goblin King, with Sarah's baby brother making his way around what appeared to be a very dangerous set. We called it the 'Esher Set' stairs, as they were going nowhere and had to look as though they were upside-down, as well as right side up and combined with arches, which was extremely complicated!

Production Designer Elliot Scott had worked on it for quite some time, but was unable to solve the problem of the intricacies of the design, so he passed it on to me. I could only manage up to three sets of stairs, as it was totally impossible to make it work with any more, so we eventually solved it by using strategically placed mirrors. It ended up as quite a big set, reaching 30ft high.

Again, this was a film that tested everything we knew about design and construction. That's the nature of working in film, as every day brings a new challenge.

Sketch of the Labyrinth *staircase showing the complicated design issues.*

Miniatures and Perspective

If you have to devise a convincing set in an extremely restricted space, you may decide to make use of miniatures in addition to the 'normal' set with actors. In the sketch shown here, the area of action is full size. To give the impression of the path running slightly upwards, the set is running very slightly downwards. The maximum available area of tank is used and the mooring posts are designed around the tank. The boat is put in full size and level. The near posts are full size, but the further ones are much shorter in order to force the perspective.

The buildings at the rear of the set are painted cut-outs. A police car that drives on to set at the rear in front of the pub is, in fact, a model car of about 1ft in height. All the painted cut-outs are to a forced perspective running away from the camera.

REVERSE ANGLES

The planning of reverse angles is an important aspect of design. Reverse-angle shots are always useful in giving more visual variety to a sequence and, when planned well, they can have other advantages. Perhaps their chief virtue is giving perceived space to an essentially tight set.

If, for example, you are filming a couple talking in the corner of a room, then you only need to build the corner. However, if you wish to give the impression that the couple are talking in the corner of a large room, then the reverse-angle shot from the corner, shooting back into the other two walls of the room, would give the maximum value to the background without it being overpowering.

Working carefully from a camera angle, it is possible to calculate precisely how much of the background set will be revealed, therefore how much of the set needs to be built. The dressing of the background should never distract the audience from the foreground action – unless it is required in the script.

Building Reverse-Angle Sets

One way of overcoming the problem of reverse angles is to build reverse-angle sets – that part of the main set which will appear in the reverse-angle shot. The set would generally have to be of normal perspective, otherwise the shots would not cut with the master take within the 'perspectivized' set, although one could build for the reverse angle in perspective if it were justified.

Photograph of the staircase. There was a clever use of mirrors involved to create the desired effect.

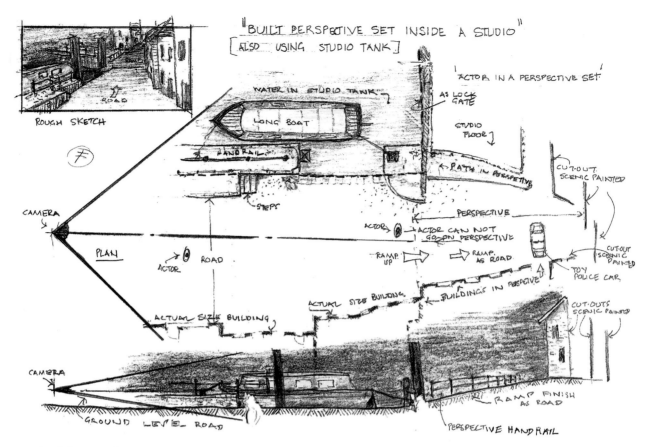

An example of the actor in a 'perspectivized' studio set using a studio tank. Note the camera angles and the toy car, which adds to the illusion of depth.

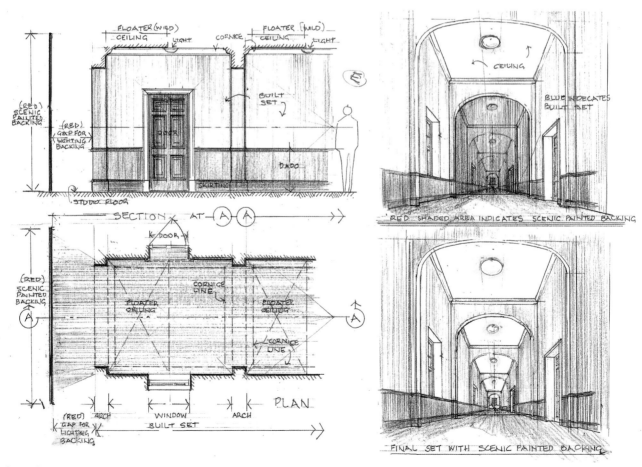

If a forced perspective set is not used, it may be replaced with a cheaper, scenic-painted backing.

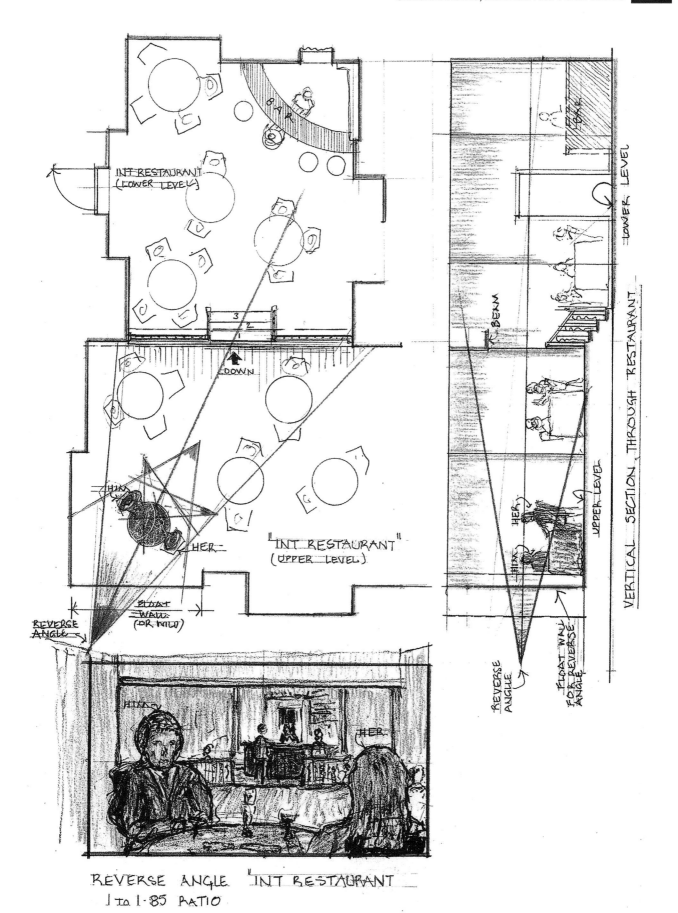

Reverse-angle diagram.

CHAPTER 6

SPECIAL PHYSICAL EFFECTS AND STORYBOARDING

During the initial reading of the script, some of the action involved might demand effects work and the Designer should discuss these sequences with the Director and Producer who may have their own ideas of how certain problems raised by the action should be solved. The Producer, who has to find the money for the production, may consider some effects too costly and require the script to be changed or other suggestions to be made. In the end, the key deciding factors for what effects, if any, will be used are the Director's visualization of the script, the budget and the Designer's concept of the final screen image.

The Designer assumes responsibility for any special effects work necessary in the production and should include the special physical (SFX) and visual effects (VFX) Departments from the outset, since the work involved will have an impact on the work of the Art Department. Although both SFX and VFX crews are highly specialized technicians, they cannot operate in a design vacuum. The VFX and SFX Supervisors will be on set before and during shooting. The SFX Supervisor is in control of the construction of all the action sets, in close co-operation with the Construction Manager. The VFX Supervisor will oversee all greenscreen and motion-capture scenes,

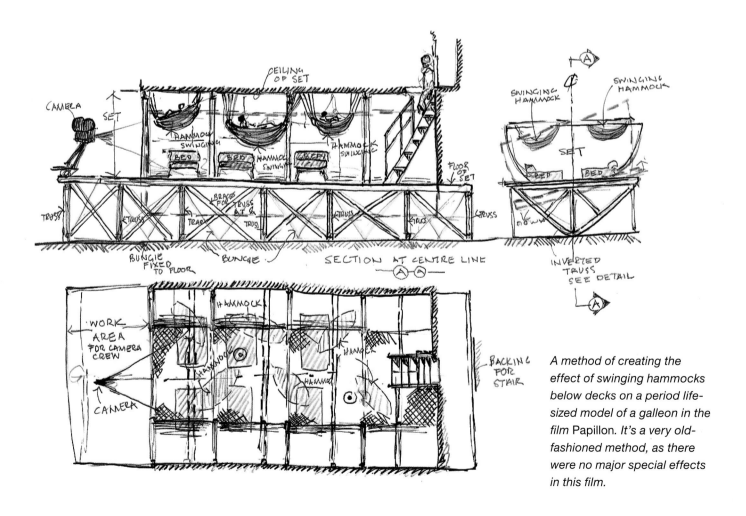

A method of creating the effect of swinging hammocks below decks on a period life-sized model of a galleon in the film Papillon. *It's a very old-fashioned method, as there were no major special effects in this film.*

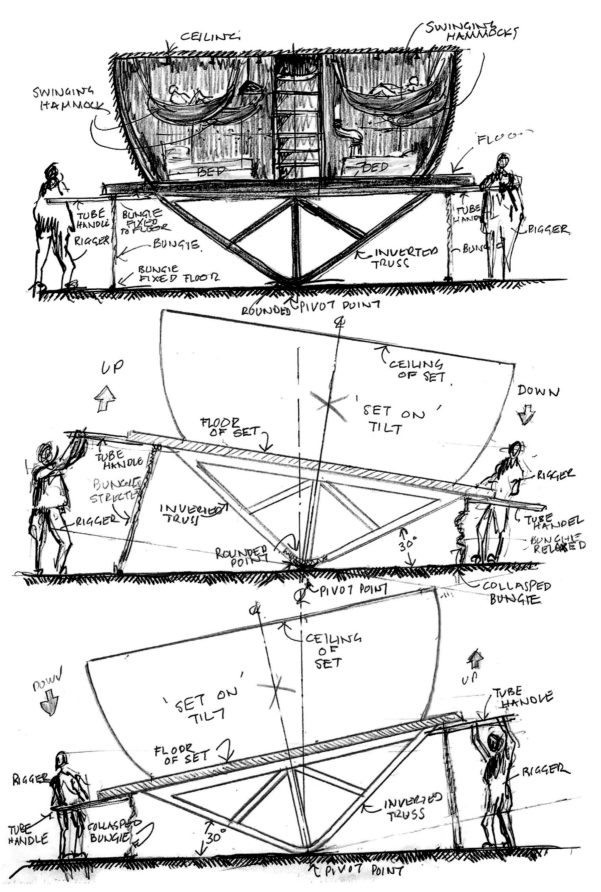

A section of the same set showing how the rocking motion is created. The rig could take the weight of actors, lights, camera crew and equipment.

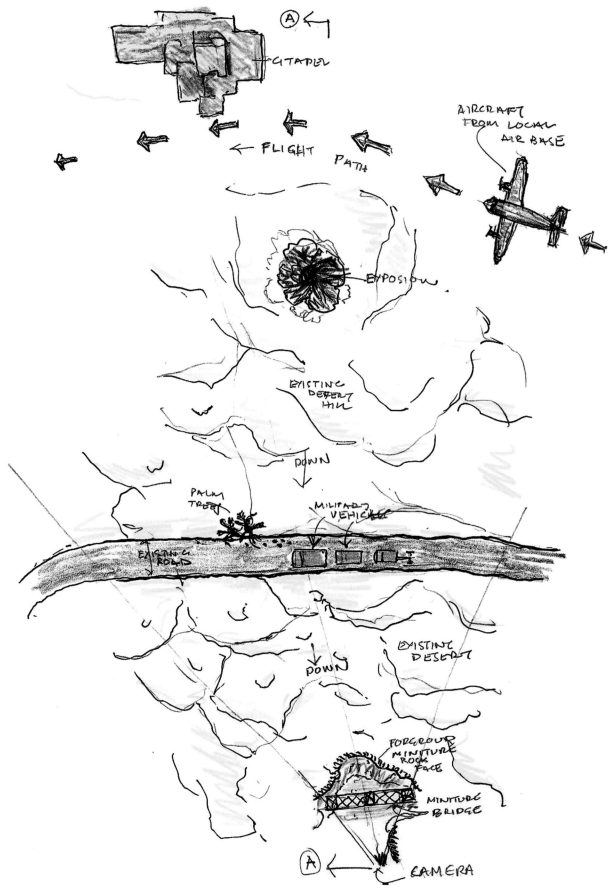

Sketch from The Living Daylights *showing the aerial view of the location for the foreground miniature shot.*

working with the Post-Production Supervisor, as much of the VFX work will take place in the post-production stages of the film.

Although the Art Department may not always be called upon to use such a complex range of effects as are seen in big-budget action and fantasy movies, it is important for the Designer and Art Director to understand the basic principles of both of the 'effects' departments and the potential of each method or technique.

THE LIVING DAYLIGHTS – JAMES BOND

On *The Living Daylights* in 1987, directed by John Glen, with Production Designer Peter Lamont, there were many techniques used by the Special Effects Department to achieve the Director's vision. One of the shots was a foreground miniature, which Art Director Michael Lamont specialized in. It was set up in the Moroccan desert with a citadel in the distance. The location was near a military air base, so we hired an aircraft for the shot, which was a massive explosion, overseen by the master of special effects, Chris Corbould.

On location in Austria, there was a scene requiring the Aston Martin to have skis, with one front nearside wheel without a tyre – just the rim, which would be used to cut the hole in the ice. The car also had to enter a shed, drive around, exit and then explode, and then, in another part of Austria, the car had

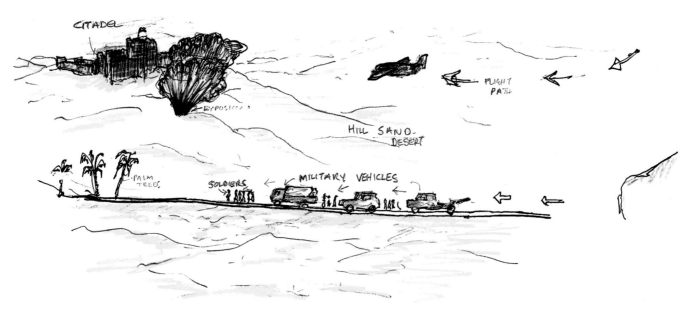

The miniature as seen by the camera. Note the citadel in the background and the military vehicles in the foreground.

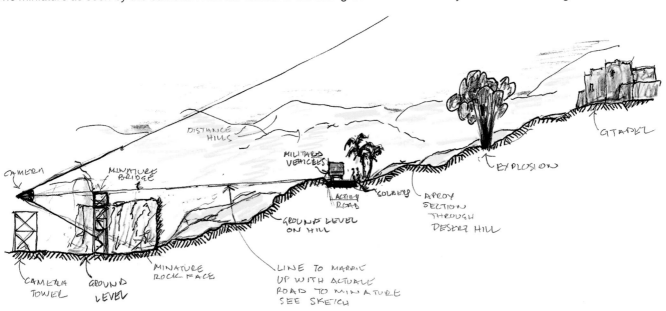

Section from the side showing the camera angle.

The final shot of the scene as would be viewed through the lens, with the bridge being a foreground miniature with the citadel and the military vehicles actual size. The 'Art of Illusion' in practice!

to mount a ramp and go through a guard house, smashing it to pieces.

The Director wanted to see the car flying through the air, so a ramp was built on the iced-over lake, though it wasn't included in the shot. The ramp was 50ft long by 12ft high at the high end. A gap of 45ft parted the ramp from the stunt boxes for the landing and the ramp was fixed to the lake with ice. The car had to travel at a speed of exactly 70mph to ensure height and accuracy when landing. However, the stunt man drove the car at 90mph and only just made contact with the stunt boxes – lucky man.

With all these scenes, the Special Effects Department did a great job.

For another scene in the film we used a Harrier Jump Jet to come out of a gasometer in Vienna. We photographed the gasometer building and enlarged the photograph back in London. At that time, the Harrier Squadron was at Whittingham Air Force base. We were given permission to photograph a Harrier doing a vertical take-off, playing the enlarged photograph of the gasometer set in front of the camera at a given distance. This was all worked out in the Art Department.

The action vehicle on the frozen lake, complete with skis.

RIGHT: *Planning the shot and making sure that the camera angle is correct.*

The vehicle hoisted by a crane ready for another shot.

The iced-over lake in Austria.

Part of the gas pipeline visible in the Harrier scene built on a glacier in Canada.

On location in Canada.

GLASS SHOTS OR GLASS PAINTING

This is one of the earliest techniques used to composite additional images on to footage. It had been perfected by the mid-twentieth century and was in global use from that time. A classic example of a traditional glass shot is the approach to the plantation in *Gone with the Wind*. The plantation and fields are all painted, while the road and the moving figures on it are filmed through the clear glass area.

Prior to the present day, if a location was perfect for shooting apart from an industrial and unattractive building spoiling the scene, a large piece of painted glass would be used as a mask between the camera and the performers. This is done by positioning a large pane of glass so that it fills the camera frame and is far enough away to be held in focus, along with the background visible through it. The entire scene is painted on the glass, except for the area revealing the background where action is to take place, which is left clear. Photographed through the glass, the live action is composited with the painted area.

The Scenic Artists doing this work are very talented, as they have not only to be painters, but also to have a full understanding of the ways in which cameras and

Testing out the Harrier in the gasometer set.

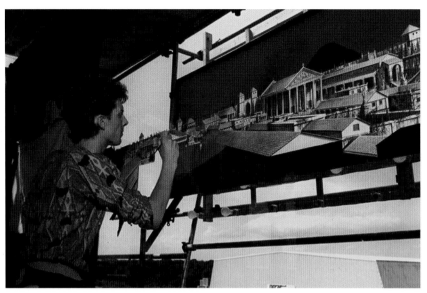

Leigh Took preparing a matte at the top of an 80ft tower for Ray Harryhausen on The Last Days of Pompeii *in 1975 in Pinewood Studios.* LEIGH TOOK, MATTES & MINIATURES VISUAL EFFECTS LTD

lenses work. The glass is painted in situ and careful note must be made of things such as the time of day that the shoot is to take place, so that any shadows are taken into consideration to make sure that the actual shot matches the painted images on the glass. These shots have to be very carefully monitored, as any unauthorized movement of the performers would ruin the shot.

This technique, like gate matting (where the work was done in the matte box on the camera) has mostly been taken over by visual effects, but every Designer and Art Director should be fully aware of these traditional processes.

For example, the Designer may decide to utilize the glass-shot technique when they need to economize in the construction of architectural detail, perhaps when a building will stand in the background of the picture. By eliminating the need to build an extensive set, the Designer can help the work of other technicians, such as the Sound Department, by giving them more flexibility in the placement of their equipment. In some films, which might normally need an extensive build but where there may not be too much action, the budget can be helped by eliminating the need for extensive and costly sets by using this technique. For the glass shot to be effective it has to be convincing in all its detail and there should be full preliminary discussions among the Designer, the Director and the Scenic Artist before work begins. The Designer will supply the Scenic Artist with very detailed sketches, which will include all the action that will take place on that set. (*See also* Leigh Took's comments below on mattes and miniatures.)

The 80ft tower where Leigh was working. LEIGH TOOK, MATTES & MINIATURES VISUAL EFFECTS LTD

The completed scene of Pompeii as seen by the camera with the matte shot. LEIGH TOOK, MATTES & MINIATURES VISUAL EFFECTS LTD

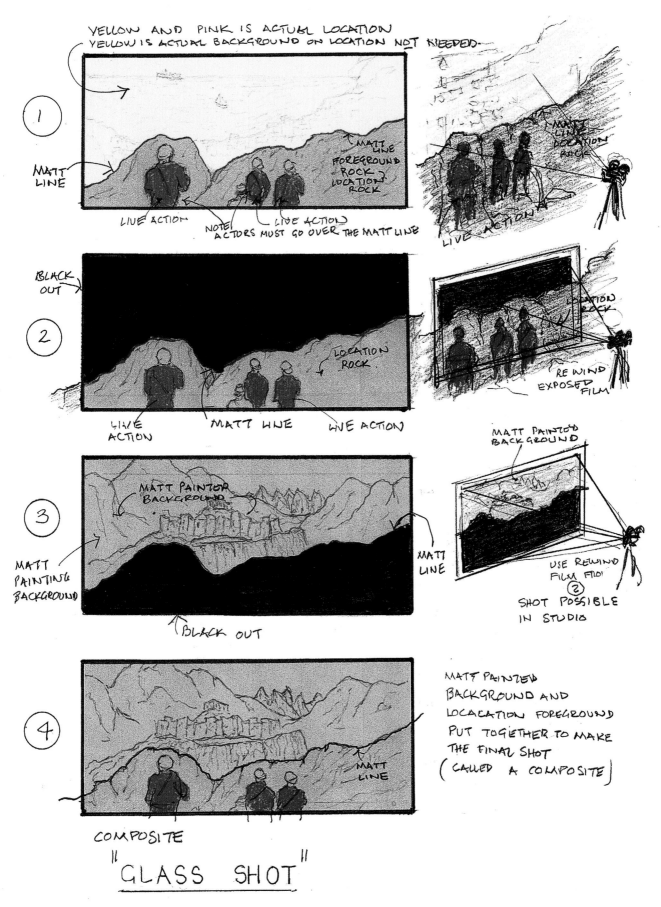

Sketch showing how a glass shot works.

MATTE PAINTING

A matte is a painted representation of a landscape, set or distant location that allows filmmakers to create the illusion of an environment that is non-existent in real life, or would otherwise be too expensive or impossible to build or visit. Historically, matte painters and technicians have used various techniques to combine a matte-painted image with live-action footage. At its best, depending on the skill levels of the artists and technicians, the effect is seamless and creates environments that would otherwise be impossible to film. In these scenes, the painted part is static and movements are integrated on to it. The first known matte painting shot was made in 1907 by Norman Dawn, who improvised crumbling buildings by painting them on glass for the film *Missions of California*.

Although you need to understand the traditional methods, these are mainly now completed within the digital processing by the Visual Effects Department (*see* Chapter 8).

The basic purpose of the travelling matte is to place a moving scene shot, usually on location, behind actors or action that takes place in the studio. The two sets of action are 'married' during processing. During the printing stage (a film laboratory if using film stock), a mask in the shape of the foreground action is used to prevent the background from 'ghosting' through the foreground action.

The blue screen method was developed in the 1930s at RKO Radio Pictures. At RKO, Linwood Dunn used an early version of the travelling matte to create 'wipes' where there were transitions like a car windscreen wiper in films such as *Flying Down to Rio* in 1933. A scene featuring a genie escaping from a bottle was the first use of a proper blue screen process to create a travelling matte for *The Thief of Bagdad* in 1940, which won the Oscar for Best Special Effects.

For decades, travelling matte shots had to be done 'locked down', so that neither the matted subject nor the background could shift their camera perspective at all. Later, computer-timed, motion-control cameras solved this problem, as both the foreground and background could be filmed with the same camera moves.

BLUE OR GREEN SCREEN TRAVELLING MATTE

Mattes are used in photography and special effects filmmaking to combine two or more image elements into a single, final image. Usually, mattes are used to combine a foreground image (such as actors on a set, or a spaceship) with a background image like a scenic vista or a field of stars and planets. In this case, the matte is the background painting. In film and stage, mattes can be physically huge sections of painted canvas, portraying large scenic expanses of landscapes.

The blue/green screen travelling matte process has two basic systems, both of them using a blue or green backing in front of which the foreground action takes place. The basic procedure for each system is as follows:

System A
Stage 1 The action is placed in front of a blue/green backing and is lit with normal studio lighting using colour negative stock.

Stage 2 Travelling Matt with a black/white master positive recording only the blue or green colour in the scene, a black/white positive results, having clear background and black image.

Stage 3 The same procedure is followed, recording only the red colours in the scene. The resulting positive has a clear image against a black background. By step-printing the positive, a high-contrast dupe is produced, with the action placed against a clear background.

Stage 4 The positive produced in Stage 2 is then printed in bi-pack with the dupe negative produced in Step 3 on to black/white high-contrast stock. The foreground image is now seen as a clear area or 'matte' against a black background. A black 'matte' can then be printed against a clear background.

Stage 5 The two mattes are then printed with the foreground action positive and the background positive, giving the required composite image.

The fault with the process is that it tends to produce haloes or black lines around the foreground action.

System B Direct Matte
Stage 1 The set-up against the blue backing is essentially the same as in the above process, except that the scene is lit with yellow light. The negative stock will show the foreground action blue against a yellow background. The negative is then printed on to black/white positive stock, giving a black foreground matte against a clear background.

Stage 2 The background has meanwhile been photographed in a normal way using colour negative stock and a colour positive print is produced. The background positive print and the foreground matte are printed together in Bi-Pack to produce a black foreground matte against a colour positive background.

Stage 3 The foreground negative is printed using a yellow filter to give a yellow positive foreground against a black background.

Stage 4 The yellow foreground positive image and the positive background image are printed together to produce a composite negative.

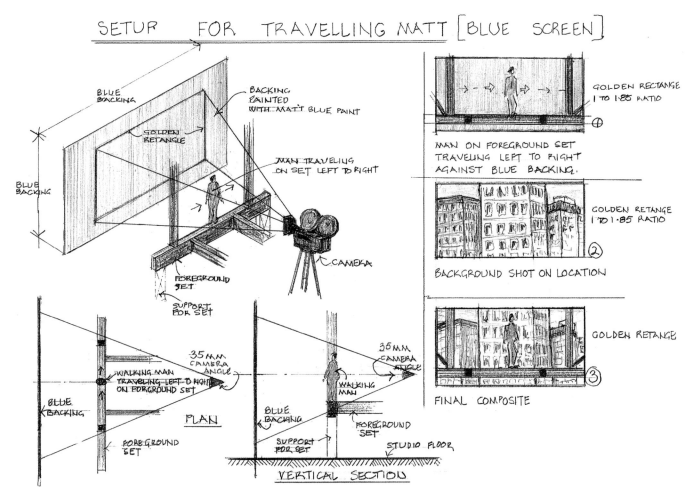

Sketch showing how travelling matte works.

Stage 5 The final composite print will show the normally lit foreground action against the location background quite convincingly.

The advantages of this process is that the haloes and black lines do not appear in this process, laboratory processing is relatively speedy, the background action can be shot at any time and the time spent on setting up in the studio is relatively short.

PLANNING FOR PROCESS SHOTS

If, on reading the script, the Designer anticipates having to use a process shot, he will normally contact the Camera Department. The Designer will have to work out precisely what background footage will be required for each shot and he will supply the Second Unit with a very detailed set of continuity sketches.

REAR OR BACK PROJECTION

Rear projection was made possible in the 1930s due to three necessary technical developments. The most important was the development of camera and projector motors that could be linked up for synchronization of their shutters, which were developed out of the unrelated needs of the 'talkies', whose timing had to be carefully controlled. Secondly, Eastman Kodak's introduction of panchromatic film stock in 1928 allowed for the camera to expose the projected background more than when using orthochromatic stocks, making it look less faint than it did before. Finally, the larger film gauges beginning to emerge in the late 1920s demanded more powerful projection lamps, which were subsequently available for making the rear-projection screen brighter and therefore more properly exposed.

Fox Film Corporation was the first to use the rear-projection technique in 1930 and was subsequently awarded a technical Oscar for its work. The technique was gradually refined as technologies and demands from filmmakers increased. The actors would stand in front of a screen, while a projector, which was positioned behind a specially constructed screen, cast a reversed image of the background. This required a large space, as the projector had to be placed some distance from the back of the screen. Frequently, the background image would appear faint and washed out compared to the foreground. The projected image could be still or moving, but was always called the 'plate'. One might hear the command 'roll plate' to instruct the stage crew to begin projecting.

These so-called 'process shots' were widely used to film actors as if they were inside a moving vehicle, but who were, in reality, in a vehicle mock-up on a sound stage. In these cases, the motion of the backdrop film and foreground actors and props was often different due to the lack of Steadicam-like imaging from the moving vehicles used to produce the plate. This was most noticeable as bumps and jarring motions of the background image that would not be duplicated by the actors.

A major advance since rear projection is front projection, which uses a special screen material to allow the plate to be projected from the front of the screen. This results in a much sharper and more saturated image. Although the technique had been used experimentally for some time, it was during the filming of *2001: A Space Odyssey* that the modern version was fully developed. In this case, it was used to avoid costly on-location shots in Africa during the opening scenes of the movie, but the effect was also used throughout the film for a variety of shots into or out of the windows of the spacecraft. The film also used rear projection to produce computer screen effects.

BACKGROUND PROJECTION

This method throws the background image on a screen behind the subjects in the foreground, while the camera makes a composite by photographing both at once. The foreground elements conceal the parts of the background image behind them. Sometimes, the background is projected from the front, reflecting off the screen but not the foreground subjects, because the screen is made of highly directional, exceptionally reflective material. (The prehistoric opening of *2001: A Space Odyssey* uses front projection.) However, rear projection has been a far more common technique.

FRONT PROJECTION

Although this system is also concerned with placing foreground action in front of a moving background plate, the method is more simple than the back-projection system and offers advantages of flexibility and economy.

The system relies on a highly reflective screen placed behind the action, with the plate projector sending its image on to the screen from the camera side of the screen. Tiny reflective glass beads, which are an integral part of cinema-projection screens, are used in front-projection material. The action takes place in

front of the reflective screen with a camera pointing straight at it. In front of the camera is a beam-splitter – a one-way mirror angled at 45 degrees. At 90 degrees to the camera is a projector that casts a faint image of the background on to the one-way mirror, which reflects the image on to the performer and the screen. The image is too faint to appear on the actor, but shows up clearly on the screen. In this way, the actor becomes his own matte. The combined image is transmitted through the one-way mirror and recorded by the camera.

The two-way mirror is set at a 45-degree angle to both the camera and the plate projector. The projected image falls on the mirror and is reflected onto the screen lying behind the action. The screen, with its highly reflective surface, reflects the image back to the mirror. This transmits the light to the camera, which is placed to photograph the action.

It will be apparent that, once the camera-projection system has been set up, the camera becomes static, since both have to maintain their precise relationship with the two-way mirror. This is one of the system's disadvantages when compared with the back-projection system, which allows the camera mobility.

Another problem which might arise is that, because a certain amount of light loss is inherent in any reflex system, dark areas in the background plates will appear even darker. Even lighting without strong shade should be used.

FOREGROUND MINIATURES

Miniatures are effectively the three-dimensional alternative to a painted matte and are used in many situations and come in various shapes and sizes. Unlike many of the historic 'effects' such as rear and front projection, the use of miniatures is still very relevant to current filming techniques. Although many effects and atmospherics are now added in post-production, there is certainly a place for using miniatures where the action requires the destruction of a building, or the sinking of a galleon at sea, or an aeroplane landing on an urban street, or an explosion on a major railway viaduct – all of which, if done in real life would cost far too much money, time and resources.

So, enter the miniature! These scale models are constructed by specialists to replicate, in exact detail, the original structure. Put into perspective, either against a natural background or in a studio setting and filmed by a Cinematographer who is expert in this field, the miniature is very often more realistic than digital effects, and, in most cases, certainly more economical.

Miniatures can be hanging, foreground, cut-outs or mobile – and all can have a part to play in a production, depending on the type of effects the Director, Designer and the Cinematographer visualize and the best way forward for the film or programme.

Miniatures are extremely detailed models of objects or

people that can be used in a film to give convincing background detail – or they can be used in foreground action when, for various reasons, it is better to use a model than the real object or person. Small 'table-top' models can be used effectively with live action when the movements of the model and the actor are carefully rehearsed.

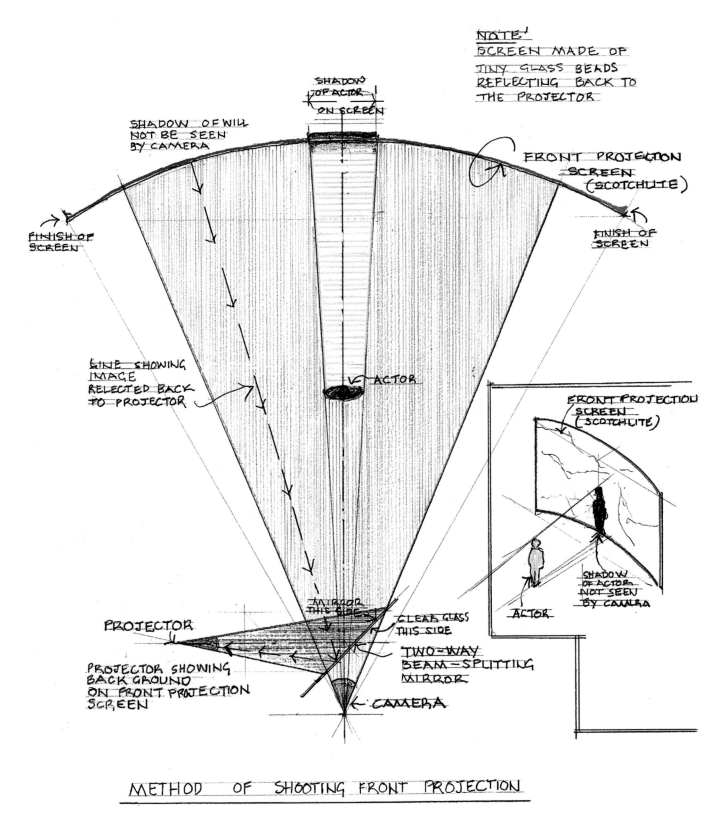

Sketch showing the method of front projection.

A table-top miniature of a petrol station.

The explosion of the miniature petrol station.

PROFESSIONAL PERSPECTIVE: LEIGH TOOK

Leigh Took. LEIGH TOOK, MATTES & MINIATURES VISUAL EFFECTS LTD

Leigh Took began his career as an apprentice in 1978 at Pinewood Studios, learning the classic techniques of matte painting under the supervision of Cliff Culley, one of the few matte painters at the time.

After working for several years with the Special Physical Effects master, Derek Meddings, on films such as *Batman* and *The Neverending Story II*, Leigh set up his own company in 1991 called Mattes & Miniatures and continued working as a Visual Effects and Models Supervisor on countless commercials, music promos, television series and feature films. Leigh Took's film credits to date include: *Kill Command; Victor Frankenstein; Bhopal: A Prayer for Rain; Filmed in Supermarionation; The Monuments Men; Dark Shadows; Ra.One; The Chronicles of Narnia: The Voyage of the Dawn Treader; The Wolfman; The Imaginarium of Doctor Parnassus; Angels and Demons; Mutant Chronicles; Stardust; The Da Vinci Code; The Descent; Ella Enchanted; Lost in Space; The Rainbow Thief; The NeverEnding Story II: The Next Chapter; Batman; The Adventures of Baron Munchausen; Hawk the Slayer; Band of Brothers; The First Men in the Moon; Highlander: The Source.*

MATTES AND MINIATURES

On a location-driven film, when is it a waterfall and when is it a working model? When is it a real backdrop and when is it a matte? This is the magic created by the skill and craft of the model and miniature effects workshop, working closely with the Production Designer and the Art Department.

Ever since I can remember I have had a keen interest in art and, of course, film, so I was lucky enough to become an apprentice to Cliff Culley, in the Special Effects Department at Pinewood Studios. The wages weren't great, but, without that initial opportunity, I doubt I would be where I am today. Amongst the first films I worked on as a trainee were *Warlords of Atlantis* in 1978 and the Ray Harryhausen film, *Clash of the Titans* in 1981, combining matte work with making miniature sets. (*See* the images illustrating the process in the 'Glass Painting' section earlier in this chapter.)

Slowly I got to do more drawing-up, or delineation of shots, blocking in colours and steadily taking on more responsibility until I reached the point where I could complete a shot from beginning to end, with Cliff adding a few dots and dashes to my work – after all, he was the boss! When we weren't so busy, I'd use any spare time I had to improve my abilities in storyboarding, designing fictitious sets, developing imaginative solutions, ways of achieving in-camera effects and optical processes in film and multiple exposures, always bearing in mind the real world of business and the budget limitations.

All this was done before the introduction of 'digital' and it was essential to be flexible and imaginative enough to come up with new techniques to achieve the desired effects for the production.

As my responsibilities increased, I learned not only how necessary it was to put 150 per cent effort into every job, but also how to handle comments from clients – whether good or bad. That feedback resulted in my wanting to do even better in the future and I think that's another thing that helps keep me going today, the desire to impress – basically, showing off!

When bidding on a film, we are usually sent pre-visuals and storyboards, with sections of script and a list of requirements. The fun starts with working out the best method of constructing a miniature, what it has to do, what scale to build it to – together with a breakdown of labour costs and materials. After the production has weighed up the methodology and costs, we wait for the go-ahead and then materials are ordered and technicians employed. Art Department drawings are provided and we are in constant contact with the Director and Art Director throughout the production. It is key to have ongoing feedback with the Art Department while we are building, as sometimes things that look okay on the drawing-board need to be modified once they are constructed as a 3D model and, of course, everyone has to be clear about the budgetary issues of any changes to original specs.

Why bother to make miniatures at all? Why not just create the whole thing in CGI? Well, miniatures offer the opportunity to have a three-dimensional artefact that can be viewed by the camera lens as 'real' and the model can be taken outside. Nothing compares to using actual daylight with a backdrop of trees and landscape in perspective with moving cloud patterns.

When I eventually come to the end of my career, nothing would please me more, as Terry is doing with this book, than to have the feeling that through my own work, I have encouraged and helped others to be able to pursue the career of their dreams and to be successful in doing so.

A miniature cathedral ready for filming with lights, camera and crew in place. LEIGH TOOK, MATTES & MINIATURES VISUAL EFFECTS LTD

A close-up of the intricate attention to detail in the vaulted ceiling of the miniature as the camera and audience would see it. LEIGH TOOK, MATTES & MINIATURES VISUAL EFFECTS LTD

HANGING MINIATURES

Miniatures placed between the camera and the 'normal' set so as to appear on screen as part of the normal set are termed 'hanging miniatures'. Although they often serve a similar purpose to the glass painting, they have an enhanced, three-dimensional quality that gives a more acceptable and convincing illusion.

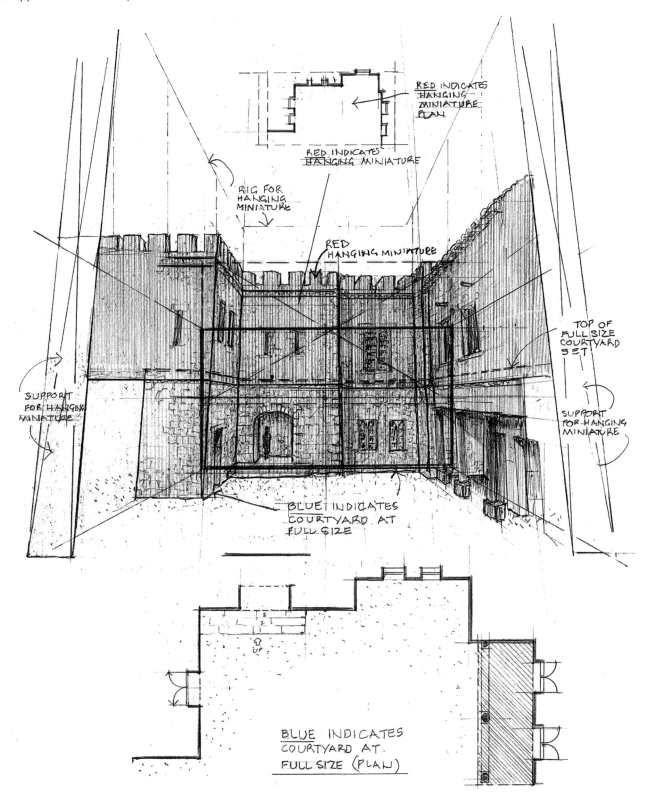

Sketch showing how a full-sized set and hanging miniature work together. The blue section is full size at ground level and the pink section is the hanging miniature in the foreground.

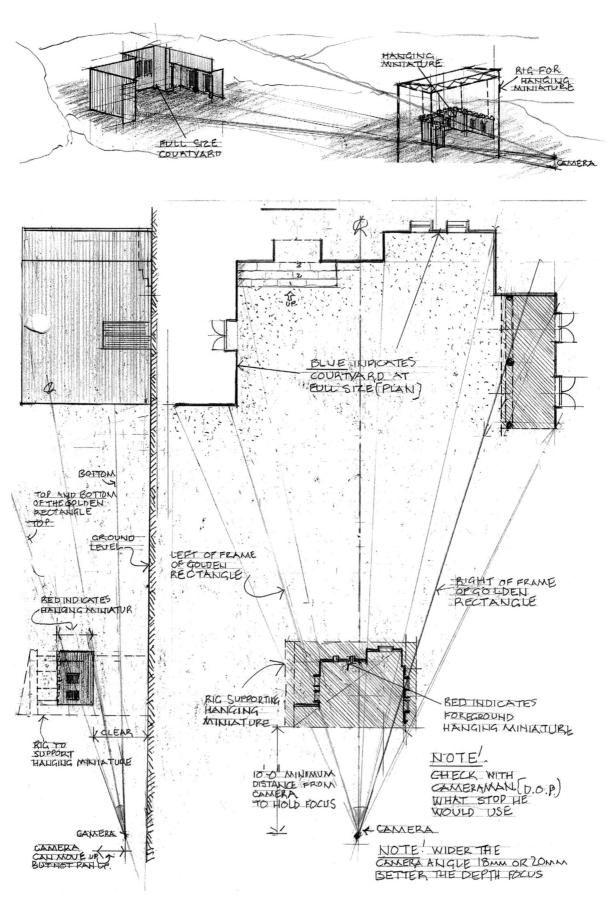

Sketch showing an overhead view of the same hanging miniature scene.

STUDIO EXTERIOR TANK

Some film studios have large exterior water tanks primarily for model ship work. They are usually 4ft deep with a feather-edge horizon spill edge set 12ft from the backing. Wave machines can be set up inside the tank to be used in conjunction with wind and smoke machines to make moving clouds. Being miniature, the film is shot at speed, producing a slight slow-motion effect, which means that the size of the water particles breaking up do not appear too unnatural. The miniature vessels are designed in the Art Department and are towed across the tank by underwater runners, sometimes with frogmen inside the miniature vessels to steer them. The tank can also be used for shots of full-size vessels if carefully planned – but usually only sections of full-size vessels can be used. Most studios also have smaller tanks and heated tanks in some of the stages, which also can be used for staircase wells.

CONTINUITY SKETCHES OR STORYBOARDS

Storyboards are an extremely helpful tool when it comes to planning an action scene where special physical effects will be used. The Storyboard Artist translates sequences from a script into a series of illustrations in order to show what the Director wants to achieve, so that the Heads of Department know exactly what is required.

Superman II

In the 1980 *Superman II*, the *Daily Planet* newspaper is based in New York where Clark Kent and Lois Lane worked. However, most of the shooting was done in Pinewood Studios in England and in other locations, such as Canada, Paris and St Lucia.

The bus-crash sequence was tricky to organize. The Special Physical Effects team had to bring a crane in to slide the bus

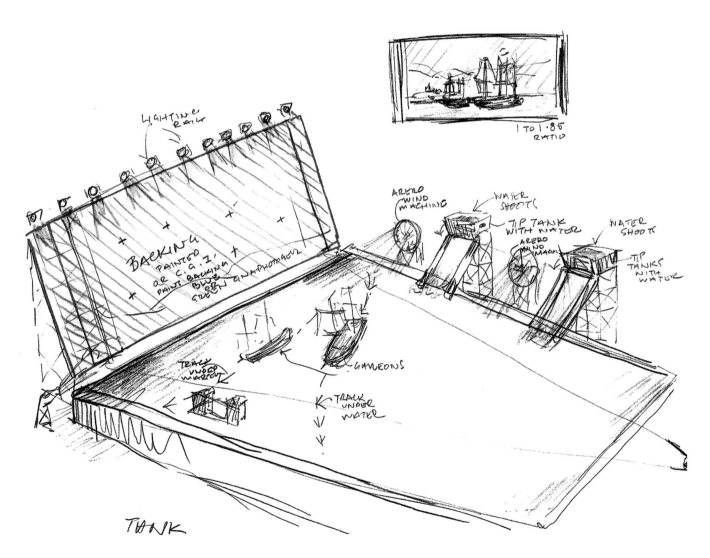

Sketch of an outdoor tank with full-sized backing to be used as green or blue screen. The vessels in the tank can be either full sized or miniatures, or a mixture of both, whichever suits the action (see also overleaf).

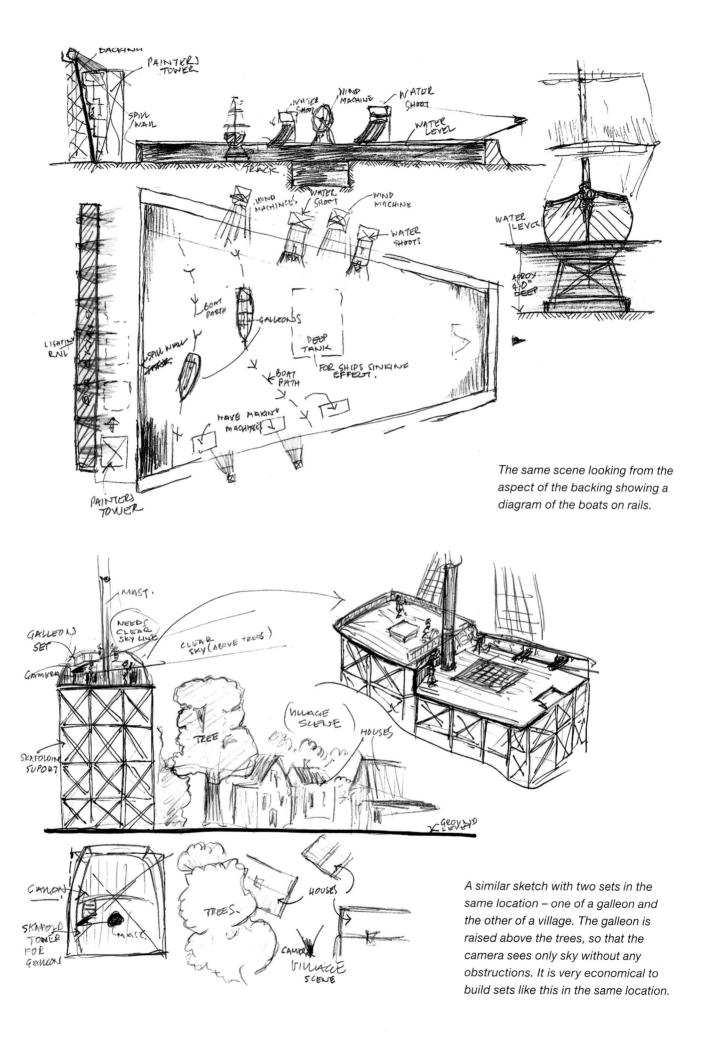

The same scene looking from the aspect of the backing showing a diagram of the boats on rails.

A similar sketch with two sets in the same location – one of a galleon and the other of a village. The galleon is raised above the trees, so that the camera sees only sky without any obstructions. It is very economical to build sets like this in the same location.

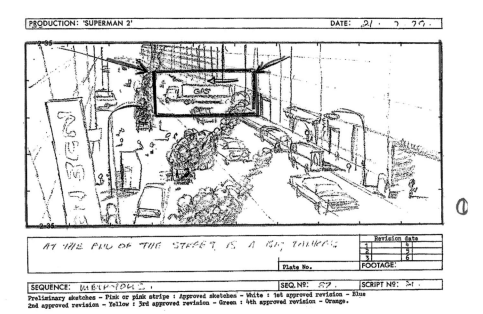

PRODUCTION: 'SUPERMAN 2'　　　　　　　　　　DATE: 21 . 3 . 79 .

AT THE END OF THE STREET IS A GAS TANKERS

	Revision date	
1		4
2		5
3		6

Plate No.　　　FOOTAGE:

SEQUENCE: METROPOLIS .　　　SEQ. Nº: 87 .　　　SCRIPT Nº: 34 .

Preliminary sketches – Pink or pink stripe : Approved sketches – White : 1st approved revision – Blue
2nd approved revision – Yellow : 3rd approved revision – Green : 4th approved revision – Orange.

PRODUCTION: 'SUPERMAN 2'　　　　　　　　　　DATE: 21 . 3 . 79

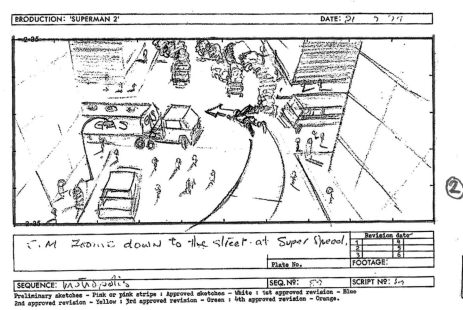

S. M. Zooms down to the street at Super Speed.

	Revision date	
1		4
2		5
3		6

Plate No.　　　FOOTAGE:

SEQUENCE: Metropolis　　　SEQ. Nº: 82　　　SCRIPT Nº: 34

Preliminary sketches – Pink or pink stripe : Approved sketches – White : 1st approved revision – Blue
2nd approved revision – Yellow : 3rd approved revision – Green : 4th approved revision – Orange.

Superman II *crash sequence storyboards. Note and match the red and blue references to the crash sequence draft sketch of the streets.*

PRODUCTION:　　　　　　　　　　DATE: 21 . 3 . 79

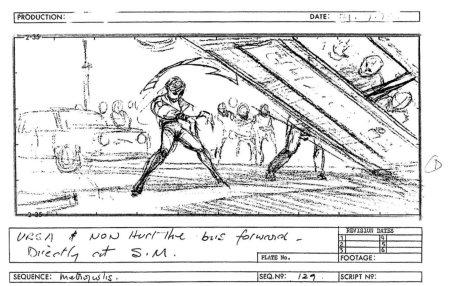

URSA & NON Hurl the bus forward –
Directly at S.M.

	REVISION DATES	
1		4
2		5
3		6

PLATE No.　　　FOOTAGE:

SEQUENCE: Metropolis .　　　SEQ. Nº: 129 .　　　SCRIPT Nº:

Preliminary sketches – Pink or pink stripe : Approved sketches – White : 1st Revision – Blue : 2nd Revision – Yellow
3rd Revision – Green : 4th Revision – Orange

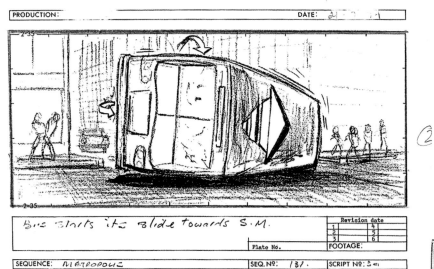

PRODUCTION:		DATE:		

Bus starts its slide towards S.M.

	Revision date		
	1	4	
	2	5	
	3	6	
Plate No.		FOOTAGE:	

SEQUENCE: METROPOLIS	SEQ. Nº: 131.	SCRIPT Nº: 3a

Preliminary sketches – Pink or pink stripe : Approved sketches – White : 1st approved revision – Blue
2nd approved revision – Yellow : 3rd approved revision – Green : 4th approved revision – Orange.

PRODUCTION: 'SUPERMAN 2'		DATE: 21·7·79		

THE BUS FLIES DIRECTLY towards SM. AND hits him squarely –

	Revision date		
	1	4	
	2	5	
	3	6	
Plate No.		FOOTAGE:	

SEQUENCE: METROPOLIS	SEQ. Nº: 132.	SCRIPT Nº: 54

Preliminary sketches – Pink or pink stripe : Approved sketches – White : 1st approved revision – Blue
2nd approved revision – Yellow : 3rd approved revision – Green : 4th approved revision – Orange.

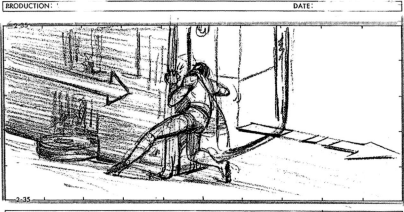

PRODUCTION:		DATE:		

HE tries to ABSORb AS much of the impact as possible.

	Revision date		
	1	4	
	2	5	
	3	6	
Plate No.		FOOTAGE:	

SEQUENCE: METROPOLIS.	SEQ. Nº: 133.	SCRIPT Nº: 3a

Preliminary sketches – Pink or pink stripe : Approved sketches – White : 1st approved revision – Blue
2nd approved revision – Yellow : 3rd approved revision – Green : 4th approved revision – Orange.

across the street in exactly the right place. The process of storyboarding was absolutely essential for this scene.

When we built the street scene for the action sequence, we had to find American street dressing items such as traffic lights, road markings, American vehicles and, of course, a New York telephone booth. We had one or two sponsors like Sony and Ferrucci to help with the window dressing. Clark and Lois's office had to have a ceiling made out of mirrors so that it looked like a very large New York press office.

For one sequence, Superman spins a hole in the road. For this, we built a section of road on a very high rostrum. When it was finished, it was so lifelike that one of the painters walked across the road, over the hole – and down he went!

There is also a scene where Superman knocks the villain through an office window and up through the ceiling. In order to achieve this, the set was built on a rostrum with a very large hinge and the set was then pivoted to create the required illusion.

Superman II crash sequence storyboards. Note and match the red and blue references to the crash sequence draft sketch of the streets.

PRODUCTION: DATE:

The force of this enormous object pushes him back —

	Revision date		
	1		4
	2		5
	3		6

Plate No.

FOOTAGE:

SEQUENCE: METROPOLIS.   SEQ. Nº: 134   SCRIPT Nº: 34

Preliminary sketches – Pink or pink stripe : Approved sketches – White : 1st approved revision – Blue
2nd approved revision – Yellow : 3rd approved revision – Green : 4th approved revision – Orange.

PRODUCTION: DATE:

A.S. S.M struggles to get himself free and help the people : —

	Revision date		
	1		4
	2		5
	3		6

Plate No.

FOOTAGE:

SEQUENCE: METROPOLIS.   SEQ. Nº: 136.   SCRIPT Nº:

Preliminary sketches – Pink or pink stripe : Approved sketches – White : 1st approved revision – Blue
2nd approved revision – Yellow : 3rd approved revision – Green : 4th approved revision – Orange.

Superman II *crash sequence
storyboards. Note and match the
red and blue references to the crash
sequence draft sketch of the streets.*

S.M. rights the bus and shouts- "Thats a lot of Hot air"

	Revision date		
	1		4
	2		5
	3		6

Plate No.

FOOTAGE:

SEQUENCE: METROPOLIS.   SEQ. Nº: 137.   SCRIPT Nº:

Preliminary sketches – Pink or pink stripe : Approved sketches – White : 1st approved revision – Blue
2nd approved revision – Yellow : 3rd approved revision – Green : 4th approved revision – Orange.

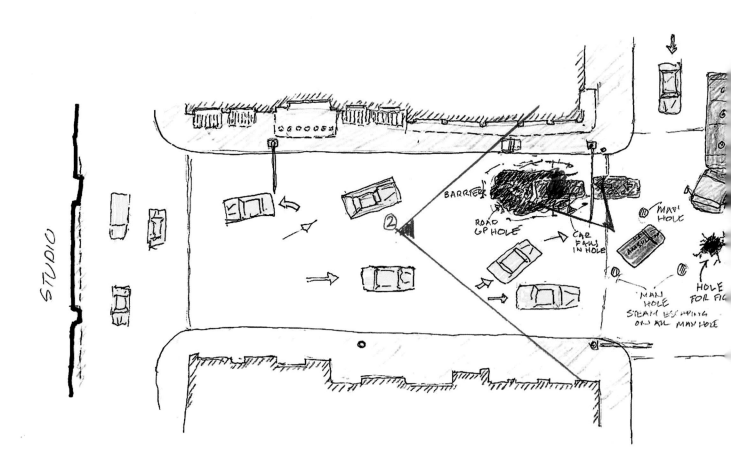

Two draft sketches of the Superman II *crash sequence showing the position of the vehicles, the explosion and the camera angles.*

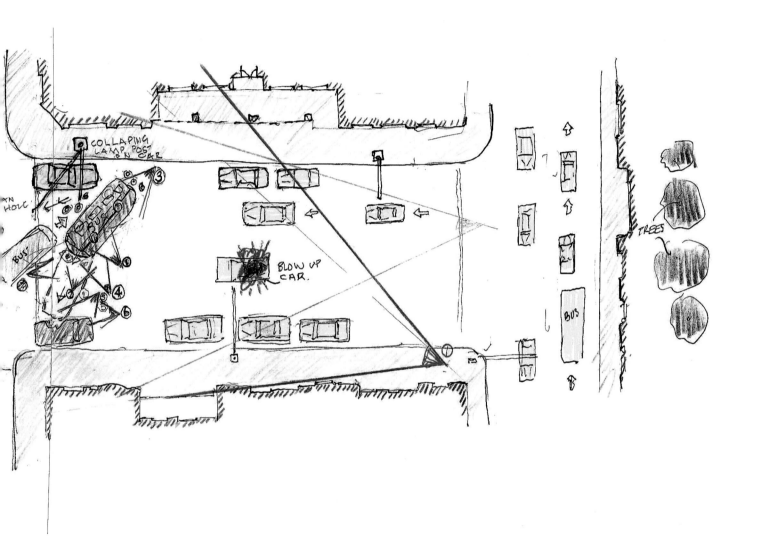

ABOVE: The finished set ready for action.

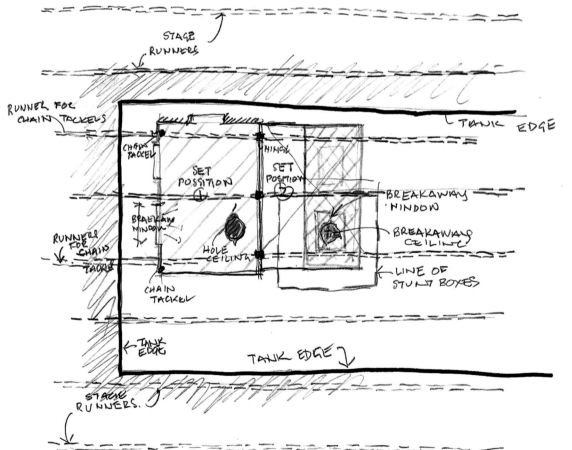

Overhead sketch of the set in the tank showing how the set is able to be moved and manipulated.

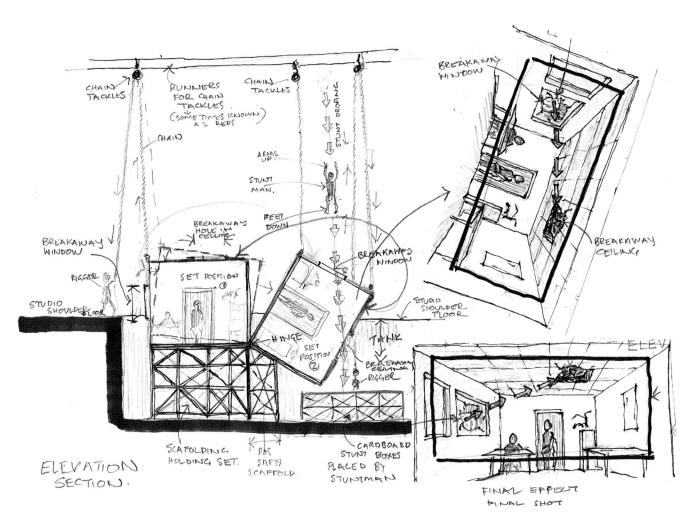

An elevation section of the breakaway room showing exactly how the action will take place.

PROFESSIONAL PERSPECTIVE: MARTIN ASBURY

Martin Asbury.

Martin Asbury was commissioned by the *Daily Mirror* for the cartoon adventure strip Garth, which he drew and wrote for over twenty years. It is still reprinted and syndicated all over the world. At the same time, he started working in the film industry as a top Storyboard Artist.

After a period of designing greetings cards, Martin started at D.C. Thomson, drawing for comics such as *Bunty* and *Hotspur*, before moving to TV Century 21, drawing 'Joe 90' and the football strip 'Forward from the Back-Streets' in 1969. He then drew 'Captain Scarlet' for *Countdown*, starting in 1971. From there, he moved to Look-in where he drew more strips based on television shows, including popular runs on 'Kung Fu' and 'The Six Million Dollar Man' until 1981. He also drew 'Doctor Who' for *TV Comic* in 1975 and a 'Star Wars' strip for the *TV Times* in 1982.

Is was then that Martin took over as the artist on the *Daily Mirror*'s long-running science fiction strip, 'Garth', following Frank Bellamy's death in 1976. He drew and wrote it until it finished in 1997. In 1994, he was invited to storyboard the film *GoldenEye*, which signalled the resurgence of the James Bond franchise and starred a new Bond in the shape of Pierce Brosnan.

He continues to work as one of the world's foremost Storyboard Artists in the feature film community.

His credits to date include: *Edge of Tomorrow; Maleficient; 47 Ronin; Skyfall; Paranorman; Snow White and the Huntsman; Captain America: The First Avenger; Harry Potter and the Deathly Hallows: Part 1; Harry Potter and the Chamber of Secrets; Quantum of Solace; Casino Royale; Die Another Day; The World is not Enough; Tomorrow Never Dies; GoldenEye; Star Wars: Chapter 8; Annihilation; Beauty and the Beast; Batman Begins; Troy; Alien 3; Interview with the Vampire; Fred Claus; Children of Men; The Da Vinci Code; The Hours; Chicken Run; Entrapment; Fierce Creatures; White Hunter Black Heart; Willow; Labyrinth; Legend.*

STORYBOARDS

In the past, the making of a film was governed by the script. It was honed and nurtured and worked upon, rewritten and rewritten. When completed to everyone's satisfaction, it was almost set in concrete. It became the Bible. But these days there appear to be more impediments and pitfalls than ever to this process. Constant writing and rewriting of the script through the prep period can only increase the budget and cause wasted effort. I tell stories in pictures – I have told stories in pictures for all my life. So, if I were asked to direct a film, I would for sure write or draw down what I wanted to do before shooting any sequence – a shot list or stick figures. It is common sense. Nobody in their right mind would walk on to a set with no preparation and no plan.

All those people waiting – all the actors, the Producers, the First, Second, Third, Fourth, Fifth, Sixth and Seventh Assistant Directors, the Lighting Cameraman, the Gaffers, the Stage Hands, the Assistants, the Standbys. Well, you know how it is, you are there with nothing in your head, everyone looking – it doesn't bear thinking about! So, the need for storyboarding becomes obvious.

Over the years, storyboards have been used extensively, from *Gone with the Wind* to virtually every film since. On the basis that one picture tells a thousand words, a finished board shows everyone what the Director has planned, what they have to do, where they have to be and what they are going to try to achieve.

Storyboards are not gospel. They serve as a starting point. They can be, and often are, discarded when events or maybe better options present themselves on the day. They can show what to do, but, more importantly, what not to do. A whole 360-degree set might not be necessary to build. A scene can possibly be cut without detrimental effect to the story, or can be revealed as being too costly. They can show set or location, when explosions and other special effects might occur, or how, for example, to shoot the double of the star in one location, whilst at the same time the star himself is shooting on another set elsewhere. They can show how to heighten drama with cunning angles and camera moves and, of course, are almost indispensable to the ubiquitous car chase. They save time, they save money.

A successful storyboard will reflect the Director's vision, the concept that he has nursed for many months, and translate it into usable workable drawings that the whole of the production team will understand, so it means that everyone is hopefully singing from the same song sheet. To achieve this, the artist should try to get inside the Director's head, not to second-guess him, but to realize his dream for the first time in a visual way. That sounds grandiose, but nevertheless is essentially true. The storyboard is the very first time the script is translated into pictures.

Every Director is different and every Director wants something different. Some will be most specific about the way they see a sequence, down to precise angles, framing and composition. Others will talk you through the scene, detailing particular shots they are anxious to include; a pan here, a track there, low or top shots, the lens to be used, the composition needed. The Storyboard Artist will then make the smooth transition and join up the dots. Other Directors will allow complete carte blanche and the artist can make his own individual pass at the scene, presenting his own take to the Director for perusal and criticism. Rarely in such a case does the Director accept the offer-up completely and he might not like it at all. Usually much more discussion follows until he is satisfied. He may accept some of it, alter and revise bits or just cherry pick what he wants. All the time, though, he is the sole arbiter of what is finally presented to the film's producers and the rest of the unit.

The Storyboard Artist is to the Director what the Concept Artist is to the Designer. He is a utensil, pure and simple. If he is worth his salt, the Storyboard Artist will support and aid the Director in all his endeavours. If successful, his boards can save a huge amount of money and prevent an equal amount of heartache. If nothing else, they can offer up a backstop – a safety net if you will – and provide the building blocks to gain the most out of any given sequence, starting-off discussion or decision.

Nowadays, with the advent and growth of the use of PreVis, the line between the two approaches has become somewhat blurred. PreVis is fantastic; it can be totally accurate in that it can demonstrate what any scene will look like from any given camera position, any lens, any lighting source. Clearly a wonderful tool for any Director. At the moment it is expensive and takes quite a while to produce, but I am sure all that, in time, will change. When that day happens, maybe storyboards per se will cease to exist – but I hope not. I still feel that the immediacy of drawing to the Director on the spot cannot be substituted. A sudden change to shooting requirements can necessitate an instant storyboard. The good artist can block out a whole sequence in a couple of days and provide a cost-effective kick-start for the whole creative process.

A good Storyboard Artist has to know, understand and love film. He has to think like a camera and draw pictures as stills of movement. He has to tell you all you need to know about what you will see on screen, but leave that little bit out for the imagination and invention. An accomplished storyboard is good for what it tells you. If it is drawn well with excitement, feeling and vigour, then all to the good, but it is all about information and communication. That is why we are all involved in this business. We inform, we communicate, we tell stories – and all in pictures.

The Storyboard Artist translates screenplays or sequences into a series of illustrations in comic-book form. These illustrations have two functions – to help the Director to clarify exactly what he wants to achieve and to illustrate to all other Heads of Department exactly what is required, for example Make-up, Costume, Art Department Props, Special and Visual Effects, Stunts and so on.

In many ways, comic books are the art form that most closely resemble cinema. They both tell stories in a primarily visual form, involving discrete, framed images linked sequentially to convey information, and through this concept it is possible to develop complex sequences in films, which require careful planning and cannot or should not be left to on-set improvisation.

Basic technical knowledge of film cameras and lenses, combined with a working knowledge of the Director's role in the filmmaking process, are invaluable. Key skills include the ability to think cinematically, excellent drawing skills, excellent communication skills, the ability to visualize perspective and three-dimensional space and be able to interpret other people's ideas visually.

CHAPTER 7

WORKING WITH PUPPETRY AND ANIMATION

If you take your career in the Art Department seriously, you will no doubt one day be asked either to design or work on set for a film or programme that will include characters who are puppets or animatronics. Perhaps you might think that everything these days can be taken care of by digital technology, but think for a moment about the much-beloved Wallace and Gromit films, or anything that includes Miss Piggy or Kermit the Frog. They need specialist knowledge and equipment to make them seem alive or an integral part of the action.

PUPPETRY

Puppetry is the making and manipulation of puppets for use

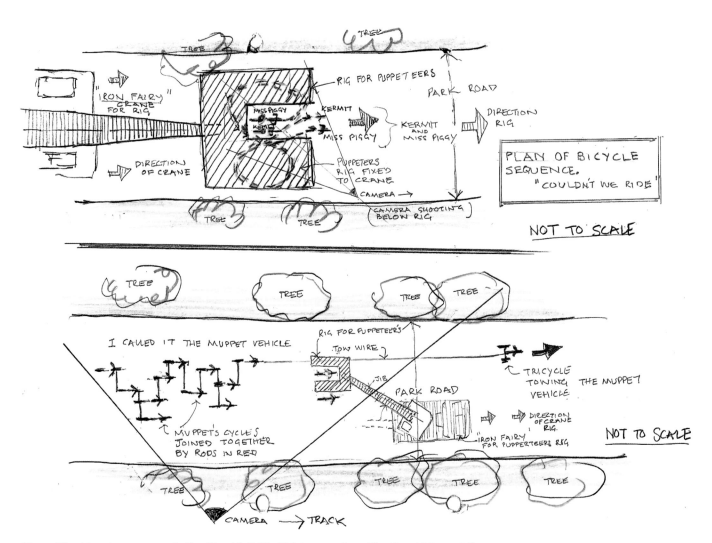

Plan of the bicycle sequence in the 'Couldn't We Ride' scene from The Great Muppet Caper.

JIM HENSON

Puppeteer Jim Henson and his wife, Jane, founded their company in 1958. Jim was recognized worldwide as an innovator in his field and is best known for creating the Muppets (now owned by Disney), who evolved as characters in their own right from Henson's children's television series, *Sesame Street*. Other children's television series produced by the company included *Fraggle Rock* and the cult science-fiction series *Farscape*.

Jim Henson's legacy includes iconic films such as *The Dark Crystal* and *Labyrinth*, as well as the Muppet movies. The Jim Henson Company, under the leadership of Jim and Jane's children, continues to remain as an established children's entertainer.

in some kind of theatrical show. A puppet is a figure – human, animal or abstract in form – that is moved by human, and not mechanical, aid.

Puppets have been used as a form of entertainment since

entertainment was invented! From basic glove puppets to the likes of Punch and Judy, who have entertained and scared children since the seventeenth century, to marionettes that are operated from above with strings, through to the almost life-size puppets devised by Jim Henson for the much-loved *Sesame Street* and *The Muppets*.

The Great Muppet Caper

In *The Great Muppet Caper* in 1981, I worked with Harry Lange. The first problem I was confronted with was trying to work out the mechanics of the sequence for the song 'Couldn't We Ride', in which Jim Henson required all the puppets to cycle together. We solved this by fixing rods to the axles to keep them in line, which were then towed by a man on a tricycle out of shot.

Another problem was the bicycles themselves. They all had to be custom-made to fit each of the characters, so we had to start from scratch as there was no way we could convert regular cycles from a showroom.

Jim wanted Miss Piggy and Kermit to do a figure of eight together on their bikes – not too complicated you would think, but it needed another big rig for the puppeteers. We fixed this rig to a crane called 'The Iron Maiden' (*see* photographs) and

Storyboards, numbered 1 to 47, outlining the full Muppets' cycling sequence. This demonstrates the value and importance of the storyboard artist to the Art Department.

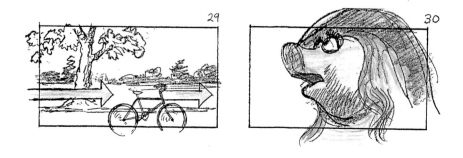

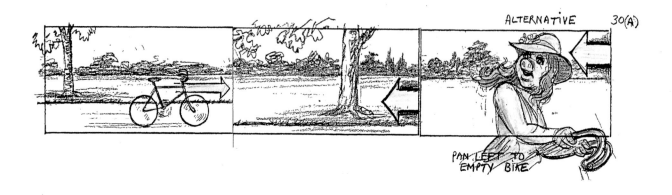

ALTERNATIVE 30(A)

PAN LEFT TO EMPTY BIKE

PIGGY'S P.O.V.

KERMIT'S P.O.V.

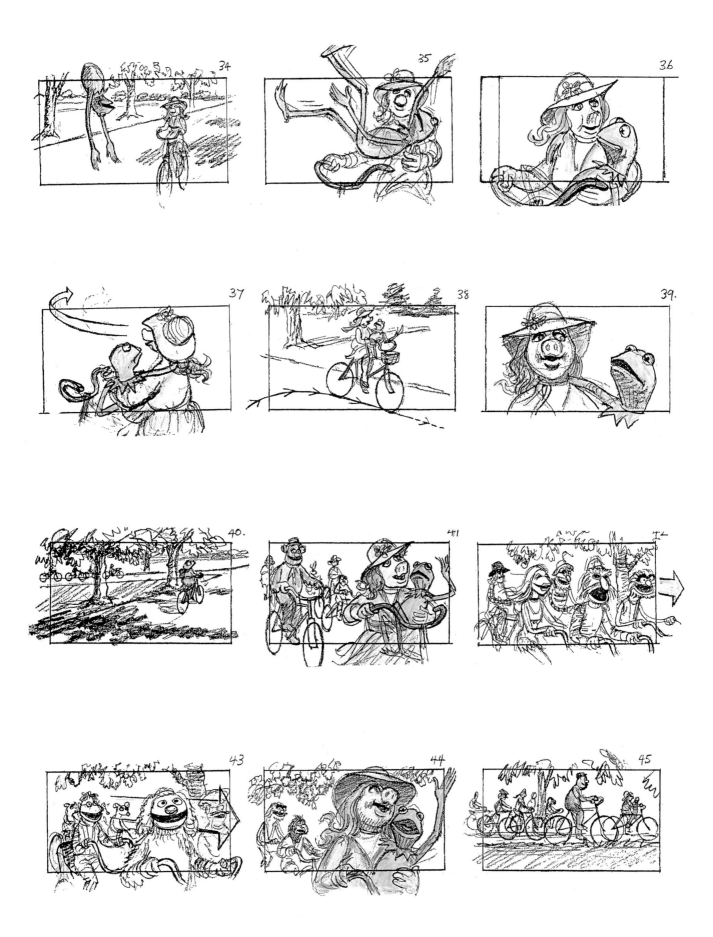

Jim suggested, in order to make it more mobile, we should mount it on a golf cart. I knew it would be top-heavy and topple over – which it did! However, it was only another problem to be solved on the day.

The opening 'balloon' sequence of *The Great Muppet Caper* was filmed in New Mexico. This involved Fozzie Bear crash-landing in the street, with live action involving cars, painters who are working on a building and a basketball game.

The first test of the 'cycling' rig. Note the puppeteer standing on the gantry.

Showing the rig on 'The Iron Maiden' crane.

Showing the rig on the crane ready for the outdoor sequences.

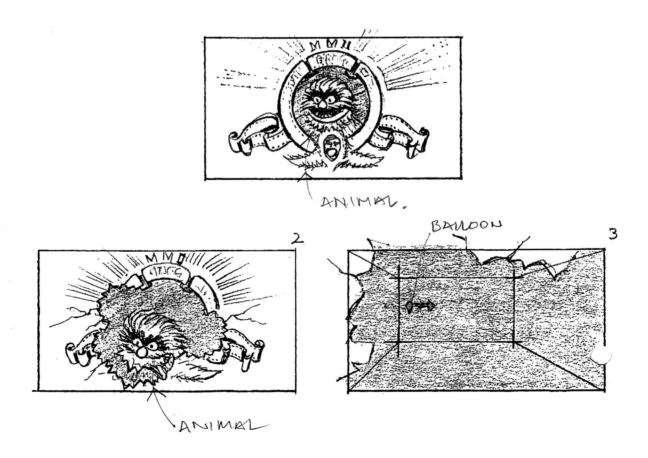

Storyboards for the opening sequence of The Great Muppet Caper *filmed in New Mexico.*

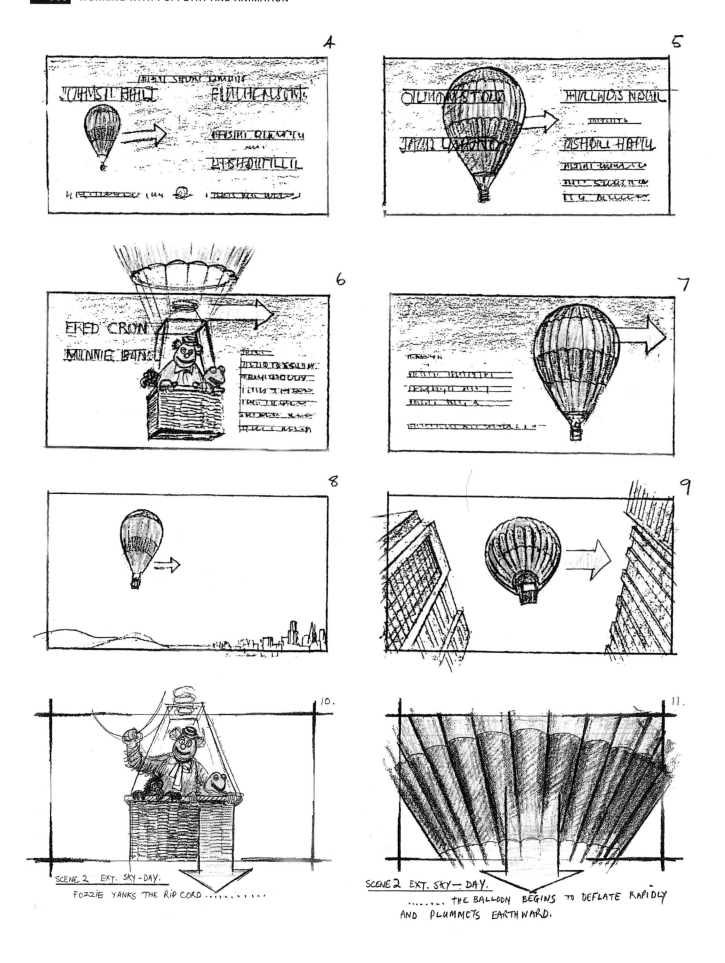

SCENE 2 EXT. SKY – DAY.
FOZZIE YANKS THE RIP CORD . . . .

SCENE 2 EXT. SKY — DAY.
. . . . THE BALLOON BEGINS TO DEFLATE RAPIDLY
AND PLUMMETS EARTHWARD.

SCENE 3 — EXT. STREET—DAY.

IT LANDS WITH A WHOOSH ON A STREET IN A
METROPOLITAN CITY............

SCENE 3 — EXT. STREET — DAY.

.... COVERED IMMEDIATELY BY THE LARGE DEFLATED
BALLOON.

Storyboards for the opening sequence filmed in New Mexico.

SCENE 3 EXT— STREET.

AS BASKETBALL DROPS INTO PAIL PAINTER DOES
BACKWARD SOMERSAULT FROM CRADLE TO GROUND
FOZZIE SINGS : — "THERE'll BE HEROES BOLD"
"THERE' ll BE COMEDY"

SCENE 3 EXT. STREET — DAY
AS FOZZIE SINGS " .... AND ME !" — BASKETBALL PLAYER
JUMPS AND "SCORES" DROPPING BALL INTO PAINT PAIL

The street complete with painters as outlined in storyboards 18 and 19.

PROFESSIONAL PERSPECTIVE: GERRY ANDERSON (1929–2012)

MARIONETTES; EXTRACTS FROM AN INTERVIEW CONDUCTED IN 2009

Gerry Anderson pictured with 'Thunderbird 2'. DAVE FINCHETT

Gerry Anderson and his team became leading exponents of working with marionettes. Having started his career as a trainee with the Colonial Film Unit in the 1940s, Gerry became very comfortable with all aspects of feature film production. He started his own production company in the 1950s and was offered a script for a children's series called *Twizzle.*

We were over the moon, our big chance to show what we were made of – then she [Roberta Leigh] dropped the bombshell, it was a puppet show – but, we were hungry for work and even the modest budget and the tight schedule didn't put us off.

Having not been impressed with puppet shows he'd seen on television, he and his team worked on the puppets to make them behave in a more realistic manner.

I hated what I had already seen on television as puppet shows and we decided to add a few 'film' techniques to make the sets more realistic with cut-outs in mid- and foreground to add depth.

Around 250 set-ups were needed for each half-hour episode, so the miniature sets were built on movable stages that could be wheeled in and out very quickly.

Every episode we made we got a little better at it. Christine Glanville was the chief puppeteer and made the heads herself from cork dust, glue and methylated spirits, which was infinitely better than the original papier mâché, as they could be sanded down to a smoother finish. Eventually all the puppets would be made of fibreglass.

So successful was their approach that they were offered another new series, *Torchy the Battery Boy*. The budget was increased substantially so that they could greatly improve the look and 'workability' of the puppets, with springs in the jaw to simulate speaking without the head bouncing up and down, which was eventually controlled by an electro-magnetic device. So innovative was this work that they came up with the name 'Supermarionation', which is still used to this day.

We were working on 35mm film with a Mitchell camera and I wanted to see what the TV audience would be viewing as we were working. I bought a lightweight video camera and fixed it to the Mitchell camera we were using so it looked directly down the lens, linking to a monitor and giving us a constant picture. This Video Assist technique was soon adopted by the film industry worldwide.

The reason the Mitchell was, and still is, so very good at this type of work is its precise, gear-driven mechanism. The next series was *Four Feather Falls*, then *Supercar*, which was broadcast very successfully coast to coast in America, followed by *Fireball XL5* and *Stingray*, shot in colour and likely one of the first puppet series to entertain both a children's and an adult audience. Then came the iconic *Thunderbirds* and *Captain Scarlet and the Mysterons*.

While Stingray *was still in production, I was writing a new series which eventually would be called* Thunderbirds. *Public response when the series was aired was phenomenal!*

Major developments and change have always been an essential part of the industry. Puppet work has been superseded by CGI and we dipped our toe in the water with Lavender Castle *and remade* Captain Scarlet *in 2005 using the latest software – except that I still worked with film people for storyboards and set design to make sure that it had that '3-dimensional' film feel.*

The technology and techniques during my career have changed so much and continue to evolve, so it makes each fresh project an exciting and rewarding challenge.

Thunderbirds *puppet Alan Tracy holding a picture of Anderson's original puppeteer, Christine Glanville.*
ANDERSON ENTERTAINMENT/ THE GERRY ANDERSON ESTATE

Gerry Anderson made a significant contribution to the field of puppetry and marionettes. The characters he created were loved by a whole generation of fans and the impact of his innovative work continues to be felt to this day in the film industry.

Gerry Anderson's credits include: *Thunderbirds; Stingray; Captain Scarlet and the Mysterons; Space Precinct; Terrahawks; Destination Moon Base Alpha; Space 1999; UFO; Joe 90; Fireball XL5; Supercar; Four Feather Falls; Torchy the Battery Boy; The Adventures of Twizzle).*

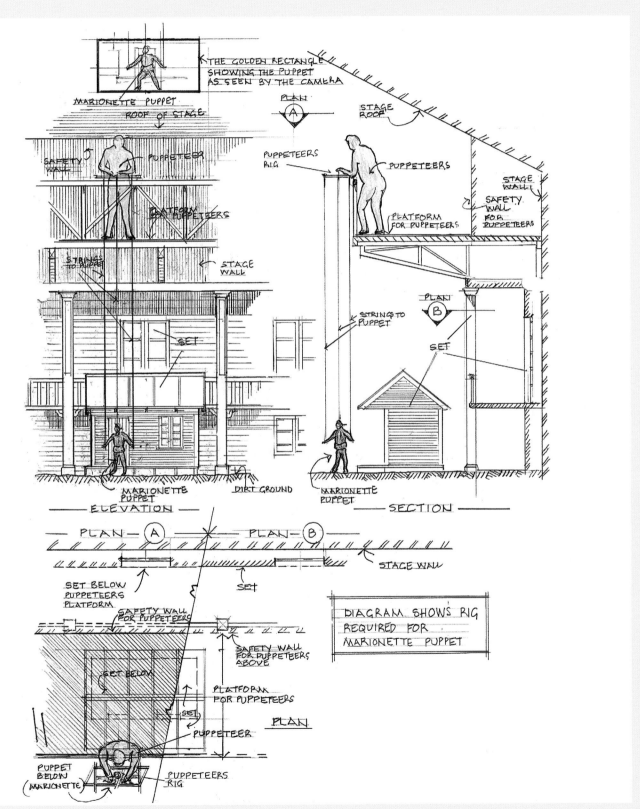

A diagram showing the type of rig required for marionettes. ANDERSON ENTERTAINMENT/THE GERRY ANDERSON ESTATE

PROFESSIONAL PERSPECTIVE: DAVID SPROXTON

David Sproxton.

David Sproxton is Co-Founder of the award-winning company, Aardman Animations.

Aardman's credits include: *Early Man; Flushed Away; Chicken Run; The Curse of the Were Rabbit; Shaun the Sheep; Arthur Christmas; The Pirates! In an Adventure with Scientists!; The Wrong Trousers; A Grand Day Out; A Matter of Loaf and Death; A Close Shave; Creature Comforts.*

STOP-FRAME MOTION

Stop-frame sets are generally of a smaller scale to those used in puppetry, as the animatable puppets need to be of a moderately small size to avoid being too heavy to bear their own weight. Gravity is the limiting factor with stop-frame models. Aardman generally uses puppets about 8–9in high for human figures, but often smaller if they are animals. Shaun the Sheep stands less than 3in high when on all fours and Morph is about 3.5in, although he lives in the 'real' world. This means that the sets are scaled down – typically about one-sixth or one-eighth life size.

False or forced perspective is often used in 'external' sets to increase the sense of space and distance, although this can prove problematic if shooting in 3D stereo. The logistics of the production often means that multiple versions of the same set need to be built. The kitchen scene where the Pirate Captain and Queen Victoria have a fight in *The Pirates! In an Adventure with Scientists!* was reproduced six times to make the logistics of the shoot work.

The use of CAD systems and cutting machinery, together with Rapid Prototyping technology, ease the problems of multiple sets considerably at this scale. Skies and other elements may be added in post-production, so green and blue screen techniques are often combined with fully built sets. Continuity of lighting is therefore important.

A key factor with stop-frame sets is rigidity and lack of movement. The sets may be up for a considerable length of time and a single shot may take several days to shoot, so the sets need to be built very solidly and not be prone to shifting or distorting over time, or with temperature or humidity changes. As a safety measure, 'background plates' are frequently shot as a separate element, so that,

On the small but perfectly formed sets of Aardman's A Matter of Loaf and Death *starring Wallace and Gromit, showing the scale of the sets. The skills and attention to detail involved in producing the sets and the characters are extremely specialized.* AARDMAN ANIMATIONS 2008

should a set shift during shooting, a clean and static set can replace the shifting set in post-production.

The animated models often need mechanical rigs to hold them in position, particularly if the character is off the ground, jumping or flying. Consideration needs to be given to these rigs when designing the sets. Further, large sets with lots of animated elements need to have access points for the animators, which must also be built into the design.

Setting up the lighting rigs for Aardman's Shaun the Sheep. *The techniques involved in filming these miniaturized sets take lighting and camerawork to a whole new level of expertise.* AARDMAN ANIMATIONS 2014

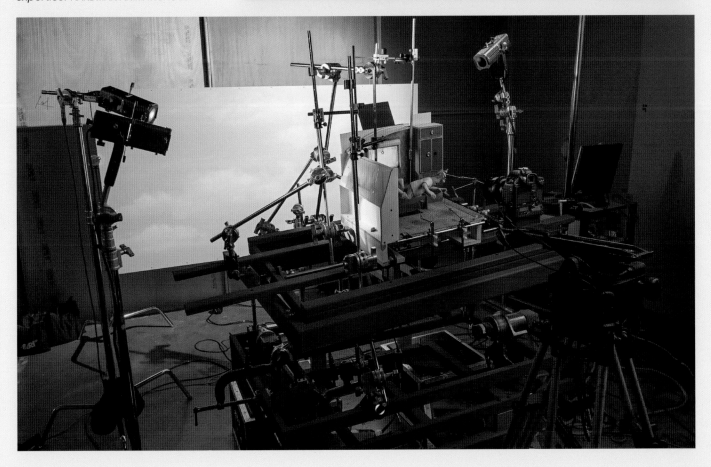

STOP MOTION

Stop motion is an animation technique whereby physical objects or puppets are manipulated or moved on a frame by frame basis so that on the screen they appear to move on their own. The objects or models could range from just a simple lump of modelling clay to a sophisticated model with a complex metal skeleton or armature that can be moved in minute increments between frames to give the model very sophisticated expressions. Often the models are animated by the process of shooting two frames at a time, but for faster movement and smoother animation, single frame shooting is preferred.

Stop-motion animation has a long history in film and was often used to show objects moving as if by magic. Possibly the first time it was recorded was in the 1898 film, *The Humpty Dumpty Circus*, credited to Albert Smith and Stuart Blackton, in which a toy circus of acrobats and animals comes to life. One of the earliest clay animation films was *Modelling Extraordinary* in 1912 and the first woman animator, Helena Smith Dayton, started experimenting with clay stop motion.

Willis O'Brien's animation work on *The Lost World* in 1925 and *King Kong* in 1933 was much admired and was all made possible by stop motion. His protégé and successor was the legendary Ray Harryhausen, whose work, including *Mighty Joe Young*, *It Came from Beneath the Sea*, *Jason and the Argonauts*, *The Golden Voyage of Sinbad* and *Clash of the Titans*, became his legacy to film animation between 1949 and 1981.

The first stop-motion film to win an Oscar was the 1975 *Closed Mondays* by filmmaker and clay animation experimenter Will Vinton, who joined with sculptor Bob Gardiner to create this experimental film. This was followed with several other successful short films, which were each nominated for Academy Awards. In 1977, Vinton made a documentary about the process and style of his animation, which was titled *Claymation*. Soon after this, the term was trademarked by Vinton to differentiate his team's work from others who were beginning to do clay animation. The word has stuck and is often used to describe clay animation using the stop-frame technique.

At around the same time as the invention of Claymation, Peter Lord and David Sproxton were forming Aardman Animations in the UK. One of their first creations was the character of Morph, a 3.5in high figure made from a British modelling clay called plasticine. Morph appeared as an animated sidekick to the television presenter Tony Hart on his BBC television programme *Take Hart*. From the start, Peter and David were interested in developing an adult audience for model animation. A series called *Conversation Pieces*, commissioned by Channel Four Television in 1982, enabled the pair to develop their innovative technique of animating puppet characters for real-life conversations. With films like *Early Bird* (set in a local radio station), Aardman demonstrated that real people could be characterized with insight, humour and sensitivity.

Peter and David met Nick Park at the National Film and Television School when he was working on his Oscar-winning, BAFTA-nominated, student film, *A Grand Day Out*, and he joined Aardman full-time in 1985. They then started on a series of animated films, using the same process, but this time made for a more general audience.

ANIMATRONICS

An animatronic is a very sophisticated, mechanized puppet that can be pre-programmed, controlled remotely or moved by a combination of mechanics, electronics and human performers – so it can be capable of either very simple movements, or be very complex and versatile. Animatronics were used in filmmaking a long time before digital effects came into being, for example the realistic shark in Jaws, the dinosaurs in *Jurassic Park* and the not so realistic creatures in *Labyrinth* and *The Dark Crystal*.

The skilled actors who are in control of the device are called puppeteers. These puppeteers will spend a lot of time with the animatronic figure, working out its range of movements and determining which movements, emotions and moods are called for in the script to make the animatronic look realistic.

So, how are they built? Like everything else connected to the Art Department, it all starts with a pencil and paper and the vital preliminary sketches and drawings. Everything that follows relies on the accuracy of these designs. When the Director and Designer are satisfied with the final design, a miniature model called a maquette is created, possibly out of clay, which is used to make sure that the design on paper is accurate and workable. Any problems and it's back to the drawing board!

Once the sketches and models are completed to everyone's satisfaction, the build will begin. Before digitization, the full-size creature would be crafted or sculpted by hand, which was a long process. Now laser scanners will take a high-resolution image of the maquette. After scanning, the computer model is used to mill the life-sized creature from polyurethane foam by a CNC machine. The animatronics sculptors then hand-carve the sculpture until they are satisfied that the creature looks the way it should, then a set of epoxy moulds are cast, from which the sculptors and artists work in a variety of ways to create the creature, whether or not it needs skin or scales or feathers.

The Dark Crystal

The set of *The Dark Crystal* in 1982 was a whole new concept for Production Designer, Harry Lange, and his team in order to accommodate the puppets and the puppeteers. The sets had to be built on a rostrum constructed out of modules, so that they were at 4ft 6in above the ground in order that the puppeteers could operate the creatures from below and out of sight of the cameras (see diagram).

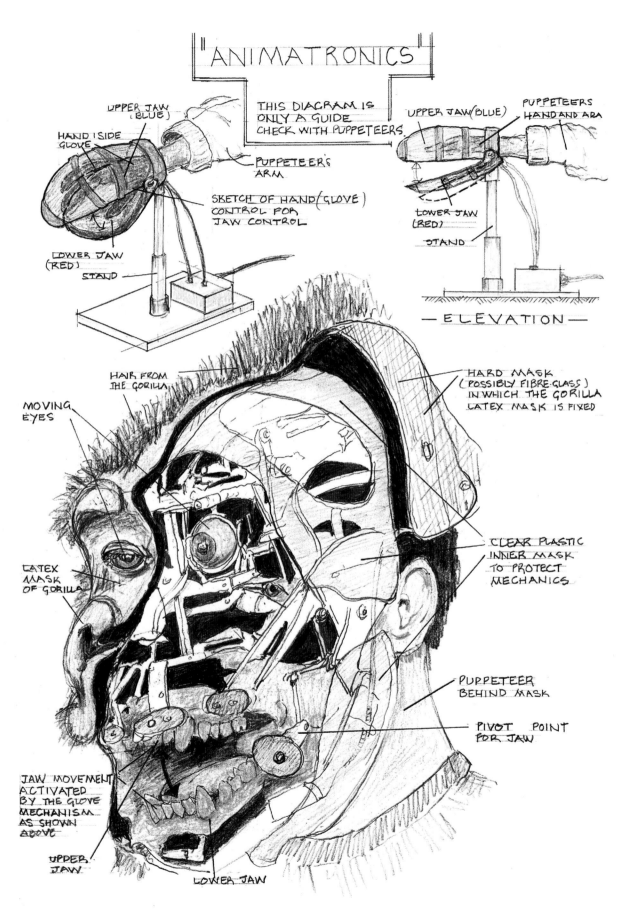

"ANIMATRONICS"

THIS DIAGRAM IS ONLY A GUIDE CHECK WITH PUPPETEERS

UPPER JAW (BLUE)

HAND I SIDE GLOVE

PUPPETEER'S ARM

SKETCH OF HAND (GLOVE) CONTROL FOR JAW CONTROL

LOWER JAW (RED)

STAND

UPPER JAW (BLUE)

PUPPETEERS HAND AND ARM

LOWER JAW (RED)

STAND

— ELEVATION —

HAIR FROM THE GORILLA

MOVING EYES

HARD MASK (POSSIBLY FIBRE-GLASS) IN WHICH THE GORILLA LATEX MASK IS FIXED

LATEX MASK OF GORILLA

CLEAR PLASTIC INNER MASK TO PROTECT MECHANICS

PUPPETEER BEHIND MASK

PIVOT POINT FOR JAW

JAW MOVEMENT ACTIVATED BY THE GLOVE MECHANISM AS SHOWN ABOVE

UPPER JAW

LOWER JAW

A guide to how an animatronic puppet works.

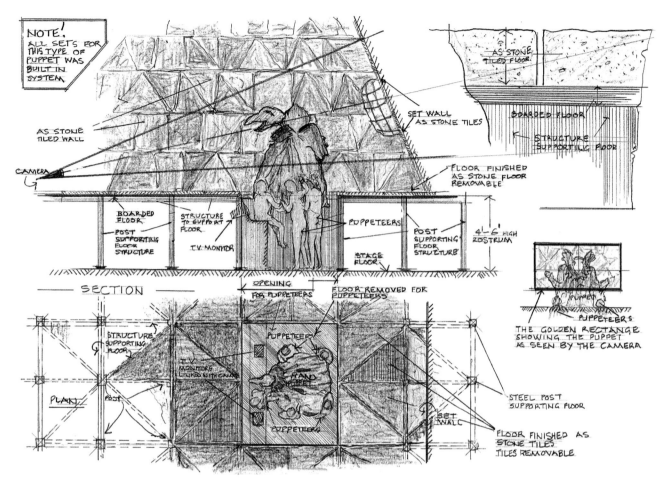

A plan of a section of the type of rig used for animatronics.

We didn't have anything to do with the creatures themselves – that was down to Jim Henson and his team, with Conceptual Designer Brian Froud designing the puppets. (Brian was also the Costume Designer!)

The actual 'Dark Crystal', also called the 'Crystal of Truth', was around 8ft tall and constructed of fibreglass. We tried to build it out of perspex, but that didn't work as we could always see the edge of the perspex on each facet of the crystal. On the screen, the crystal looked as though it was coloured purple and white. The Director of Photography, the wonderful Ossie Morris BSC, came up with a tricky use of a lighting pattern with the help of Lighting Gaffer John Harman.

One of the major sets we had to build was the one that contained 'Aughra's Orrery'. (Aughra was a wise but mysterious character who understood both science and spiritual matters.) The Orrery was a very complicated, intricately revolving apparatus that represented the motions of the planets in their solar system and was built by the Special Physical Effects Department.

All in all, this was a really enjoyable film to work on, as it was so different to anything else I had done in the past and it tested all of our ingenuity and skill to the utmost!

Although the Production Designer, Art Director and the Draughtsmen do not need to know the minutiae of all the technical details, it's essential that they have an understanding of the processes involved. How a creature, or a puppet, is going to be constructed and fit into the scenario will determine the size and layout of the set you're going to design.

A photograph of the 'Orrery' under construction from the back of the set.

A still image of the set as seen by the camera.

The crew of The Dark Crystal all assembled on part of the set.

CHAPTER 8

VISUAL EFFECTS

The influence of digital technologies has changed the way in which creative people involved in film, games and television production approach every new project.

Visual effects (VFX) are essentially a highly useful story-telling tool. They are the process by which imagery is created and/or manipulated following a live action shoot, during the post-production period. This imagery is blended back into the film at the final edit and grading phases. Although VFX are still largely a post-production process, planning for their inclusion begins at the earliest stages of pre-production and continues in some form right through the project. Please take careful note, visual effects are very different from special physical effects (action sequences, explosions, fires) and getting this terminology wrong will get you much criticized by your peers!

VFX are a part of nearly every film these days, to differing degrees. They could range from a simple and relatively 'invisible' requirement of removing some modern pylons from the background of only twenty shots in a historical drama, right through to a 'VFX heavy' project, where the visual effects are a major and noticeable feature of the film. Most of the modern blockbuster superhero films fall into this latter category and may involve complex CG characters and elaborate CG environments, which will be seen in something like over 2,000 shots.

Although working in the Art Department doesn't necessarily mean that you will have to get physically involved in doing any of this work, it is more than essential that you fully understand exactly how your designs and ideas will be handled by the extended film production processes, both before the work comes to you and after it leaves your hands.

DESIGNING FOR DIGITAL PRODUCTION

Digital filmmaking has led to the rewriting of some job descriptions, but the Art Department is still the central point around which the *imagery* of filmmaking revolves. Whether footage is originated digitally or on film stock, the Digital Intermediate (DI) process means that what was once done in the laboratory or the optical house can now be done by an artist working on a computer in a facilities house. With the increasing mixture of computer-generated imagery and live action in film, the Visual Effects Supervisor is a key part of the production team right from the start, working with the Director and Production Designer, regardless of the amount of visual effects in the film.

Visual effects are most effectively used when they tell an aspect of a story that is impossible or impractical to capture in live action. Most Directors with experience of using visual effects will appreciate that 'if you can shoot it for real, you should shoot it for real'. There is very little point in creating a table in visual effects if you can simply obtain a real table, as long as it doesn't need to do anything unusual, such as turn into a dragon! Visual effects are best used when the story calls for something that is impossible to shoot for real – for example, the CG characters and magic effects in films such as the *Harry Potter* franchise. Visual effects are also frequently used when there is a Health and Safety threat to the crew or talent, perhaps involving a giant fire or an explosion. Even CG animals have been used in situations where the animal's welfare could have been at risk – a wolf biting a horse, for example. Visual effects are also very effective in situations where the Special Physical Effects teams need a helping hand, such as the demolition of a whole building, or the collapse of a whole mountainside.

The VFX Supervisor will work closely with the Director, Production Designer, Art Director and Producer in the planning stages of a film to discuss and advise on the most effective and visually compelling approach to solving these visual challenges. The VFX Supervisor works closely with the Art Director and Production Designer in particular to review the artistic concepts and to decide on what should be created for real, what would be best created using physical effects and what should be created using visual effects. They work to find a good balance, which gives the highest visual impact for the best possible use of the budget.

The Visual Effects Supervisor, with the help of a small team of artists, will take the designs created by the Art Department and convert them into CG versions, animatics (test animations) and Previsualization. These will help the Director and Production Designer to visualize these elements more fully within the story and to decide on the best method for creating them in the film.

During the pre-production planning, the VFX Supervisor will also request bids or quotes from various VFX companies (often called 'VFX vendors') for various parts of the film that will have been flagged as requiring visual effects. They are normally sent as 'packages' or sets of sequences. All companies may be asked to bid on all packages or only a select set, based on that company's prior experience. For example, if a company has done a lot of complex CG character work, it may only be asked to bid on a package that includes this.

The VFX Supervisor, during the shooting process, will collaborate with the Production Designer and all the departments involved, as he or she has to make sure that all equipment and technologies, such as blue or green screen and motion-capture facilities, are organized and to ensure that the filming is being done in a way that makes the post-production process as efficient and cost-effective as possible. Many film projects in the past have not shot the scenes in a conducive way for the visual effects process and this actually ends up costing a lot more money to fix later on, so the role of the VFX Supervisor in the planning stages is vital. Prevention is always better, and cheaper, than the cure!

MOTION CAPTURE

Motion or performance capture (MoCap) is the technical process that is used to translate an actor's performance into a digital character. It can capture realistic movement very quickly and easily, although is not entirely a replacement for animation that is done by a skilled animator. MoCap is effectively 'locked' to a particular performance, thus an obvious benefit of 'manually created' animation is that it is entirely modifiable and easy to change the performance. It is still a useful tool and is used on occasion.

The performer, working in a specialized studio, wears markers, either as a tightly fitting suit and head cap, or individually placed, so that all subtle body movement and facial expressions are recorded by a specialist array of cameras. The equipment captures 360 degrees of any movement, which allows for 'real-time' interaction between the Director and the actors, giving the digital character a lifelike movement with which the audience can fully engage. In post-production, the Visual Effects Artists will add skin, hair, clothing and anything else necessary to create either the surreal creature or the lifelike figures used in the games marketplace, or in films such as *Avatar* or *John Carter*, which rely heavily on semi-human characters.

A motion-capture headcam. THE IMAGINARIUM, FOUNDED BY ANDY SERKIS AND JONATHAN CAVENDISH

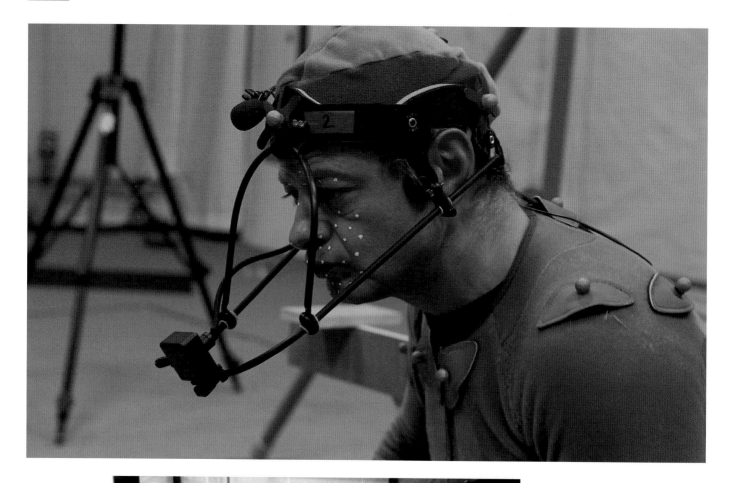

Andy Serkis, well known for taking performance capture to new levels in roles such as Gollum in The Lord of the Rings *and the title character in* King Kong. THE IMAGINARIUM, FOUNDED BY ANDY SERKIS AND JONATHAN CAVENDISH

Facial capture in the studio. THE IMAGINARIUM, FOUNDED BY ANDY SERKIS AND JONATHAN CAVENDISH

Motion-capture studio testing. THE IMAGINARIUM, FOUNDED BY ANDY SERKIS AND JONATHAN CAVENDISH

Members of the Imaginarium ensemble. THE IMAGINARIUM, FOUNDED BY ANDY SERKIS AND JONATHAN CAVENDISH

Motion-capture movement in the studio. THE IMAGINARIUM, FOUNDED BY ANDY SERKIS AND JONATHAN CAVENDISH

VFX are actually a combination of many sub-disciplines:

• Matchmoving or tracking
Creating a CG camera that exactly matches the real camera for every shot, so that CG can be made to 'stick' to live action. It uses a lot of information from the shoot.

• Previsualization (PreVis)
A small team of animators and VFX technical advisors who work on the initial pre-production planning and design of important VFX sequences in the film.

• Modelling
Creating the objects in CG, maybe a character, a building or an aircraft.

• Texturing
Quite simply, the digital painting of the models.

• Rigging
Adding a skeleton to a CG character or creature, which the animators use to make it move.

• Animation
Specialists who make anything move, from a giant CG monster through to a CG car. They are the digital actors of visual effects.

• Lighting
Artists who add CG lights to a scene to make it match the look and feel of the filmed scene.

• Effects
Clever technical people who create CG explosions, destruction, debris, giant waves, fiery landscapes, misty magical effects and any other required simulations.

• Matte painting
The digital equivalent of the glass painters on a set, who make elaborate backgrounds for shots.

• Rotoscoping
Digital matte creators, who make masks that allow visual effects to be inserted in and around the live action. While today's Rotoscope Artist works almost exclusively with computers and continuously evolving software, the fundamentals of

the art remain the same as a century ago. Rotoscope Artists provide traced outlines (mattes) so that live-action objects can be integrated into layers for films, television shows and video games. Today, instead of manually tracing each frame by hand, a computer and complex software are used to make the process more time-efficient. Invented at the beginning of the twentieth century by Max Fleischer, he was the master of the art of combining animation and live action, using an easel, a pen, a projector and a glass pane.

• **Compositing**
The team who put all of the above together, colour-match everything and blend it into the live action. Pre-digital compositing techniques go back as far as the late nineteenth century.

MATTES

Traditionally, matte paintings were made by artists using paints or pastels on large sheets of glass for integrating with the live-action footage (see also Chapter 6). Throughout the 1990s, traditional matte paintings were still in use, but were becoming more integrated with digital compositing. One of the first films to use digitally composited live-action footage with a traditional glass matte painting that had been photographed and scanned into a computer was the last scene in *Die Hard 2* (1990), which took place on an airport runway.

By the end of the decade, the time of hand-painted mattes was drawing to a close, although as late as 1997 some traditional paintings were still being made, notably for the rescue ship in James Cameron's *Titanic*.

Painting with a brush has now been superseded by 'digital paint' images created using photo references, 3D models and drawing tablets, with modern matte painters combining their digitally painted textures within computer-generated environments. Although much of this work is done on computer, there is still a very valid place for physical mattes using paint and canvas that can capture a less stylized image and can then can be digitized, giving a more realistic finish to the scene.

Advantages of Digital Mattes
Digital matting has replaced the traditional approach for two reasons. In the old system, the five separate strips of film (foreground and background originals, positive and negative mattes and copy stock) could drift slightly out of registration, resulting in halos and other edge artefacts in the result. Prepared correctly, digital matting is perfect down to the single-pixel level. Furthermore, in traditional methods using film, the final dupe negative would be a third- or perhaps a fourth-generation copy and, as film loses quality each time it is duplicated, the results would often be less than perfect, so digital images that can be copied multiple times without loss of quality are a great time and money saving advantage.

BLUE SCREEN/GREEN SCREEN

Chroma key compositing, or chroma keying, is a visual effects technique for compositing or layering two images or moving image streams together based on colour or chroma range. The technique has been used heavily in many fields to remove a background from the subject of an image, particularly in the news-casting, motion picture and videogame industries. A colour range in the foreground footage is made transparent, allowing separately filmed background footage or a static image to be inserted into the scene. The chroma keying technique is commonly used in film and television production and post-production.

This technique is also referred to as colour keying, colour-separation overlay, or by various terms for specific colour-related variants, such as green screen and blue screen. Chroma keying can be done with backgrounds of any colour that are uniform and distinct, but green and blue backgrounds are more commonly used because they differ most distinctly in hue from most human skin colours. No part of the subject being filmed or photographed may duplicate the colour used as the backing, so Production and Costume Designers have to be very aware of this technology.

In television studios, blue or green screens create a backdrop to news readers, allowing the compositing of stories behind them, more noticeable perhaps in the weather reports.

Virtual sets in filmmaking mean that composited backgrounds are combined with actual sets – both full-size and models, vehicles, furniture and other physical objects that enhance the reality of the composited visuals. Sets of almost unlimited size can be created digitally. Most common of all, perhaps, are set extensions, or digital additions to actual performing environments.

Performances from different takes can be composited together, which allows actors to be filmed separately and then placed together in the same scene. Chroma key allows performers to appear to be in any location, without actually leaving the studio.

Current computer technology has made it easier to incorporate motion into composited shots, even when using handheld cameras. Reference points can be placed on to the coloured background (usually as a painted grid, Xs marked with tape, or equally spaced tennis balls attached to the wall). In post-production, a computer can use the references to compute the camera's position and thus render an image that matches the perspective and movement of the foreground perfectly. Modern advances in software and computational power have eliminated the need for accurate placement of the markers – the software figures out their position in space. A perceived disadvantage of this is that it requires a large camera movement, possibly encouraging modern film techniques where the camera is always in motion (see also Chapter 6).

PREVISUALIZATION

PreVis, short for Previsualization, is a technique that allows filmmakers to plan parts of the script quickly so as to solve any problems and make the planning and execution easier. Very useful for any special physical effects or visual effects sequences, it is almost exactly the same function as that carried out by the Storyboard Artist, but created on computer as opposed to pencil and paper.

The PreVis Artist, just like the Storyboard Artist, has to be able to visualize the set as if looking through the lens of a camera. They not only have to have skills in digital art and animation, but also have to be extremely familiar with all aspects of film production and able to understand the Director's ideas, translating them into viable 3D images of any given set-up.

The PreVis Artist will probably need to create several options of the same sequence. They may work from already produced storyboards that the Director will have been working from, but expand these into animated sequences with colour detail and texture. The PreVis Artist will visualize the Director's intentions, paying close attention to animatic sequences, incorporating virtual camera movement and framing, creating the whole environment with character modelling and animation. These animations are not detailed and intended only to illustrate the technical aspects of a scene to inform the crew on set of the aspects of the sequence.

PROFESSIONAL PERSPECTIVE: DAYNE COWAN

Dayne Cowan.

Dayne Cowan has over twenty years' experience in the film industry as a Visual Effects Artist and Visual Effects Supervisor. His broad experience includes over ten years at Double Negative as the Head of 3D, Development Manager at Cinesite, VFX Supervisor and Head of VFX at Molinare. He has served on the board of the Visual Effects Society. He has also worked for major post-production companies in Australia and Asia. More recently, he has been the Vice President for VFX at Infinite Studios and is currently the Vice President of Film Visual Effects at VHQ Media in Singapore.

Dayne Cowan's credits include: *Chronicles of the Ghostly Tribe; Wolf Totem; Krrish 3; John Carter; Paul; Batman Begins; Dead Mine; Stranger Than Fiction; 10000 BC; Harry Potter and the Order of the Phoenix; Harry Potter and the Half-Blood Prince; Scott Pilgrim vs. the World; Batman: The Dark Knight; Battle for Lost Angeles; The Bourne Ultimatum; The Da Vinci Code; Mee-Shee: The Water Giant; Batman Begins; Thunderpants; Blade II; The Beach;* and the Academy Award winning film *The Reader.*

VISUAL EFFECTS

The Art Director and VFX Supervisor work very closely in the pre-production stages of a film. The digital visuals that the VFX Supervisor will have to create will always be conceptually driven by the Art Department. One of the VFX Supervisor's tasks is to ensure that the look and feel, or essence, of the original concepts are faithfully adhered to, right through the post-production process. Visual continuity must be maintained.

The VFX Supervisor will always seek to form a good working relationship with both the Art Director and the Production Designer as early in a project as possible. The more that they instinctively understand each other, the more successful the final result will be.

Whilst the relationship with the Production Designer is more about determining what should be created in VFX and what should be created for real, the relationship between the Art Director and VFX Supervisor is all about what the visuals should look like. It is a very direct connection, with the Art Director advising and guiding the VFX Supervisor on how everything should be created. Once concepts and looks are agreed, these will be passed on to the various VFX facilities companies working on the film as the master template for them to follow. The Art Director's role is thus very critical in this process.

During the pre-production phase, it is quite common for the VFX Supervisor's team to work closely with the Art Department to convert drawings, sketches and even sculptures into a sort of prototype digital version of the object. Test work can be done on these models, to make them move and interact, which gives everyone an insight into how they will appear in the final result. They can help to bring this artwork 'to life' quickly and fairly easily. It is such a useful part of the design process that many Art Departments actually employ a small team of VFX artists themselves, so that the two disciplines are tightly connected throughout the production.

Although an Art Director's involvement on a film usually ends at some point during the filming phase, it is becoming more common to see them involved through the post-production period as well, to help steer and advise on the look of the visual effects in the film's final creation stage.

CONCLUSION

So, as Wendy said in the Preface – what does illusion mean and how does it translate into film production? If you've read through all the chapters in this book and you've reached this point, you will undoubtedly understand its meaning exactly!

The ethos which drives film and television production hasn't changed much since the early days. In fact, if you've fully understood what I've been teaching you, you will have realized that, apart from the enormous advances in the technologies that are currently used, the passion that drives the whole of the Art Department – and the entire film crew – is very simple. Everyone is intent on getting the very best image on to the screen, not to get the awards or accolades (although they're very nice when they come along), but to create a couple of hours of entertainment that transports the audience out of their day to day lives.

There are so many nuances involved in production, particularly in feature films and television dramas, which change from project to project. Everyone involved, no matter what their age or experience, will approach each new venture with a degree of eager anticipation, knowing that it will test their skill and imagination to the absolute limit. It's very similar to having a life-long apprenticeship. Each job will add to your list of skills and experience, which is why people like me, who have worked for so many years and encompassed so many changes in technology, are honour-bound to pass on any tips and tricks we can to the up and coming film and programme makers, so that they, in their turn, can extend their knowledge to future generations with confidence.

In his 1943 lecture entitled 'The Art and Technique in Set Designing', Edward Garrick (son of Edward Gordon Craig, known as the father of modern theatre) addressed an audience of both film professionals and the general public, asserting that the need for adaptability and imagination is a constant in production:

Art is artifice – tricks – and it is the knowledge of the tricks of the trade that is so useful to the artist. In the early days of film, when big expenses in set construction were first encountered and costly effects were required at small outlay, these difficulties were got over by the artist-technician using his brains and ingenuity, with the result that so many devices and patents have been invented for use in film-making so that nothing is now beyond our scope if only we were to use them and use them properly. Except for a few specialists, the general knowledge of effect and trick work amongst Directors, Art Directors and cameramen is very low indeed. Lack of knowledge and experience has been the cause of all the failure in the technical execution of these methods.

This lack of 'trick work' in production has been overcome as technology and techniques have developed and matured over the decades since Garrick's experiences in the 1940s. The modern Designer not only has the luxury of computer technology at his or her fingertips, but the technicians, on and off set, are now past masters at all kinds of 'trick work' that has been fine-tuned by each generation of practitioners.

At the end of his lecture, Garrick said the following:

What we all lack at this stage in film history is a film school, where we can all become acquainted with old and new methods and get together over the inventing of new ideas for tackling this greatest of all arts; the making of films.

This is exactly why I started Film Design International and why I was driven to write this book. It is essential, if you're going to be able to do your job properly, that you understand the basis on how each job in the Art Department has developed since the invention of the moving image by the innovators who stretched the boundaries and, in doing so, have developed the techniques and technologies that are used today. Now it's your turn to carry the torch for the Art Department by fully appreciating the basic methods, whilst stretching your abilities as far as they will go to achieve the best possible results.

From the moment the Production Designer sits down with the Director and the other Heads of Department to discuss the script in order to design the entire production – whether it be a feature film or a television drama – it becomes a team effort. If you want to work as a creative in the Art Department you need one important faculty – a very fertile imagination, combined with the ability to translate that imagination, using your skills, into a tangible product.

TECHNICAL EXERCISES

The following exercises are designed to enhance your design skills and techniques, as well as to familiarize you with the level of detail required in technical sketches for a feature film. For each exercise, there is a basic-level task and an extension to encourage progression.

DOOR STAGES EXERCISE

Flush Door

- Draw a vertical rectangle of your desired width and height. These measurements will depend on the purpose and period of the door.

- Label each of the four corners as A, B, C and D.
- Draw a line between the two diagonally opposite points from top to bottom. In the illustrated case A to D and B to C.
- Where these two lines intersect will give the dead centre of the width and height of the door.
- This method of finding the centre will apply to any door you draw except the futuristic door example.

Four-Panel Door

- Obviously all period panel doors are different in terms of design and spacing of the panels, but they will generally follow the rules given here. In this case, the door is 7ft high

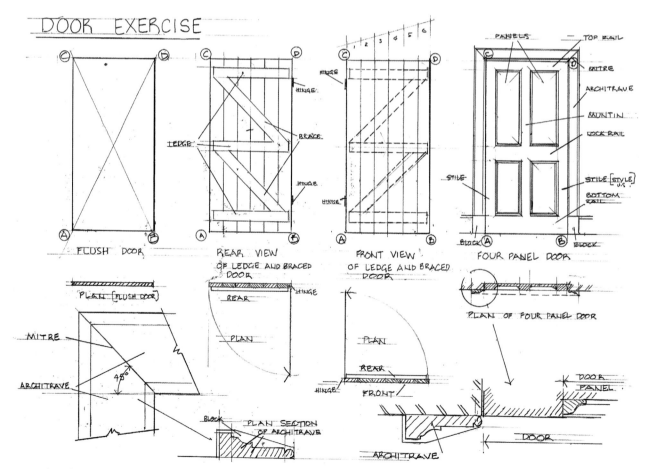

Door exercise showing examples of flush and four-panel doors.

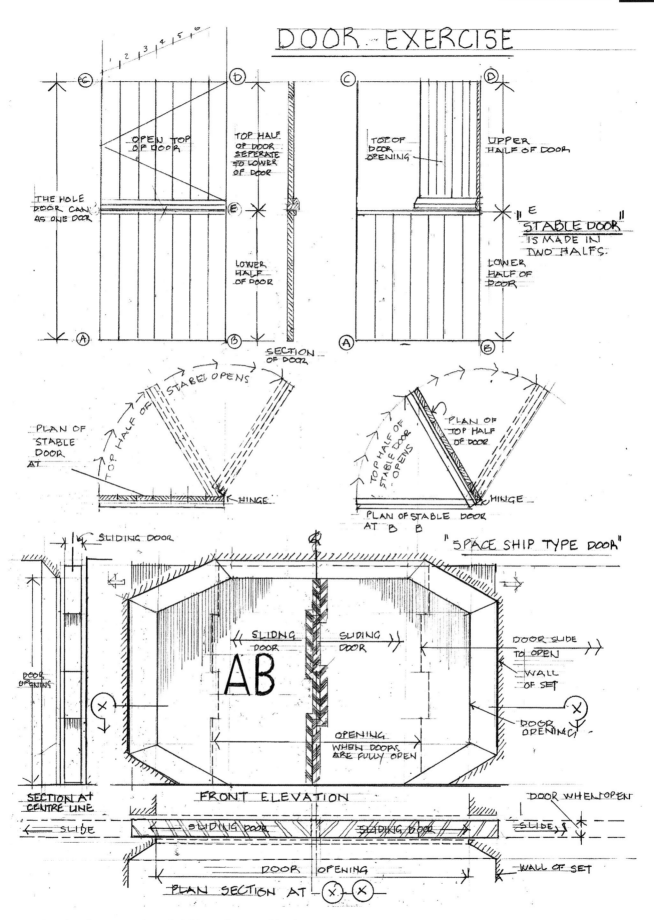

Door exercise showing examples of stable and spaceship doors.

and 2ft 9in wide (this measurement is for the door only and does not include the height of the architrave).

- Draw a vertical rectangle to the above measurements. Use a suitable scale to the purpose of your drawing.
- As you can see from the illustration, the door is divided into a bottom rail, a lock rail, a top rail, stiles and panels.
- The bottom rail is typically the deepest of the rails. In this example the bottom rail will be 9in.
- The locking rail is called such because it is at the same height as the door handle and consequently the lock. This rail is typically 6in wide. The height of the top line of this rail would be 3ft from the floor in this case.
- The top rail is the same width as the stiles, which run vertically. This measurement will be 4in.
- Use the diagonal method to find the dead centre of the door.
- Measure in and draw all of the different types of rails and stiles.
- Once you have marked the centre, you can easily determine the position of the panels.

STAIRCASE DETAIL STAGES EXERCISE

There are many different styles of staircase the Designer may be asked to replicate, but each structure has to conform to certain dimensions and building regulations and be strong enough to be used by the performers and crew on set.

As an exercise, take measurements of as many staircases as you can and try to replicate the example sketches to scale, but using your own accurate dimensions.

ARCH DETAIL STAGES EXERCISE

Trammel Arch
- First draw a horizontal line and label it XX. This will be the spring line – the point at which the arch begins to curve.
- Draw a vertical line through the XX line. This will be the centre line. Label the centre line B.
- Above the intersection of the two lines you have drawn, make a mark where you would like the crown/head of the trammelled arch. Label this point A. This is on the blue line of the example drawing.
- Decide the span (width) of the arch. Draw vertical lines on the horizontal line equidistant from each other to the centre line. These lines will represent the walls of the arch.
- On the left-hand wall you have just drawn mark the point at which it intersects the spring line as A. This is represented on the example drawing on the red line.
- With a straight strip of plain card, place it flush to the XX line.
- Mark the red A and the centre intersect B on the card. These marks will be the same distance apart as half of the arch's span.

- Now turn the strip of card 90 degrees clockwise and line up vertically on the blue line. Match the first A mark on the card with the A on the blue line. Once in this position, mark the position of B on the card.
- You will now have three marks on the card. Label the first mark on the left A, the middle mark B and the final mark on the right C.
- Return the card to the original horizontal position on the red line. Make sure to line up the first mark labelled A to the red A on the drawing. Subsequently the mark you have labelled C will line up with the centre point marked as B on the drawing.
- In small stages, rotate clockwise the strip of card from this starting position, ensuring that the points B and C remain on their corresponding line (red for B and blue for C). At each small movement of the card as it is rotated clockwise, make a mark at point A.
- These dots will form the outline of the curve. At the finishing point of rotation. The A point on the card will be at point A on the vertical blue line and point B on the card will be at the centre line intersect at point B.
- Join these dots up freehand.
- Repeat the process to form the opposite curve of the arch.

Equilateral Arch
Unlike the Trammel Arch this exercise uses a pair of compasses.

- Draw a horizontal line. This will be the spring line. Name this line XX.
- Draw a vertical line through the horizontal line at 90 degrees. This is now the centre line.
- Decide the width of the arch by drawing vertical lines an equal distance away from the centre line. This has now become the span of the archway.
- Where the vertical wall lines intersect the horizontal XX line label B and B.
- The points B and B are the compass points from which you will draw the curvature of the arch. Place the point of the compass on the left-hand B and the pencil of the compass on the right-hand B. Draw a line upwards until the centre line is intersected. Without altering the compass, place the point on the right-hand B and draw a line up to the centre line. This has now formed the curvature of the arch.

Venetian Gothic Arch
- Draw a horizontal line. Label this line CC. This is the spring line.
- Draw a vertical line through CC. This is the centre line.
- Decide on the span (width) of the arch by drawing two vertical lines an equal distance apart from the centre line at a 90-degree angle to the spring line.

"STAIR EXERCISE"

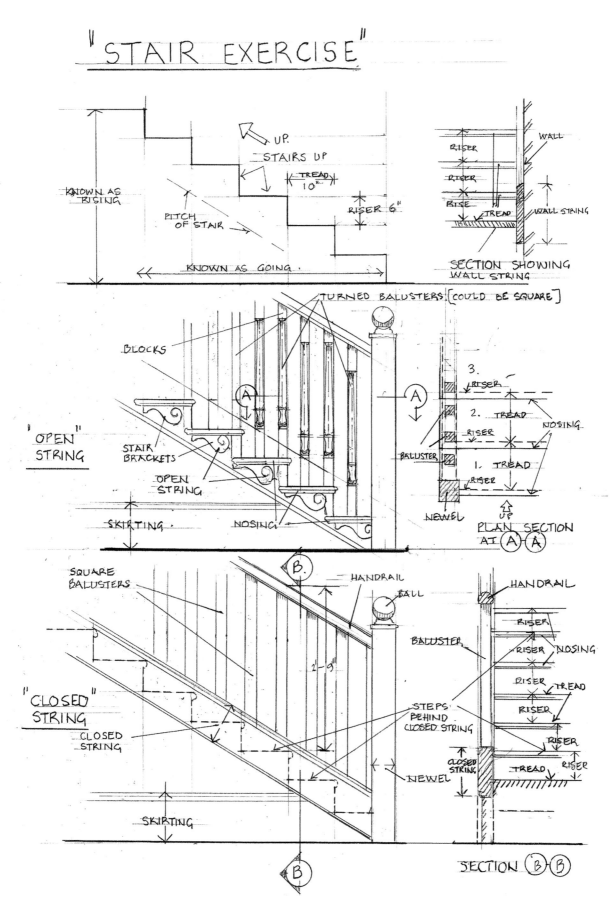

Stair exercise showing examples of wall, open, and closed string staircases.

TYPES OF STAIRCASES

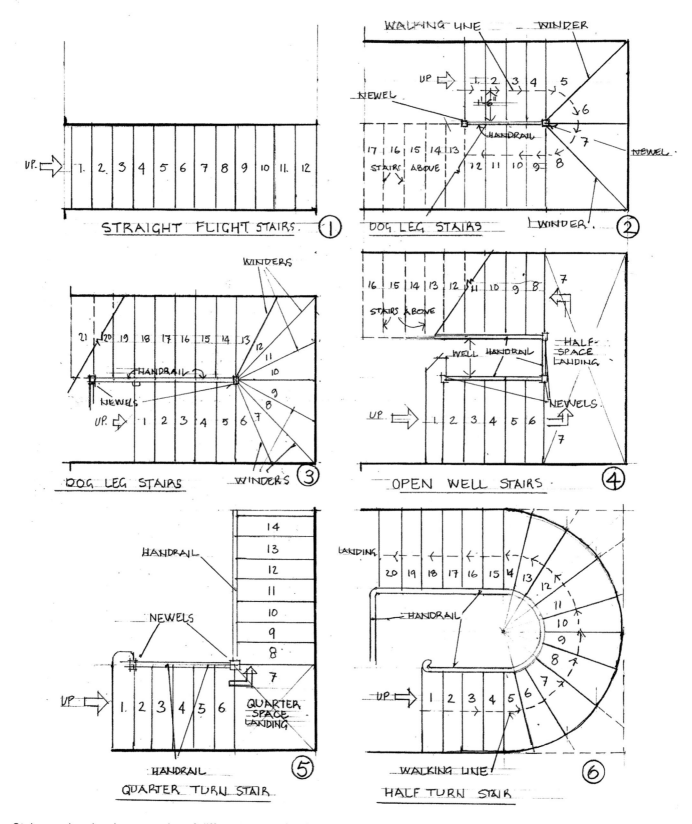

Stair exercise showing examples of different types of staircases.

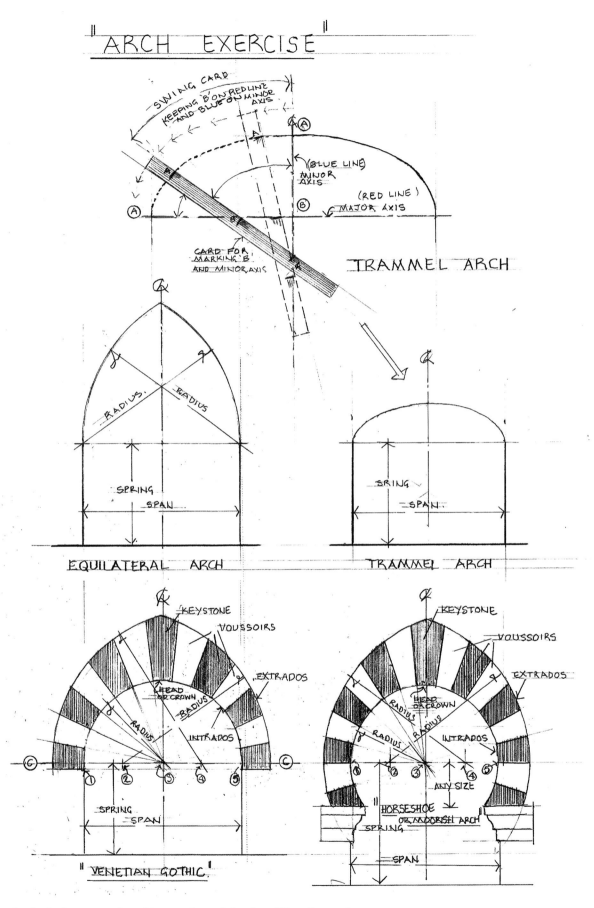

Arch exercise including examples of trammel, equilateral and Venetian arches.

- Divide the span equally into four vertical segments using the centre line so that there are two equal parts either side of it.
- This will produce five points on the spring line. At point 1 is the wall intersect, 2 illustrates the first quarter, point 3 is the centre line, point 4 is the third quarter and point 5 is the right-hand side of the arch's wall intersect. Label these as such.
- From point 3 on the centre line place the compass point.
- Line up the pencil of the compass with point 1 and draw a semicircle from point 1 to point 5. This has produced the intrados of the arch.
- Decide on the width of the arch by making a mark on the external side of the semicircle along the spring line CC. Repeat this same distance on the other external side on the CC line and make a mark. Label both of these marks as X.
- Place the point of the compass on point 4. Adjust the compass so the pencil point is now on the left-hand side X point.
- Draw a compass line from X to the top of the centre line clockwise.
- Repeat on the right-hand side using point 2 as the compass point position and without adjusting the compass place the pencil point on the right-hand side X. Draw a compass line anticlockwise up to the centre line.
- This has now produced the extrados of the arch.

Horseshoe or Moorish Arch

- Draw a horizontal line. Label this line CC. This is the spring line.
- Draw a vertical line through CC. This is the centre line.
- Decide on the span (width) of the arch by drawing two vertical lines an equal distance apart from the centre line at a 90-degree angle to the spring line.
- Divide the span equally into four vertical segments using the centre line so that there are two equal parts either side of it.
- This will produce five points on the spring line. At point 1 is the wall intersect, 2 illustrates the first quarter, point 3 is the centre line, point 4 is the third quarter and point 5 is the right-hand side of the arch's wall intersect. Label these as such.
- From point 3 on the centre line place the compass point.
- Line up the pencil of the compass with point 1 and draw a semicircle from point 1 to point 5. This is the same process for the Venetian arch up to this point. Instead of ending the semicircle at the spring line points, carry the compass line on below the spring line. This is at the drawer's discretion, but it should not ideally exceed 35 degrees from the horizontal line.
- This has produced the intrados of the arch.
- Decide on the width of the arch by making a mark on the external side of the semicircle along the spring line CC. Repeat this same distance on the other external side on the CC line and make a mark. Label both of these marks as X.

- Place the point of the compass on point 4. Adjust the compass so the pencil point is now on the left-hand side X point.
- Adjust the compass so that the compass point is on point number 4 and the pencil is on X. Set the compass and take it down to where the intrados line intersects the compass pencil point. Draw a line up to the centre line.
- Repeat on the right-hand side using point 2 as the compass point position and without adjusting the compass place the pencil point on the right-hand side where the intrados line intersects the pencil point of the compass. Draw a compass line anticlockwise up to the centre line.
- This has now produced the extrados of the arch.

WINDOW DETAIL EXERCISE

Windows come in many different styles and sizes, so take the opportunity to have free artistic rein for this exercise. The windows shown are a sash window example (double hung – USA) and a casement window example:

- Similarly to finding the dead centre of a door, mark the four corners of the window with A, B, C and D.
- Draw a line between the diagonally facing corners. The point at which they intersect will be the dead centre.

Note in the vertical section view of the sash window example that it does not include the weights and pulleys to aid the opening and closing of the window. As we are drawing for film and television a working window is rarely used. This dummy construction, known as 'non-practical', saves money on the budget. If a window is to be filmed as open, a screw either side is ample enough to achieve this.

FANLIGHT AND COLUMN STAGES EXERCISE

Fanlight Exercise

- Place the compass point on A.
- Adjust the compass to the half width of the door frame. This will give the radius.
- Draw a semicircle above the door.
- The outside and inside lines can be whatever width you like, but ensure the compass point is on point A.

Column Exercise

- Draw a circle the same desired diameter of the base of the column you would like to draw. Do not alter the radius of the compass once set, as you will need it on the elevation.
- On a horizontal line, in this case XX, follow up the diameter of the circle you have drawn below and make two marks to represent the width of the column. These will be named A and B.

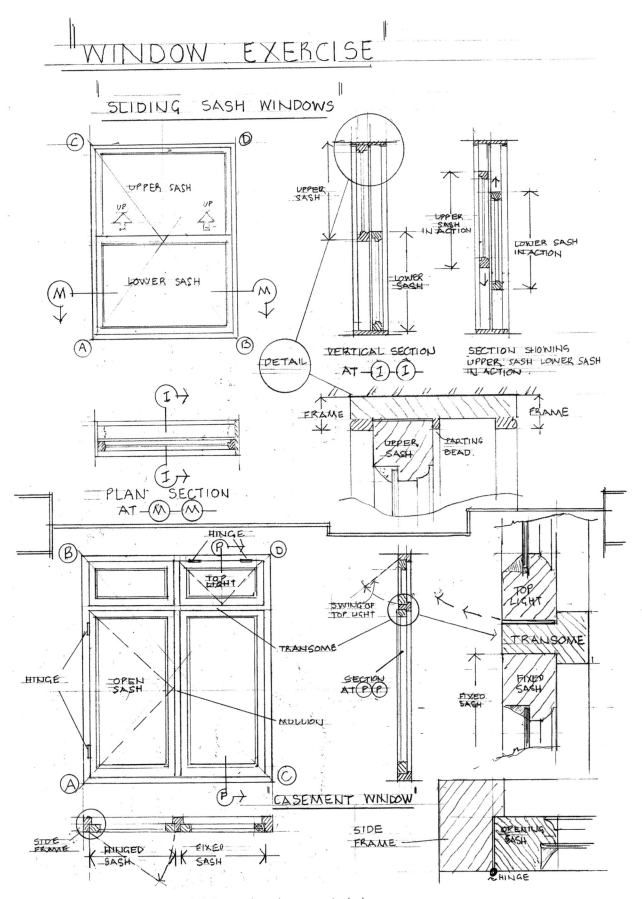

Window exercise showing examples of sliding sash and casement windows.

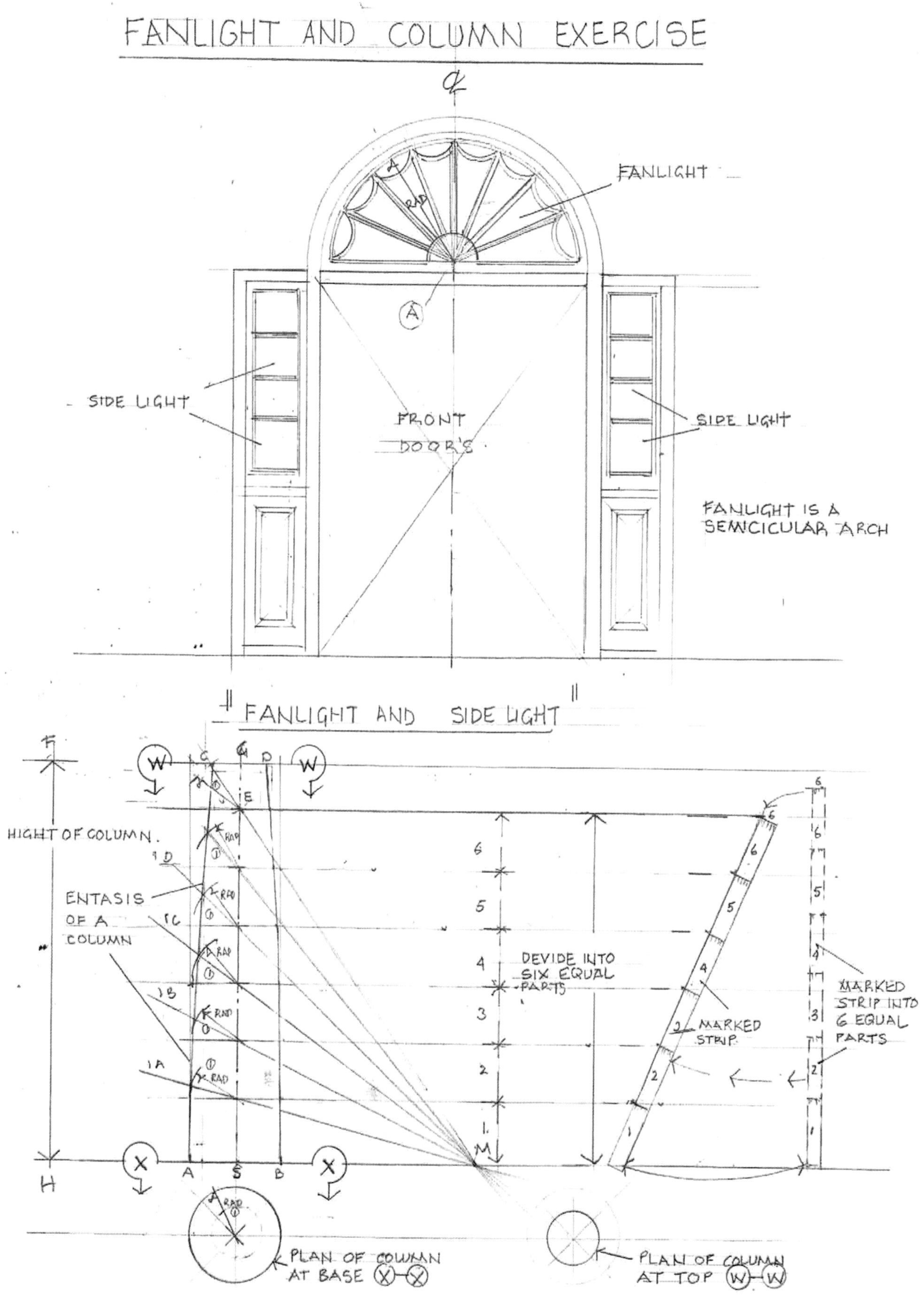

FANLIGHT AND COLUMN EXERCISE

FANLIGHT

SIDE LIGHT

SIDE LIGHT

FRONT DOOR'S

FANLIGHT IS A SEMICICULAR ARCH

FANLIGHT AND SIDE LIGHT

HIGHT OF COLUMN.

ENTASIS OF A COLUMN

DEVIDE INTO SIX EQUAL PARTS

MARKED STRIP.

MARKED STRIP INTO 6 EQUAL PARTS

PLAN OF COLUMN AT BASE (X)-(X)

PLAN OF COLUMN AT TOP (W)-(W)

Fanlight and column exercise showing dimensions.

- Draw a line vertically dead centre between points A and B. This will be the centre line; name the line S.
- Decide the height of the column. Make a mark on the centre line (S) to the desired height. This point will now be known as G. As a result, the centre line is now S-G.
- At the top of the centre line parallel to mark G, plot the width of the top of the column. Ensure the distance is equal both sides of point G. Name these points C and D.
- From the base line either left or right of your column, draw a height line using arrows to indicate where the line starts and ends. Name this line F-H.
- Place the unaltered compass point on point C. Draw a line with the compass to cross the centre line. Where these lines intersect will represent point E. Point E must be on the centre line.
- Draw a line connecting point C through point E right down to the base line. This point at the base line becomes point M.
- From point S (on the base line) to point E further up the centre line divide the space in-between these two points into six equal parts. This can be achieved either by measuring, or a simpler and quicker way is to angle your ruler between S and E, turning off the vertical until six equal units fit perfectly at an angle – this method is illustrated. Mark off each equal part off the ruler.
- From these equal marks draw a horizontal line through line S-G. Where the horizontal lines intersect the centre line, S-G represents the point at which the unaltered compass is placed.
- Draw a line from M to where each of these intersections meets. You will have a total of six lines from point M.
- You will now have three lines on each of the six equal

sections that intersect. These are the lines you have just drawn from the M point, the centre line S-G and the horizontal lines. At this tri-intersect, place the unaltered compass and draw a line with the compass that intersects the M line on the opposite side of the column to the M point.
- Join the six points you have created by using the compass and the M point. This line will create the entasis of the column. Repeat the process for the opposite side.

FIGURE DIMENSIONS

In order to appreciate fully how the human body will fit into the finished set and to ensure that the dimensions of your sketch or drawing are realistic, insert a figure into the sketch using the examples in the figure dimensions image.

CREATING A MOTIF TO SCALE

In creating a motif for a complex decoration or construction, sketch or draw it to scale using a graph so that it can be easily and accurately expanded to full size.

REPRODUCING ARTWORK

The sketches reproduced for this section are the work of several well-respected Production and Set Designers and are all good examples of the differing methods and personalities involved.

Copy these sketches as closely as possible at first and, as you progress, you can start to add in new detail or modify your drawing to subtly change the composition. This will help you to begin developing and perfecting your own personal style.

Figure dimensions exercise showing examples of differing stances and how they would fit with furniture on set.

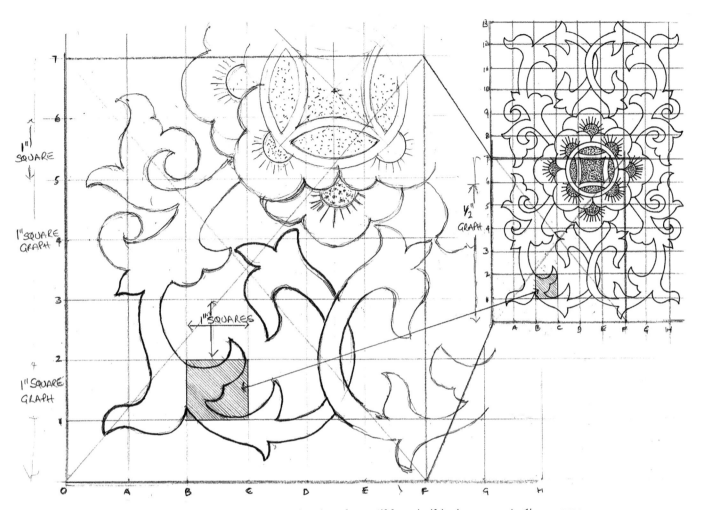

Motif exercise to show the use of a graph to increase the size of a motif from half-inch squares to 1in squares.

Sketches and designs from several Production and Set Designers showing alternative styles and methods.

Sketches and designs from several Production and Set Designers showing alternative styles and methods.

PAN

Sketches and designs from several Production and Set Designers showing alternative styles and methods.

UNIT LIST TITLES FOR UK AND USA

Department	UK Title	USA Title
Production	Producer	Producer
	Director	Director
	Executive Producer	Executive Producer
	Unit Manager	Unit Production Manager
	Production Supervisor	Production Supervisor
	1st Assistant Director	1st Assistant Director
	2nd Assistant Director	2nd Assistant Director
	3rd Assistant Director	3rd Assistant Director
	Floor Runner	Offset 2nd Assistant
		Crowd 2nd Assistant
		Key On Set PA
	Production Coordinator	Production Coordinator
	Production Secretary	Production Secretary
	Production Runner	Production Runner
	Accounts Clerk	Accounts Clerk
		Payroll (outside company)
Art Department	Production Designer	Production Designer
	Supervising Art Director	Supervising Art Director
	Art Director	Art Director
	Set Decorator	Set Decorator
	Draughtsman	Set Designer/Drafter/Draftsman
	Junior Draughtsman	Junior Draftsman/Drafter
	Concept Artist	Illustrator
	Storyboard Artist	Storyboard Artist
	Art Department Assistant	Art Department Assistant
	Art Department Runner	Art Department Runner
	Art Department Coordinator	
Camera	Director of Photography/Cinematographer	Director of Photography/Cinematographer
	Camera Operator	'A' Camera Operator
	1st AC/Focus Puller	'A' Camera 1st AC
	2nd AC/Clapper Loader	'A' Camera 2nd AC
	Specialist Camera Operators	'B' Camera Op and Steadicam
	Camera Assistant/Trainee	
	Digital Assist Manager	Digital Assist Manager

Department	UK Title	USA Title
(Grips)	Key Grip	Key Grip
	Best Boy Grip	Best Boy Grip
	Camera Assistant/Trainee	
	Digital Assist Manager	Digital Assist Manager
	Camera Car Driver	Camera Car Driver
(Electrics and Lighting)	Lighting Gaffer	Lighting Gaffer
	Chargehand Rigger (Electrics)	Rigging Gaffer
	Best Boy	Best Boy Electrics
	Electrician (Sparks)	Electrician
	Lighting Console Operator	Console/Board Operator
Hair and Make-up	Hair and Make-up Designer	Hair and Make-up Designer
	Special FX and Prosthetics	Special FX and Prosthetics
Costume	Costume Designer	Costume Designer
	Costume Dept Coordinator	Costume Dept Coordinator
Construction	Construction Manager	Construction Manager
	Construction Coordinator	Construction Coordinator
	Construction Buyer	Construction Buyer
	Heads of Department (HOD)	General Foremen
	Carpenter	Carpenter
	Standby Carpenter	
	Chargehand Stagehand	Lead Stagehand
	Stagehand	Stagehand
(Plaster)	Master Plasterer	Head Plasterer
	Chargehand Plasterer	Plaster Foreman
	Standby Plasterer	
	Plasterers	Plasterers
(Scenic)	Scenic Artist	Head Scenic
	Master Painter	Scenic Foreman
	Chargehand Painter	Set Finisher
	Standby Painter	
	Painters	Set Painters
	Painter's Labourer	Brush Hand
(Sculpting)	Head Sculptor	Head Sculptor
	Sculptor	Sculptor
(Rigging – Steel)	Master Rigger	Master Rigger
	Outside Contract	
Rigging	Key Rigger/Rigging Gaffer	Master Rigger
	On Set Rigger	On Set Rigger

Department	UK Title	USA Title
	Chargehand Rigger	Rigging Foreman
	Rigger	Rigging Grip
Location	Location Manager	Location Manager
	Unit Manager	Asst Location Manager
	Location Scout	Location Scout
Props	Property Master	Property Master
	Property Buyer	Property Buyer
	Armourer	Armourer
	Standby Props	Standby Props 1 and 2
	Prop Dressers	Prop Dressers
	Prop Maker	Prop Maker
	Green's Chargehand	Green's Chargehand
	Greensman	Greensman
Post-Production (Picture)	Post-Production Supervisor	Post-Production Supervisor
	Visual Effects Supervisor	Visual Effects Supervisor
	Assistant Editors	Assistant Editors
Sound Production and Post	Sound Designer/Supervising	Sound Designer
	Sound Editor	
	Sound Mixer	Sound Mixer
	Boom Operator	Boom Operator
	Assistants	Assistants

USEFUL WEBSITES, PUBLICATIONS AND BIBLIOGRAPHY

WEBSITES

AMPAS – American Motion Picture Arts and Sciences
www.oscars.org

BAFTA – British Academy of Film and Television Arts
www.bafta.org

BECTU (the media and entertainment union)
www.bectu.org.uk

Below the Line – Find Film Work   www.findfilmwork.com

British Film Designers Guild   www.filmdesigners.co.uk

Filmmakers Alliance (USA)   www.filmmakersalliance.org

Graphic Artists Guild (USA)   www.graphicartistsguild.org

IMDB – Internet Movie Database (cast lists for all films)
www.imdb.com

Kays Directory   www.kays.co.uk

Network Nine News (for information on all skills and crafts)
www.networkninenews.com

Production Base   www.productionbase.co.uk

Shooting People   www.shootingpeople.org

Soho Runners   www.sohorunners.com

Sundance Institute (USA)   www.sundance.org

WFTV – Women in Film and Television   www.wftv.org.uk

PUBLICATIONS

3D World   www.3dworldmag.com

4RFV – Regional Film and Video (online publication)
www.4rfv.co.uk

Concept Art World   www.conceptartworld.com

Hollywood Reporter   www.hollywoodreporter.com

Imagine (the magazine for animation professionals)
www.imagineanimation.net

Imagine FX   www.imaginefx.com

Moviescope (for filmmakers)   www.moviescopemag.com

Production Wizard   www.productionwizard.com

Screen International   www.screeninternational.com

Sight and Sound (available through the BFI website)
www.filmstore.bfi.org.uk

The Stage (the newspaper for performing arts industries)
www.thestage.co.uk

The World of Interiors   www.worldofinteriors.co.uk

Variety (weekly publication for film, television, music,
interactive)   www.variety.com

BIBLIOGRAPHY

Amery, C., *Period Houses and their Details* (Whitney Library of Design, 1974)

Antonov, V., *Concept Art: Digital Artists Masterclass* (d'artiste) (Ballistic Publishing, 2006)

Ascher, S. and Pincus, E., *The Filmmaker's Handbook: A Comprehensive Guide for the Digital Age* (Plume, 2013)

Calloway, S. (ed.) *The Elements of Style: An Encyclopedia of Domestic Architectural Detail* (Mitchell Beazley, 1991)

Carley, R., *The Visual Dictionary of American Domestic Architecture* (Holt Paperbacks, 1994)

Chiang, D., *Mechanika: How to Create Science Fiction Art* (Impact Books, 2008)

Cruickshank, D. (ed.), *Sir Banister Fletcher's A History of Architecture: Twentieth Edition* (Architectural Press, 1996)

Drpic, I., *Sketching and Rendering Interior Spaces* (Whitney Library of Design, 1988)

Ettedgui, P., *Production Design and Art Direction* (Focal Press, 2001)

Frayling, C., *Ken Adam: The Art of Production Design* (Faber and Faber, 2005)

Gibbs, J., *Interior Design* (Portfolio) (Laurence King Publishing, 2009)

Honthaner, E.L., *The Complete Film Production Handbook: Fourth Edition* (Focal Press, 2010)

Hudson, J., *Interior Architecture: From Brief to Build* (Laurence King Publishing, 2010)

Jones, O., *The Grammar of Ornament* (reissue) (Princeton University Press, 2016)

Katz, S.D., *Film Directing Shot by Shot* (Michael Wiese Productions, 1991)

King, B.L., *Big Screen, Little Screen: Career Opportunities Inside the Art Department in Film and Television* (ePub, 2009)

LoBrutto, V., *By Design: Interviews with Film Production Designers* (Greenwood Press, 1992)

LoBrutto, V., *The Filmmaker's Guide to Production Design* (Allworth Press, 2002)

McCurdy, K.M., *Shoot on Location* (Focal Press, 2011)

McKay, W.B., *Building Construction Volumes 1–4* (Pearson Education)

Morgan, M., *Calligraphy: A Guide to Hand-Lettering* (New Holland Press, 2001)

Neumann, D. (ed.), *Film Architecture: From 'Metropolis' to 'Blade Runner'* (Prestel Publishing, 1996)

Neville, P., Robertson, S., Belker, H., Goerner, M., *Concept Design 2* (Titan Graphic Novels, 2006)

Pile, J.F., *Perspective for Interior Designers* (Whitney Library of Design, 1986)

Plunkett, D., *Drawing for Interior Design* (Portfolio Skills) (Laurence King Publishing, 2009)

Preston, W., *What an Art Director Does: An Introduction to Motion Picture Production Design* (Silman-James Press, 1994)

Rice, M., *Rice's Architectural Primer* (Bloomsbury, 2009)

Rickitt, R., *Special Effects: The History and Technique* (Aurum Press, 2006)

Rizzo, M., *The Art Direction Handbook for Film* (Focal Press, 2005)

Seger, L. and Whetmore, E.J., *From Script to Screen – The collaborative art of filmmaking* (Lone Eagle Publishing, 2004)

Simon, D., *Film and Video Budgets: 5th Edition* (Film and Video Budgets) (Michael Wiese Productions, 2010)

Speltz, A., *The Styles of Ornament* (Dover Pictorial Archive, 2000)

Tangaz, T., *The Interior Design Course: Principles, Practices and Techniques for the Aspiring Designer* (Thames & Hudson: 2006)

Taschen, *Interiors Series* (Cologne, Germany: Taschen)

Thornton, P., *Authentic Decor: The Domestic Interior 1620–1920* (Weidenfeld & Nicolson, 1984)

Wilhide, E., *The Interior Design Directory: A Sourcebook of Modern Materials* (Quadrille, 2009)

Winslow, C., *Handbook of Set Design* (The Crowood Press, 2006)

Woodbridge, P., *Draughting for the Entertainment World* (Focal Press, 2000)

GLOSSARY

Action Vehicle: any car which moves in a shot.

Act of God: a natural phenomenon such as extreme weather conditions, fire or flood, which might close down production for a length of time.

Apple Boxes: sturdy wooden boxes used in film, video, photo, stage and studio grip equipment. Great for raising a prop, table, person, dolly track, camera and more.

Archivist or Digital Asset Manager: an Art Department position for one who labels, organizes, stores and manages digital information and images.

Armature: the wire or metal frame used for any object, either inanimate to allow a larger structure to be self-supportive such as a manufactured tree or statue, or for a character puppet to allow movement when covered with a substance, which, in itself, needs support, such as plasticine or other modelling clays.

Art Director: the person responsible for the production's setting, Art Department budget, construction and the Art Department crew, plus Art Department scheduling.

Aspect Ratio: the height and width of the image frame as used in film and television. There are several standards globally.

Backdrop/Backing: a painted cloth hung at the back of a set.

Barn Doors: designed to be attached to the front of spotlights and so on to give the photographer the ability to shape the light and how it falls on the subject.

Below the Line: above and below the line describes the divisions in the film crew. Above is the Producer, Director, Cinematographer and performers. Below is everyone else, the full working crew including the Art Department.

Best Boys – Grips and Lighting: the First Assistant to the key grip or the Lighting Gaffer. The Best Boy is in charge of the pre-lighting of the set, which is then handed over to the Gaffer. The term applies to both male and female practitioners.

Billing: names and roles on promotional posters and DVD/ Blu-ray covers.

Blocking: how a Director physically places performers on set as they play a scene.

Blocks or 2.4.6: 2, 4 and 6in blocks used by the Props Department to 'block' or raise the height of, or level out, items on set.

Blue Screen (*see also* **Green Screen**): where actors perform in front of an evenly lit blue or green background. In post-production the background is replaced by computer-generated images (*see also* **Chroma Key**).

Bounce: a lighting term meaning any surface used to reflect or 'bounce' light on to a subject.

Breakaway: glass objects, windows, wine glasses, bottles, plates used for stunts or gags in a scene. Can also mean destroyable scenery or costumes that can be ripped.

C-47(USA) Crocodile Clip (UK): a wooden clothes peg, metal in the UK, used by the Sparks (electricians) to clip gels and diffusers to a hot lamp's barn doors.

CAD: the generic term for Computer-Aided Design.

CAD/CAM: Computer-Aided Design/Manufacturing, a system that can be used both for designing a product and for controlling the manufacturing process.

CADD: Computer-Aided Design and Draughting specifically refers to architecture or scenery.

Call Sheet: contains all the information relevant to the day's shoot (*see also* **Call Time** and **Wrap**).

Call Time: the specific time people are expected to begin work on set. This is indicated on the **Call Sheet**.

Camera Angle Projection: perspective drawing for cinematography where the dimensions of a drawing are processed according to the camera angles, lens, aspect ratio and so on.

Camera Dolly: a movable camera support, either on wheels or on tracks, used by the Grip Department.

Camera Wrap: the camera crew may be finished, but the cast and crew may still have to do wild tracks (sound) or stills.

CGI: Computer-Generated Imagery.

Chroma: a colour attribute derived from splitting a beam of light with a prism, producing the colours of the rainbow. The light primaries are red, blue, green and the pigment primaries are red, blue, yellow.

Chroma Key: a visual effects post-production technique for compositing (layering) two images or video streams together based on colour hues.

Cinema: originally spelt 'kinema' in the UK from the original Greek for 'motion', but later popularized as 'cinema' by Lumière in 1896 – *see* following.

Cinematographe: patented by the Lumière brothers as a machine combining camera, printer and projector, later improved by Edison as the Kinetoscope.

Colourtrans: a large-scale colour photograph printing on translucent material, a category of photographic backdrop able to be lit from front or back.

Composite: the process of combining two images on to a single piece of film. Typically foreground action with background acquired elsewhere, which involves mattes.

Consumables (UK), Expendables (USA): materials such as tape, gels and so on that are used and discarded.

Convergence: single point perspective where all object outlines meet at the same vanishing point on the horizon. Also the name of the equipment invented in the 1970s that allowed pictures on video footage to be seen when running backwards. Previously the images could only be seen running forwards.

Counter-Track: where the camera moves in the opposite direction to the subject.

Credits: the name and title within the credit lists on a film or television programme.

C-Stand: an item of grip equipment that combines the use of an adjustable clamp on a metal tripod.

Cutaway: usually a shot of an inanimate object to be used as a fill when needed, such as a bowl of flowers on a table (*see also* **Insert**).

Cyclorama: usually shortened to 'cyc' – a continuous length of fabric or a scenery wall used as a fixed backdrop to suggest volumes of space used in all areas of photography and cinematography.

Dailies: the day's shoot by principal and other units. If originated on film, the footage is shown the next morning, having been processed overnight; if originated digitally, it is shown as soon as the Director requires (*see also* **Rushes**).

Descenders: an American term to indicate free-fall/high-fall stunts.

Digital Intermediate: a motion picture post-production process that classically involves digitizing footage shot either digitally or on film and manipulating the colour and other image characteristics.

DoP: Director of Photography.

Double-Up Schedule: mostly for television where two crews shoot separate episodes on the same day.

Dupe or Duplicate: refers to the copy of a photographic image. Used primarily when shooting with film stock.

Electrician (Practical): works with the everyday electrics, particularly alongside the Props Department.

EPK/Electronic Press Kit: a one- or two-person crew shooting the 'Making of …' footage.

Exposition: the initial plot layout of a film revealed within the first ten minutes as an emotional 'hook' to capture the attention of the audience.

Finger Wedges: small wedges used to prop up sets.

Flat: a scenery wall.

Floating (UK): a piece of scenery in a set that is designed to be moved, removed and replaced as needed to allow lighting and shooting needs.

Four-Waller: usually in the UK, a studio stage that is rented out as a four-wall space that allows the production to install its own crews and set builds.

Frames per Second/FPS: the rate at which film is run through the camera, for example 24fps.

Fringing: non-registration or haloing of film images, usually a product of early film cameras.

FSD or Full-Size Detail: a drawing in actual size showing close-up detail for exact building purposes.

Gaffer: the title that is used for the Heads of Department for the Lighting and Rigging crews on a film, usually assisting the Director of Photography.

Gimbal: the mechanism, using the working principles of a gyroscope, to spin or rotate a room or scenery piece on set.

Golden/Magic Hour: the hour before and until sunset.

Green Light: the formal instruction given by the producer to begin the pre-production process once the money is released.

Greens: deals with living or artificial plants or trees for dressing the set.

Green Screen: (*see also* **Blue Screen**) where actors perform in front of an evenly lit blue or green background. In post-production the background is replaced by CGI (*see also* **Chroma Key**).

Grip(s): the equipment used to move the camera(s) around the set or on location and the expert crew who use this specialist equipment.

Hero: any set, set piece, prop, item of set dressing or vehicle relating directly to the actors (also known as action props).

Highly Directional: the reflective quality of a front-projection screen, the material has the ability both to reflect and transmit light.

HOD/Head of Department: each department of a film crew has its own head, who is in complete charge of his or her own crew and their work.

Honey Wagon: the toilets!

Horse Master: person in charge of horses and stunts involving horses (*see also* **Wrangler**).

Hot Set (USA): a set or location actively being used by the shooting crew.

Hue: the attribute of a colour from splitting a beam of light with a prism producing the colours of the rainbow.

In-Camera: refers to any processing or optical work that is done within the body of the camera, usually using mattes, mirrors and other devices to overlay pieces of film to create a composite image.

Insert: can be a close-up shot of an actor or prop shot out of sequence and inserted into the main footage (*see also* **Cutaway**).

Interpolation: the process of filling in frames between key frames in animation, which was originally done by hand, but now computerized.

Key Frame: a single shot of a sketch or model used in Previsualization as a template.

Key Grip: the head of the Grips Department who has responsibility for the movement of all cameras and camera equipment on set or location.

Kinemacolor: from the Greek *kinema*, this was the first successful motion picture process.

LCD or Liquid Crystal Display: a monitor screen that uses liquid crystal technology to produce images.

Lights: many names for lights to become familiar with – baby, blonde, brute, chimera, dedo, inky, kino, midget, redhead and many more.

Location Scout: looks for suitable locations for a film shoot.

Locked Off: a static camera on a tripod or pedestal base.

Magazine: a reel of film stock loaded on to the camera.

Marking: done with coloured tape, different for each actor, placed on the studio or stage floor to indicate where the actor has to be to deliver the lines.

Martini Shot (USA): the last shot of the last scene, just before wrap time.

Master: a shot that lasts the length of the entire scene.

Matte Box: a camera accessory.

Matte Shot: the optical process of combining separate shots of foreground and background by masking off part of the frame area. It is a technique by which a glass painting from a matte artist is combined with live-action footage (*see also* **Split Screen**).

Meme: a behaviour or style which spreads involuntarily throughout all those present; an example is a yawn.

Miniature: intricate small-scale models photographed in such a way that they give the illusion of full-size buildings or vehicles.

Mise en Scène: from the French, literally meaning 'putting in the scene'; staging action usually in a long shot to include both technical and non-technical elements that make up the scene's look and feel.

Motion Capture or MoCap: motion capture tracks and computerizes the movements of an actor by sensors placed over the surface of a tightly fitting suit and head cap; this information can then be digitally manipulated.

NTS: not to scale.

Onion Skin: or tracing paper/sketch pad used to sketch ideas quickly in the design process.

Optical Printing: there are two ways of printing an image – contact printing by placing a negative against a piece of photographic paper and optical printing, which is effectively taking a picture of a picture. Contact printing is putting two strips of film, emulsion to emulsion, in a process or optical camera.

Paganini: pieces of wood of varying depths, secured by a central pole, with each piece added to the correct height used by grips to level the camera track on uneven terrain.

Per Diem: payment for overnight locations to cover food costs.

Performance Capture: *see* **Motion Capture**.

Persistence of Vision: the afterimage within the human eye, which is estimated to persist for around one-twenty-fifth of a second.

Photoplay: a stage play altered for the movies, first used in the 1920s.

Pick-Up Shots: additional photography for previously shot scenes, which usually happens after principal photography (*see also* **Reshoot**).

Picture Plane: the imaginary plane or frame of sight through which an audience views a scene.

Plaster Shop (UK), Staff Shop (UK): in the UK all studios are '**Four-Wallers**' and each production brings in its own plaster crew. The plaster shop is where they fabricate, mould and sculpt all items needed for the construction of the sets.

Post-Production: the process of editing all footage and sound, when all sound design and visual effects take place.

Pre-Production: the planning stage of a film before photography begins.

Process Camera: the camera used to facilitate **Optical Printing**.

Production: 'the production' refers to the film itself, 'production' refers to the process of making the film.

Production Design: the overall design, look and feel of the film, including colour palette, graphics, construction, costumes and make-up.

Production Designer: is entirely responsible for designing the look and the feel of the film to the Director's instruction.

Raked or Raking: a floor surface angled up and away from the camera.

Raw Stock: unexposed film or tape.

Recce: short for reconnoitre, is what the Location Scout and team do to find suitable locations to satisfy the Director, Production Designer and Art Director.

Reds/Runners: RSJs which run across the ceilings of studio sets with laterally moving chains to attach and support scenery.

Reshoot: additional photography for previously shot scenes, which usually happens after principal photography (*see also* **Pick-Up Shots**).

Retrofit: specific physical changes to a location or set to make sure that the design concept is believable.

Rigger: is essentially a scaffolder with extended skills who works within the Construction Crew, erecting the essential structural skeletons on which the set is supported.

Rights: legal and business terms negotiated by the Producer and the owners of any copyrights.

Rotoscoping: a method of tracing each frame of live action and then hand-painting in the silhouette, which was used by early cartoonists and animators but is now mainly digitized.

Runaway Production (USA): in the 1990s American producers took advantage of a failure to negotiate jurisdiction by the Screen Actors Guild and moved productions to other countries.

Rushes: the day's shoot by principal and other units. If originated on film, the footage is shown then next morning, having been processed overnight; if originated digitally it is shown as soon as the Director requires (*see also* **Dailies**).

Screenplay: the written form of a film, including acting instruction, which is effectively the working script for the film.

Second Unit: a separate full shooting crew that is either assigned to work on location whilst the main action is taking place in the studio, or to work with the Special Physical Effects Department to film all the action shots.

Sequence: a number of shots or scenes to be joined together in the edit.

Set-Up: when the camera is being repositioned.

SFX/Special Physical Effects: specifically referring to mechanical or physical effects used within a scene such as stunts and action sequences, pyrotechnics with small or large explosions, gunshots and building fires. This skillset is never to be confused with Visual Effects.

Sharp: in focus.

Soft: out of focus.

Sparks: the UK term for a film lighting technician as well as a practical electrician.

Split Screen: the optical process of combining separate shots of foreground and background by masking off part of the frame area. It is a technique by which a glass painting from a matte artist is combined with live-action footage (*see also* **Matte Shot**).

Stage/Studio: any building in which sets are built ready for filming.

Stagehand: a stagehand's work, whether in film, theatre or television, is working alongside construction, props and set dressers, assisting with everything from hanging backdrops and moving heavy props to taking care of transport.

Stage Layout (UK), Spotting Plan (USA): a ground plan for a set 'spotting' or indicating a special relationship with doors and distance from existing walls or other sets sharing the same space.

Standby Art Director: a Junior Art Director who monitors the Art Department's work on set during filming on behalf of the Art Director.

Standby Props 1 and 2: no.1 stays with the camera crew organizing any adjustments to the set dressing to the camera crew's requirements, checking the positioning of props on a monitor. Standby no.2 is his assistant and undertakes any alterations necessary. They are also available to advise the performers on the use of any specific prop.

Standbys: in the Construction Crew Standbys are highly experienced practitioners who are available on set or location during shooting and are responsible for dealing with any changes or improvements to the set that may be required during a film shoot

Stand-In: actors who fit a similar sex, body weight, size and colour of the lead actors, whose purpose is to replace the principal performer for lighting and blocking purposes.

Step Printer: a photographic apparatus that develops film from a reflex camera or a movie camera.

Stop-Motion or Stop-Frame Animation: a technique where models or items are shot one frame at a time and repositioned between each frame, so that when the footage is run in real time, the figures appear to come to life.

Storyboard: a series of sequential illustrations of proposed events on set as if looking through the camera lens, taking the form of a cartoon strip. They are used by the Director, Designer, Stunt Co-ordinator and Cinematographer to map out certain sequences, particularly action shots.

Strips: a term for the production boards used for the shooting schedule before the advent of budgeting and scheduling software.

Swing Set (UK) or Swing Stage (USA): a recurring set is placed on a 'swing stage', which is mainly used in episodic television programmes.

Telecine: the technology that enables the images captured on film to be viewed and transferred to video. This has been mainly superseded by the **Digital Intermediate** process.

Translite: a large-scale colour photograph printing on translucent material, a category of photographic backdrop able to be lit from front or back.

Trope: a universally identified image imbued with several layers of context, creating a new visual metaphor.

Turnaround: the time between wrap and call the following day.

Undercrank: shooting the film at slow speed so that it plays back as fast motion.

Unit Base/Base Camp: where all the trailers, trucks, honey wagons and catering vehicles are parked.

VFX or Visual Effects: visual and fantasy effects, which cannot be accomplished under normal circumstances. This incorporates techniques and technologies such as blue and green screen, chroma key and motion capture and is used in fantasy and science-fiction films. This technology is never to be confused with special physical effects.

Video Village: on-set video playback area.

Walk-Through: the Director, Cinematographer and anyone else involved in a scene walking through the action before shooting.

Wedge (Finger): used by the Props Department to place various items, for example mirrors, or levelling a wobbly table.

Wedge (Grips): used to level camera tracking or any other equipment.

Wedge (VFX): a visual effects term for compositing layers or 'wedges' per frame.

White Card Models: models used in the development and concept stages of film design used by the Art Department.

Wild (USA): a piece of scenery in a set that is designed to be moved, removed and replaced as needed to allow lighting and shooting needs.

Wild Tracks: a sound track recorded without picture on a film in order to provide ambient background to be used in post-production.

Wind Bags: large, lightweight canvasses used as scenery.

Wrangler: animal manager (*see also* **Horse Master**).

Wrap: either the formal end to shooting of a production, or the time the crew stops shooting on any given day.

INDEX